About This Book

Why is this topic important?

Organizational consulting generally has a broader focus than training. Whereas a trainer might develop people's understanding of team roles, a consultant might help a dysfunctional team function. Similarly, a trainer might deliver a workshop on developing good time management and productivity skills, whereas a consultant might be contracted to analyze and recognize workflow through a team or through an entire division or operating unit. There are clearly similarities between training and consulting—and the terms are often used interchangeably—but each has a unique focus and requires divergent approaches, tools, and techniques.

What can you achieve with this book?

Offering entirely new content each year, the Pfeiffer *Consulting Annual* showcases the latest thinking and cutting-edge approaches to organization development and performance improvement contributed by practicing consultants, organizational systems experts, and academics. Designed for both the dedicated consultant and the training professional who straddles both roles, the *Annual* presents a unique source of new knowledge and ideas, as well as practical and proven applications for facilitating better work processes, implementing and sustaining change, and improving organizational effectiveness.

How is this book organized?

The book is divided into four sections: Experiential Learning Activities (ELAs); Editor's Choice; Inventories, Questionnaires, and Surveys; and Articles and Discussion Resources. All the material can be freely reproduced for training purposes. The ELAs are the mainstay of the *Annual* and cover a broad range of training topics. The activities are presented as complete and ready-to-use designs for working with groups; facilitator instructions and all necessary handouts and participant materials are included. Editor's Choice pieces allow us to select material that doesn't fit the other categories and take advantage of "hot topics." The instrument section introduces proven survey and assessment tools for gathering and sharing data on some aspect of performance. The articles section presents the best current thinking about workplace performance and organization development. Use these for your own professional development or as resources for working with others.

About Pfeiffer

Pfeiffer serves the professional development and hands-on resource needs of training and human resource practitioners and gives them products to do their jobs better. We deliver proven ideas and solutions from experts in HR development and HR management, and we offer effective and customizable tools to improve workplace performance. From novice to seasoned professional, Pfeiffer is the source you can trust to make yourself and your organization more successful.

Essential Knowledge Pfeiffer produces insightful, practical, and comprehensive materials on topics that matter the most to training and HR professionals. Our Essential Knowledge resources translate the expertise of seasoned professionals into practical, how-to guidance on critical workplace issues and problems. These resources are supported by case studies, worksheets, and job aids and are frequently supplemented with CD-ROMs, websites, and other means of making the content easier to read, understand, and use.

Essential Tools Pfeiffer's Essential Tools resources save time and expense by offering proven, ready-to-use materials—including exercises, activities, games, instruments, and assessments—for use during a training or team-learning event. These resources are frequently offered in looseleaf or CD-ROM format to facilitate copying and customization of the material.

Pfeiffer also recognizes the remarkable power of new technologies in expanding the reach and effectiveness of training. While e-hype has often created whizbang solutions in search of a problem, we are dedicated to bringing convenience and enhancements to proven training solutions. All our e-tools comply with rigorous functionality standards. The most appropriate technology wrapped around essential content yields the perfect solution for today's on-the-go trainers and human resource professionals.

Pfeiffer *Essential resources for training and HR professionals*
www.pfeiffer.com

The Pfeiffer Annual Series

The Pfeiffer Annuals present each year never-before-published materials contributed by learning professionals and academics and written for trainers, consultants, and human resource and performance-improvement practitioners. As a forum for the sharing of ideas, theories, models, instruments, experiential learning activities, and best and innovative practices, the *Annuals* are unique. Not least because only in the *Pfeiffer Annuals* will you find solutions from professionals like you who work in the field as trainers, consultants, facilitators, educators, and human resource and performance-improvement practitioners and whose contributions have been tried and perfected in real-life settings with actual participants and clients to meet real-world needs.

The Pfeiffer Annual: Consulting
Edited by Elaine Biech

The Pfeiffer Annual: Leadership Development
Edited by David Dotlich, Ron Meeks, Peter Cairo, and Stephen Rhinesmith

The Pfeiffer Annual: Management Development
Edited by Robert C. Preziosi

The Pfeiffer Annual: Training
Edited by Elaine Biech

Michael Allen's e-Learning Annual
Edited by Michael Allen

Call for Papers

How would you like to be published in the *Pfeiffer Training* or *Consulting Annual*? Possible topics for submissions include group and team building, organization development, leadership, problem solving, presentation and communication skills, consulting and facilitation, and training-the-trainer. Contributions may be in one of the following three formats:

- Experiential Learning Activities

- Inventories, Questionnaires, and Surveys

- Articles and Discussion Resources

To receive a copy of the submission packet, which explains the requirements and will help you determine format, language, and style to use, contact editor Elaine Biech at Pfeifferannual@aol.com or by calling 757–588-3939.

Elaine Biech, EDITOR

The *2009* Pfeiffer ANNUAL

CONSULTING

Pfeiffer
A Wiley Imprint
www.pfeiffer.com

ISBN: 978-0-4703-7143-5
ISSN: 1046-333-X

Acquiring Editor: Holly Allen
Director of Development: Kathleen Dolan Davies
Development Editor: Susan Rachmeler
Production Editor: Dawn Kilgore
Editor: Rebecca Taff
Editorial Assistant: Marisa Kelley
Manufacturing Supervisor: Becky Morgan

Printed in the United States of America

Printing   10 9 8 7 6 5 4 3 2 1

Contents

Experiential Learning Activities

** Talent Management Topics

Editor's Choice

Inventories, Questionnaires, and Surveys

** Talent Management Topics

Articles and Discussion Resources

** Talent Management Topics

** Talent Management Topics

Preface

The 2008 Training and Consulting *Annuals* were the first to focus on a specific theme, that of "change." The themed *Annuals* were so successful with our readers and our authors alike that we decided to present a theme for this year. The 2009 *Annual* theme is "talent management."

The *Training Annual* presents eight talent management submissions and the *Consulting Annual* provides you with ten talent management submissions. Both *Annuals* continue to present our other popular topics: team building, leadership, communication, problem solving, and so forth. The talent management theme is an added bonus to concentrate some of our great contributors' talents in one year. Please let us know what you think of the idea of the topic-focused *Annuals*.

Why talent management? Organizations throughout the world are finding it difficult to hire the talent required to conduct business. The competition for talent is keen. To be successful, organizations of the 21st Century must have a clear vision; understand the competencies required to achieve the organizational vision; and acquire and retain a talent pool of people who possess the required competencies.

Strong forces are hampering many organizations' ability to attract and retain the talent required to meet the organizations' strategic vision. Some of these forces include:

1. A critical talent shortage that has been fueled by the retirement of the Baby Boomers. Estimates as high as 50 and 60 percent of the managers in some companies will be eligible to retire in the next five years.

2. The challenge of attracting, retaining, and engaging critical talent. U.S. organizations have not kept up with hiring and retention tactics that are attractive to a diverse population. In addition, employee loyalty and the value of tenure are decreasing.

3. Some talent such as scientists, engineers, and technicians will soon be in critically short supply. Highly skilled, techno-savvy individuals are always in demand, but a tighter supply is expected.

4. The lack of transferring critical knowledge throughout the organization. Most organizations' knowledge management efforts have been heralded by a few forward-looking souls, but fallen on deaf ears and languished by the wayside.

5. A need to develop a global workforce. Again, most organizations have ignored the seriousness of this issue, an imperative in a global business world.

What is talent management? The meaning of talent management has grown and changed over the past dozen years from a narrow focus to a broad and integrated plan. Talent management processes are treated as a whole system of interrelated aspects that provide the assurance that an organization will be able to strategically leverage its talent. The integration provides organizations with the ability to attract, develop, promote, engage, and retain talent to meet their strategic imperatives. Organizations are starting to structure talent management goals that are directly connected to their business strategies.

The aspects that make up what is called talent management may vary from organization to organization. They may include some of the following: recruiting talent, retaining talent, developing the workforce, planning for high-potential employees and leadership development, addressing performance management, implementing knowledge management systems, providing feedback and metrics, conducting annual workforce planning, forecasting employee placement and succession planning, supporting mentoring and coaching, offering career planning, conducting job analysis, measuring employee engagement, strategizing for replacement planning, investing in diversity efforts, and managing culture and value expectations. Organizations may combine several of these under one heading. Most organizations create a process in which human resources is a player, but may share the lead.

As you can see, many elements make up the broad theme of talent management. Many organizations have claimed for years that their people are their "greatest asset." Few demonstrate it. A strategic talent management plan must work in tandem with the business strategy in order for today's organizations to succeed. A well-designed talent management strategy will result in a workforce that goes beyond simply completing the job. It generates a workforce that is committed to improving the overall performance of the organization. Many organizations have a huge task ahead of them. They will face keen competition for the workers who are available. We hope that the ELAs, articles, and inventory that address talent management will fill a need for you.

The 2009 *Training Annual* includes a wonderful array of tools to help you with talent management. You'll want to check out the two diversity ELAs by Dennis Gilbert and M.K. Key. The ELA for interviewing by Peter Garber is also useful for those of you wrapped up in your talent management efforts. Talent management articles are presented by well-known author Jean Barbazette; long-time contributor Homer Johnson; Ajay Pangarkar and Teresa Kirkwood; Richard Rees, Allen Minor, and Paul Gionfriddo; and Yusra Visser and Ryan Watkins.

The 2009 *Consulting Annual* also includes talent management tools. Check out the ELA by long-time contributor Bob Preziosi. Two talent management ELAs are by authors you know: Thiagi and Len and Jeanette Goodstein. We are excited to have Nancy Kristiansen as a first-time author. Check her ELA out; it's creative and one you'll want to try. Talent management articles are presented by two former authors, Andy Beaulieu and Mohandas Nair, well-known Julie O'Mara and Alan Richter, and Ajay Pangarkar and Teresa Kirkwood. The *Consulting Annual* has also published an inventory by James Moseley, Sacip Toker, and Ann Chow.

This year the famed Marshall Goldsmith joins us as a contributor. We have one of his articles in each *Annual*. Thumb through the table of contents in each volume. I think you will be pleasantly surprised about the large number of experienced authors who have contributed for 2009. And you will be delighted with the exciting new ELAs, articles, and inventories you'll be able to use.

What Are the Annuals?

The *Annual* series consists of practical materials written for trainers, consultants, and performance-improvement technologists. We know the materials are practical, because they are written by the same practitioners who use the materials.

The *Pfeiffer Annual: Training* focuses on skill building and knowledge enhancement and also includes articles that enhance the skills and professional development of trainers. The *Pfeiffer Annual: Consulting* focuses on intervention techniques and organizational systems. It also includes skill building for the professional consultant. You can read more about the differences between the two volumes in the section that follows this preface, "The Difference Between Training and Consulting: Which Annual to Use."

The *Annuals* have been an inspirational source for experiential learning activities, resource for instruments, and reference for cutting-edge material for thirty-seven years. Whether you are a trainer, a consultant, a facilitator, or a bit of each, you will find tools and resources that provide you with the basics and challenge (and we hope inspire) you to use new techniques and models.

Annual Loyalty

The Pfeiffer *Annual* series has many loyal subscribers. There are several reasons for this loyalty. In addition to the wide variety of topics and implementation levels, the *Annuals* provide materials that are applicable to varying circumstances. You will find instruments for individuals, teams, and organizations; experiential learning activities to round out workshops, team-building, or consulting assignments; ideas and contemporary solutions for managing human capital; and articles that increase your own knowledge base, to use as reference materials in your writing, or as a source of ideas for your training or consulting assignments.

Many of our readers have been loyal customers for a dozen or more years. If you are one of them, we thank you. And we encourage each of you to give back to the profession by submitting a sample of your work to share with your colleagues.

The *Annuals* owe most of their success, though, to the fact that they are immediately ready to use. All of the materials may be duplicated for educational and training purposes. If you need to adapt or modify the materials to tailor them for your audience's needs, go right ahead. We only request that the credit statement found on the copyright page (and on each reproducible page) be retained on all copies. Our liberal copyright policy makes it easy and fast for you to use the materials to do your job. However, if you intend to reproduce the materials in publications for sale or if you wish to reproduce more than one hundred copies of any one item, please contact us for prior written permission.

If you are a new *Annual* user, welcome! If you like what you see in the 2009 edition, you may want to consider subscribing to a standing order. By doing so, you are guaranteed to receive your copy each year straight off the press and receive a discount off the cover price. And if you want to go back and have the entire series for your use, then the *Pfeiffer Library—which contains content from the very first edition to the present day—*is available on CD-ROM. You can find information on the *Pfeiffer Library* at www.pfeiffer.com.

I often refer to many of my *Annuals* from the 1980s. They include several classic activities that have become a mainstay in my team-building designs. But most of all, the *Annuals* have been a valuable resource for over thirty-five years because the materials come from professionals like you who work in the field as trainers, consultants, facilitators, educators, and performance-improvement technologists, whose contributions have been tried and perfected in real-life settings with actual participants and clients to meet real-world needs.

To this end, we encourage you to submit materials to be considered for publication. We are interested in receiving experiential learning activities; inventories, questionnaires, and surveys; and articles and discussion resources. Contact the Pfeiffer Editorial Department at the address listed on the copyright page for copies of our guidelines for contributors or contact me directly at Box 8249, Norfolk, VA 23503, or by email at pfeifferannual@aol.com. We welcome your comments, ideas, and contributions.

Acknowledgments

Thank you to the dedicated, friendly, thoughtful people at Pfeiffer who produced the *2009 Pfeiffer Annuals*: Kathleen Dolan Davies, Lisa Shannon, Marisa Kelley, Dawn Kilgore, Susan Rachmeler, and Rebecca Taff. Thank you to Lorraine Kohart of ebb associates inc, who assisted our authors with the many submission details and who ensured that we met all the deadlines.

Most important, thank you to our contributors, who have once again shared their ideas, techniques, and materials so that trainers and consultants everywhere may benefit. Won't you consider joining the ranks of these prestigious professionals?

Elaine Biech
Editor
July 2008

The Difference Between Training and Consulting

Which Annual to Use?

Two volumes of the *Pfeiffer Annuals*—training and consulting—are resources for two different but closely related professions. Each *Annual* serves as a collection of tools and support materials used by the professionals in their respective arenas. The volumes include activities, articles, and instruments used by individuals in the training and consulting fields. The training volume is written with the trainer in mind, and the consulting volume is written with the consultant in mind.

How can you differentiate between the two volumes? Let's begin by defining each profession.

A *trainer* can be defined as anyone who is responsible for designing and delivering knowledge to adult learners and may include an internal HRD professional employed by an organization or an external practitioner who contracts with an organization to design and conduct training programs. Generally, the trainer is a subject-matter expert who is expected to transfer knowledge so that the trainee can know or do something new. A *consultant* is someone who provides unique assistance or advice (based on what the consultant knows or has experienced) to someone else, usually known as "the client." The consultant may not necessarily be a subject-matter expert in all situations. Often the consultant is an expert at using specific tools to extract, coordinate, resolve, organize, expedite, or implement an organizational situation.

The lines between the consulting and training professions have blurred in the past few years. First, the names and titles have blurred. For example, some external trainers call themselves "training consultants" as a way of distinguishing themselves from internal trainers. Some organizations now have internal consultants who usually reside in the training department. Second, the roles have blurred. While a consultant has always been expected to deliver measurable results, now trainers are expected to do so as well. Both are expected to improve performance; both are expected to contribute to the bottom line. Facilitation was at one time thought to be a consultant skill; today trainers are expected to use facilitation skills to train. Training one-on-one was a trainer skill; today consultants train executives one-on-one and call it "coaching." The introduction of the "performance technologist," whose role is one of combined trainer and consultant, is a perfect example of a new profession that has evolved due to the need for trainers to use more "consulting" techniques in their work. The "performance consultant" is a new role supported by the American Society for Training and Development (ASTD). ASTD has shifted its focus from training to performance improvement.

As you can see, the roles and goals of training and consulting are not nearly as specific as they once may have been. However, when you step back and examine the two professions from a big-picture perspective, you can more easily differentiate between the two. Maintaining a big-picture focus will also help you determine which *Pfeiffer Annual* to turn to as your first resource.

Both volumes cover the same general topics: communication, teamwork, problem solving, and leadership. However, depending on your requirement and purpose—a training or consulting need—you will use each in different situations. You will select the *Annual* based on *how you will interact with the topic, not on what the topic might be.* Let's take a topic such as teamwork, for example. If you are searching for a lecturette that teaches the advantages of teamwork, a workshop activity that demonstrates the skill of making decisions in a team, or a handout that discusses team stages, look to the Training *Annual*. On the other hand, if you are conducting a team-building session for a dysfunctional team, helping to form a new team, or trying to understand the dynamics of an executive team, you will look to the Consulting *Annual*.

The Training Annual

The materials in the Training volume focus on skill building and knowledge enhancement as well as on the professional development of trainers. They generally focus on controlled events: a training program, a conference presentation, a classroom setting. Look to the Training *Annual* to find ways to improve a training session for 10 to 1,000 people and anything else that falls in the human resource development category:

- Specific experiential learning activities that can be built into a training program;

- Techniques to improve training: debriefing exercises, conducting role plays, managing time;

- Topical lecturettes;

- Ideas to improve a boring training program;

- Icebreakers and energizers for a training session;

- Surveys that can be used in a classroom;

- Ideas for moving an organization from training to performance; and

- Ways to improve your skills as a trainer.

The Consulting Annual

The materials in the Consulting volume focus on intervention techniques and organizational systems as well as the professional development of consultants. They generally focus on "tools" that you can have available just in case: concepts about organizations and their development (or demise) and about more global situations. Look to the Consulting *Annual* to find ways to improve consulting activities from team building and executive coaching to organization development and strategic planning:

- Skills for working with executives;

- Techniques for solving problems, effecting change, and gathering data;

- Team-building tools, techniques, and tactics;

- Facilitation ideas and methods;

- Processes to examine for improving an organization's effectiveness;

- Surveys that can be used organizationally; and

- Ways to improve your effectiveness as a consultant.

Summary

Even though the professions and the work are closely related and at times interchangeable, there is a difference. Use the following table to help you determine which *Annual* you should scan first for help. Remember, however, there is some blending of the two and either *Annual* may have your answer. It depends . . .

Element	Training	Consulting
Topics	Teams, Communication, Problem Solving	Teams, Communication, Problem Solving
Topic Focus	Individual, Department	Corporate, Global
Purpose	Skill Building, Knowledge Transfer	Coaching, Strategic Planning, Building Teams
Recipient	Individuals, Departments	Usually More Organizational
Organizational Level	All Workforce Members	Usually Closer to the Top
Delivery Profile	Workshops, Presentations	Intervention, Implementation
Atmosphere	Structured	Unstructured
Time Frame	Defined	Undefined
Organizational Cost	Moderate	High
Change Effort	Low to Moderate	Moderate to High
Setting	Usually a Classroom	Anywhere
Professional Experience	Entry Level, Novice	Proficient, Master Level
Risk Level	Low	High
Professional Needs	Activities, Resources	Tools, Theory
Application	Individual Skills	Usually Organizational System

When you get right down to it, we are all trainers and consultants. The skills may cross over. A great trainer is also a skilled consultant. And a great consultant is also a skilled trainer. The topics may be the same, but how you implement them may be vastly different. Which *Annual* to use? Remember to think about your purpose in terms of the big picture: consulting or training.

As you can see, we have both covered.

Introduction

to *The 2009 Pfeiffer Annual: Consulting*

The 2009 Pfeiffer Annual: Consulting is a collection of practical and useful materials for professionals in the broad area described as human resource development (HRD). The materials are written by and for professionals, including trainers, organization-development and organization-effectiveness consultants, performance-improvement technologists, facilitators, educators, instructional designers, and others.

Each *Annual* has three main sections: Experiential Learning Activities; Inventories, Questionnaires, and Surveys; and Articles and Discussion Resources. A fourth section, Editor's Choice, has been reserved for those unique contributions that do not fit neatly into one of the three main sections, but are valuable as identified by the editorial staff. Each published submission is classified in one of the following categories: Individual Development, Communication, Problem Solving, Training, Groups, Teams, Consulting, Facilitating, Leadership, and Organizations. Within each category, pieces are further classified into logical subcategories, which are identified in the introductions to the three sections.

The Training and Consulting *Annuals* for 2009 have a slightly different focus from past years. Both focus on the topic of *talent management*, a topic that permeates our organizations and pervades all that we do as professionals in the learning and consulting arena.

The series continues to provide an opportunity for HRD professionals who wish to share their experiences, their viewpoints, and their processes with their colleagues. To that end, Pfeiffer publishes guidelines for potential authors. These guidelines are available from the Pfeiffer Editorial Department at Jossey-Bass, Inc., in San Francisco, California.

Materials are selected for the *Annuals* based on the quality of the ideas, applicability to real-world concerns, relevance to current HRD issues, clarity of presentation, and ability to enhance our readers' professional development. In addition, we choose experiential learning activities that will create a high degree of enthusiasm among the participants and add enjoyment to the learning process. As in the past several years, the contents of each *Annual* span a wide range of subject matter, reflecting the range of interests of our readers.

Our contributor list includes a wide selection of experts in the field: in-house practitioners, consultants, and academically based professionals. A list of contributors to the *Annual* can be found at the end of the volume, including their names, affiliations, addresses, telephone numbers, facsimile numbers, and email addresses. Readers will find this list useful if they wish to locate the authors of specific pieces for feedback, comments, or questions. Further information on each contributor is presented in a brief biographical sketch that appears at the conclusion of each article. We publish this information to encourage "networking," which continues to be a valuable mainstay in the field of human resource development.

We are pleased with the high quality of material that is submitted for publication each year and often regret that we have page limitations. In addition, just as we cannot publish every manuscript we receive, you may find that not all published works are equally useful to you. Therefore, we encourage and invite ideas, materials, and suggestions that will help us to make subsequent *Annuals* as useful as possible to all of our readers.

Introduction

to the Experiential Learning Activities Section

Experiential learning activities ensure that lasting learning occurs. They should be selected with a specific learning objective in mind. These objectives are based on the participants' needs and the facilitator's skills. Although the experiential learning activities presented here all vary in goals, group size, time required, and process, they all incorporate one important element: questions that ensure learning has occurred. This discussion, led by the facilitator, assists participants to process the activity, to internalize the learning, and to relate it to their day-to-day situations. It is this element that creates the unique learning experience and learning opportunity that only an experiential learning activity can bring to the group process.

Readers have used the *Annuals'* experiential learning activities for years to enhance their training and consulting events. Each learning experience is complete and includes all lecturettes, handout content, and other written material necessary to facilitate the activity. In addition, many include variations of the design that the facilitator might find useful. If the activity does not fit perfectly with your objective, within your time frame, or to your group size, we encourage you to adapt the activity by adding your own variations. You will find additional experiential learning activities listed in the "Experiential Learning Activities Categories" chart that immediately follows this introduction.

The 2009 Pfeiffer Annual: Consulting includes thirteen activities, in the following categories:

Individual Development: Sensory Awareness

Encouragement: Improving One's Outlook, by Phyliss Cooke and Daniel Eckstein

Communication: Awareness

**Hide and Go Seek: Finding the Value-Added in Your Organization, by Nancy S. Kristiansen

---

** Talent Management Topics

1

Communication: Feedback

**Losses or Gains: Addressing Talent Management Opportunities, by Robert C. Preziosi

Communication: Styles

The Key to Me: Understanding Work Style and Communication Preferences, by Sara Keenan Rohling and Sheryl D. Peck

Problem Solving: Information Sharing

Speed Networking: Solving Problems Through Networking, by Richard L. Bunning

Groups: Competition/Collaboration

Bridges: Building Teamwork, by Susan K. Gerke and Karon West

Groups: Conflict

Conflict Resolve: Exploring Task and Relationship Conflict, by Tim Buividas and Vera Litcheva

Teams: How Groups Work

**Find Your Team: Improving Teamwork with Diversity, by Sivasailam "Thiagi" Thiagarajan

Teams: Roles

My Favorite Role: Exploring Team Roles, by Halelly Azulay

Teams: Feedback

What's Important? Creating a Team Assessment, by Steve Sphar

Teams: Conflict and Intergroup Issues

Communication Controversies: Clarifying Definitions for Improved Team Communication, by Lou Russell

Consulting, Training, and Facilitating: Facilitating: Skills

Facilitime: Exploring Facilitation Techniques, by David Piltz

---

** Talent Management Topics

Organizations: Vision, Mission, Values, Strategy

> **Values Consensus: Clarifying Organizational Values, by Jeanette Goodstein and Leonard D. Goodstein

To further assist you in selecting appropriate ELAs, we provide the following grid that summarizes category, time required, group size, and risk factor for each ELA.

** Talent Management Topics

Category	ELA Title	Page	Time Required	Group Size	Risk Factor
Individual Development: Sensory Awareness	Encouragement: Improving One's Outlook	13	75 minutes	Several groups of 2 or 3	Moderate
Communication: Awareness	Hide and Go Seek: Finding the Value-Added in Your Organization	23	5 hours	Up to 10 or several groups of 4 to 6	Moderate
Communication: Feedback	Losses or Gains: Addressing Talent Management Opportunities	31	Approximately 2 hours	12 to 16 supervisors or managers	Moderate
Communication: Styles	The Key to Me: Understanding Work Style and Communication Preferences	37	2 to 3 hours	Teams of 4 to16 who have been working together at least 6 months	Moderate
Problem Solving: Information Sharing	Speed Networking: Solving Problems Through Networking	43	60 minutes or more	15 to 30	Moderate
Groups: Competition/ Collaboration	Bridges: Building Teamwork	47	45 to 60 minutes	Several groups of 5 to 7	Moderate
Groups: Conflict	Conflict Resolve: Exploring Task and Relationship Conflict	55	Approximately 2 hours	6 or more participants from an intact work group	Low
Teams: How Groups Work	Find Your Team: Improving Teamwork with Diversity	59	30 minutes	10 to 100, best with 15 to 25	Low to Moderate
Teams: Roles	My Favorite Role: Exploring Team Roles	65	Approximately 70 minutes	7 to 12 from the same work group	Moderate
Teams: Feedback	What's Important? Creating a Team Assessment	71	1 to 2 hours	Up to 20	Moderate
Teams: Conflict and Intergroup Issues	Communication Controversies: Clarifying Definitions for Improved Team Communication	77	60 to 70 minutes	Any, in groups of 3 to 5	Low
Consulting, Training and Facilitating: Facilitating: Skills	Facilitime: Exploring Facilitation Techniques	81	Approximately 90 minutes	Up to 4 teams of 3 to 5	Moderate
Organizations: Vision, Mission, Values, Strategy	Values Consensus: Clarifying Organizational Values	87	Approximately 90 minutes	10 to 15 members of same organization's strategic planning group	Moderate to High

Experiential Learning Activities Categories

Note that numbering system was discontinued beginning with the 2004 Annuals.

Encouragement
Improving One's Outlook

Activity Summary

An interactive exercise to highlight the importance of encouragement as a means to improve the quality of life.

Goals

- To highlight the importance of encouragement as a means to improve the quality of our relationships with others.

- To introduce two conceptual frameworks on the topic of encouragement: The Seven Types of Encouragement and the Four Directions of Encouragement.

Group Size

A group large enough to allow for several subgroups of 2 to 3 members each.

Time Required

90 minutes.

Materials

- One copy of the Encouragement Interview Questions for each participant.

- One copy of the Encouragement: The Seven Types handout for each participant.

- One copy of Encouragement: Four Directions handout for each participant.

- A pencil for each participant.

- A flip chart and a felt-tipped marker (or a whiteboard and marker) for recording points raised.

- Masking tape for posting flip-chart sheets.

Physical Setting

A room large enough to permit some privacy for each subgroup of two to three members each.

Facilitating Risk Rating

Moderate.

Process

1. Introduce the activity by explaining that encouragement is one of the strongest interpersonal tools we have and an important part of the human experience. Positive encouragement can enrich one's life and improve one's relationships with others. Review the goals of the session and give an overview of the activity.

2. Distribute the Encouragement Interview Questions to the participants and review the form.

3. Create subgroups of two or three members each, depending on the size of the total group.

4. Tell the subgroup members that they are to use the Interview Questions while interviewing one another. If there are three in a subgroup, the members are to rotate the roles of interviewer, interviewee, and observer so that each member has an opportunity to play each role. Allow up to 5 minutes for the participants to read the questions and think about their answers. (10 minutes.)

5. Allow 5 minutes for each person to be interviewed. (15 minutes.)

6. Reassemble the total group and distribute Encouragement: The Seven Types handout. Go through the points verbally while the participants follow along.

7. Invite group members to contribute examples drawn from the interview activity. Allow 5 to 10 minutes for this, depending on response enthusiasm. (5 to 10 minutes.)

8. Distribute the Encouragement: Four Directions handout. Go through it verbally while the participants follow along. Lead the participants in providing specific examples of encouragement in each of the Four Directions:

   - Downward (the facilitator gives encouragement to group members).

   - Upward (group members give encouragement to the facilitator).

   - Across (group members give encouragement to one another).

   - Inward (the facilitator and group members take a few moments to give silent encouragement to themselves).
   (10 minutes.)

9. Reconvene the subgroups or create new ones and ask the members to discuss their reactions to learning about the Seven Types of Encouragement and the Four Directions of Encouragement. Then ask them to discuss themes that emerged during their interview sessions.
   (15 minutes.)

10. Reassemble the total group and solicit examples from the subgroup discussions of (in order) reactions, answers given, themes, and insights.
    (20 minutes.)

11. Return to Question 8 on the first handout. Ask how many responded "yes." If any participants said that they would not go back and tell the persons who encouraged them what it meant to them, ask why that was. Point out that we affect each other positively or negatively every day, in everything we do, and that thanking someone for encouragement in the past is a way of passing on the positive effects. Answer any questions and respond to comments.

12. Encourage them to state what they will do differently in the future as a result of this activity.
    (10 minutes.)

13. Provide summary comments and closure. Sample comments are:

    - It is important to realize that encouragement occurs in many ways other than just through direct interactions with people. Sights and sounds can encourage us. We can gain a sense of calm and well-being by visiting a garden, sitting and watching the ocean, or walking in a forest. Pets can provide encouragement through their unwavering affection. We can witness interactions between complete strangers that touch and encourage our spirits. Books, movies, and music can inspire us. Media stories of positive acts can inspire us to aid those in need or to take positive risks.

- It is as important to encourage those around you as it is to be a source of encouragement to yourself. As parents, teachers, bosses, and friends, we have numerous opportunities every day to encourage others. Do it often.

Variation

The conceptual inputs on the Seven Types of Encouragement and the Four Directions of Encouragement can be introduced before participants are asked to share their personal experiences.

Submitted by Phyliss Cooke and Daniel Eckstein.

Phyliss Cooke, Ph.D., *was a senior consultant with University Associates/Pfeiffer & Company and dean of its Intern Training Program. As a consultant, she specializes in the areas of small-group dynamics, organization development, training-program design and implementation, training for new trainers, and consulting skills for internal-resource personnel. In addition, she is an adjunct faculty member in the School of Psychology at Capella University. She is the author of numerous training activities and assessment instruments.*

Daniel Eckstein, Ph.D., *is an associate professor in the Center for Research and Counselor Education at Sam Houston State University, Huntsville, Texas. He is the author of Leadership by Encouragement, The Encouragement Process, and Psychological Fingerprints.*

Encouragement Interview Questions

1. Looking back on your life, who encouraged you? (Examples: a family member, teacher, friend, stranger)

2. What did this person say or do?

3. Were there factors in that situation that you think were relevant to what was said or done? (Examples: Another person present or listening? A significant event preceding or following the encouragement? An unusual setting?)

4. What was your approximate age at the time?

5. Looking back, how did this encouragement affect you? How did it affect the person you have become?

6. Has the encouragement you received inspired you to encourage others?

7. Did you ever tell the person who encouraged you about how the encouragement affected you?

8. If you did not, and it were still possible, how likely would you be to tell the person?

Encouragement: The Seven Types

1. Role Modeling

Role models can be positive or negative. By observing someone behaving in certain ways, you begin to develop a sense of how you want to be. It can be enlightening to review how you chose your role models in your formative years.

Examples

> Coach: "Although he frequently chewed me out, the coach let me know that performance matters, not excuses; that when others are relying on you, you need to contribute; and that he believed in my potential. This was what they call 'tough love.'"

> Teacher: "My teachers praised me for small achievements, encouraged me to try harder, and pointed out possibilities that I hadn't thought of."

> Film Stars: Through the roles they play in film and in real life, actors and actresses influence the popular culture, particularly teenagers and young adults.

2. Identifying Strengths and Abilities

Having one's personal qualities (e.g., sense of humor, rapport with animals, sensitivity), talents, and skills pointed out by others is a powerful form of encouragement.

Examples

> "My teacher said that I was a good writer, so I wanted to write more."

> "My grandmother said I had a green thumb, just like her."

3. Supporting Over the Long Haul

Repetition of mottos to live by serves as encouragement for certain kinds of actions from childhood on. These must be continued over an extended period to have much effect.

Examples

> "My father said that courage is not the absence of fear but the ability to carry a task through to completion."

> "Many positive statements from my friends throughout my formative years are the basis of my self-confidence."

"My parents always told me that they would support me in achieving my career goals, no matter how long it took."

4. Seeing a Person as Special

People who have low self-concepts or damaged psyches can be helped by being singled out by someone who believes in them.

Examples

"I was verbally abused at home, but my teacher paid attention to me and said I was a good person."

"My sister protected me from my brothers, who called me stupid."

5. Encouraging in Dark Times

Steadfast encouragement and loyalty is the theme here, usually during a difficult time in a person's life.

Examples

"I was unfairly accused, yet he believed in my innocence and supported me during my darkest moments."

"When I had the disease, my father said, 'I believe in you; you can fight this.' It kept me from giving up."

6. Supporting What a Person Is Interested In

A person's qualities, interests, and skills are the focus of the encouragement, whether or not the encourager has those same interests and skills.

Examples

He said, "If that is what you want to be when you grow up, we can take a trip to try it out."

"My mom drove me to all the games and intrastate tournaments, even though she had never been interested in sports."

7. Encouraging Specific Career Choices

Pointing the way toward specific career choices through influence, mentoring, etc., is a form of encouragement.

Examples

"My teacher said I had a gift for math and arranged for me to take advanced courses at the university while I was in high school."

"My father wanted me to take over his business after I graduated from college, so I majored in business."

Encouragement: The Four Directions

1. Downward

Family: Parents to children; older relatives to younger relatives/children
Work: Superior/supervisor to employee
Social: Higher formal-status person to lower formal-status person (government, police, military, committee, other title holders)

2. Upward

Family: Children to parents or older relatives
Work: Employees to superiors/supervisors
Social System: Lower formal-status person to higher formal-status person

3. Across

Family: Parent to parent, sibling to sibling
Work: Co-worker to co-worker
Social System: member to member, friend to friend, neighbor to neighbor

4. Inward

Oneself to oneself

Hide and Go Seek
Finding the Value-Added
in Your Organization

Activity Summary

An experiential activity on a talent management practice that will serve an ongoing process of discovering what constitutes "value-added" long after the class is over.

Goals

- To develop a deeper understanding of what "value-added" actually means to the people with the potential to add, *or withhold*, their value.

- To uncover and dissolve any preconceived ideas, or mental models, about why people work in professions considered outside your comfort zone, knowledge, or interest.

- To develop an inspired strategy that can be used to motivate, recognize, manage, develop, and retain the talent within your organization.

Group Size

One group of up to 10 participants, or several groups of 4 to 6 persons from within an organization.

Time Required

Approximately 2 hours prior to the event and 3 hours in the group.

Materials

- Hide and Go Seek Guidelines distributed to participants one to two weeks prior to the activity.

- Flip charts and felt-tipped markers for each group.

- Masking tape for posting flip-chart sheets.

Physical Setting

A room large enough for one group of up to 10 to be seated in a circular or U arrangement, or for several smaller groups to engage in dialogue without disturbing one another.

Facilitating Risk Rating

Moderate.

Preparation

Provide advance notification to each participant, along with a copy of the Hide and Go Seek Guidelines at least one, if not two weeks prior to the scheduled date. Include your contact information for any questions that may arise.

Process

1. Review the activity and its goals and how it ties in with other activities, objectives, or reasons for conducting the workshop. Include Margaret Wheatley's quote (from the Guidelines) or any others you may wish to add. (15 minutes.)

2. Divide participants into several small groups, depending on the number of people, and invite participants to share their interview experiences within their groups, taking turns.

   (10 minutes for each participant, divided by number of groups. 6 participants at 10 minutes each = 60 minutes divided by 2 groups = 30 minutes.)

3. Facilitate group dialogues. This may be done by a designee from within each group. The following discussion points should be raised. Consider creating a visual aid with the following questions and discussion points. Instruct each group to capture key findings and insights on their flip charts.

- How did interview subjects feel about being interviewed?

- Did you discover any surprises in the interviews you conducted?

- Did any of your interviews shed new light on your beliefs or preconceived ideas?

- Were any ill-informed mental models dissolved?

- What were the common and unique experiences among the group?

- What do your observations tell us about the nature of value-added regarding such concepts as manager-employee communication, customer service, sense of purpose and/or the various relationships involved?
(30 minutes.)

4. If small groups were used, reconvene into a single group to continue the dialogue, enriched by the experience of every participant. Ask each group to summarize their dialogue highlights and insights thus far.
(15 minutes.)

5. Deepen the dialogue by leading the discussion and capturing additional insights on flip charts. Use these questions to lead the discussion:

- Were there any differences between what your interview subjects think is the value they add to their work and *what they believe* their manager(s) think it is?

- If there were any differences, did it seem to matter to them?

- From your own experience, do you notice any differences between what you believe your own work is about and what your organization believes it is? Does it matter to you?

- When there are differences, how do these differences impact talent management strategies in your organization? Consider development or retention, for example.

- What leadership and organizational practices motivate you to realize your highest "value-added" purpose in your work?

- What management practices *inspire* individuals to effectively maximize their potential? [*Capture insights on the flip chart.*]

- What management practices *stifle* individuals from effectively maximizing their potential? [*Capture insights on the flip chart.*]
(30 minutes.)

6. Facilitate a closing discussion, using the following questions:

- What, if anything, will you *do differently* as a result of this inquiry into what constitutes "value-added"? [*Capture insights on flip chart. Seek to draw out thoughts about the following concepts in this closing discussion.*]

    - Ill effects of inaccurate assumptions about jobs or work you are not familiar with.

    - The potential to release unrealized potential when clarity of purpose is a mutual experience between manager and employees.

    - The importance of actively seeking out and listening to discover new insights and opportunities to better manage and lead processes and people.

    - High levels of "value-added" activity may be discovered in the most unexpected places.

    - Tapping into the sense of value and purpose from individuals at all levels and within all functional areas can dramatically influence individual and organizational performance through commitment, shared vision, openness and the mutual respect.

(15 minutes.)

Variations

- Class time required can be modified by adjusting the number of participants and reducing the number of interviews from three to two for each participant.

- This activity also is excellent for exploring the concept of "value-added" outside the organization.

- Use for public seminars where participants will be attending from different organizations or when there is a preference to avoid conducting the interviews with persons within the participants' organization. In either of these cases, encourage participants to choose interview subjects in unfamiliar professions. Emphasize the benefits of leaving one's comfort zone and exploring areas well outside their "usual sphere." Participants may have diverse reasons for choosing interview subjects in this context, which will add interest to class dialogues.

References

Terkel, S. (1974). *Working: People talk about what they do all day and how they feel about what they do.* New York: The New Press.

Wheatley, M.J. (2001, Spring). Innovation means relying on everyone's creativity. *Leader to Leader, 20,* 14–20.

Submitted by Nancy S. Kristiansen.

Nancy S. Kristiansen *is an independent consultant, providing a range of training, organizational development, and design services. More than thirty years in the electronics industry and a strong interest in adult and organizational learning have led her to a master's degree from Suffolk University and teaching leadership courses at Saint Joseph's College of Maine in its innovative online MBA program. She believes that effectiveness in any endeavor is achieved through balanced management of discipline and creativity.*

Hide and Go Seek Guidelines

"Our organizations and societies are now so complex, filled with so many intertwining and diverging interests, personalities, and issues, that nobody can confidently represent anybody else's point of view . . . nobody sees the world exactly the same as we do. No matter how hard we try to understand differences, there is no possibility that we can adequately represent anybody else. But there is a simple solution to this dilemma. We can ask people for their unique perspectives. We can invite them in to share the world as they see it. We can listen for the differences. And we can trust that together we can create a rich mosaic from all our unique perspectives."

(Wheatley, 2001)

This activity has been designed to provide you with an experiential opportunity to discover the meaning of "value-added" for people at any level or function within your organization. It is hoped that this activity will provide you with deep insights that will help you unlock the hidden potential in your organization. Your talent management strategies for motivation, development, recognition, retention, and even succession planning will all benefit from your sincere inquiry into the beliefs and attitudes of others concerning what constitutes "value-added."

The activity consists of two elements:

1. Pre-workshop interviews with three people within your organization to discover *their* perspectives on how they bring value to their work.

2. In-class interview summary presentations and reflective dialogues centered on your experiences.

The Interviews

To gain the most from this activity, take advantage of the opportunity to meet people with whom you might not ordinarily talk. Your primary purpose is to develop a deeper understanding of what "value-added" actually means to the people with the potential to add, *or withhold*, their value. Review the interview guidelines below to prepare for and conduct your three interviews.

Preparation

1. Identify three individuals with whom you seldom, if ever, have the opportunity to talk because their work or lifestyle is outside your usual sphere or comfort zone.

2. Contact your subjects to set up the interviews, being clear about your purpose. Ask them directly whether they would mind helping you with the assignment.

3. Schedule a mutually agreeable time and place that is conducive for conversation. You will probably need at least half an hour for each meeting. (*Note:* If you wish to record interviews, do not attempt to without first obtaining consent from the person you are interviewing.)

4. To jump-start conversations, develop a few questions or topics in advance. Use some of the questions suggested in the next step.

Conducting the Interviews

1. Invite stories. Be conversational in your approach, without being too formal. Here are some sample questions:

   - What brought you to this work or position?

   - What do you care most about?

   - Who are your customers?

   - What part of your work do you consider the most "value-added" aspect?

   - Do you think your organization or manager appreciates the purpose you bring to your work? Does it matter?

   - How do management decisions or practices influence your ability to give it your all?

2. Avoid distracting behavior by using small index cards to take notes if you will need help remembering what was said later, after the interview.

3. Be attentive and listen with an open mind. Resist any temptation to over-manage the interview.

4. Close the meeting graciously.

5. Write down as much as you remember immediately after the interview, capturing both your thoughts and feelings.

6. Continue to add your thoughts and reflections to your interview notes prior to attending our workshop.

7. Send a thank-you note or other form of appreciation to each of your interview subjects.

8. Be prepared to share a short (5- to 10-minute) summary presentation of your interviews in our workshop.

Reference

Wheatley, M.J. (2001, Spring). Innovation means relying on everyone's creativity. *Leader to Leader, 20,* 14–20.

Losses or Gains
Addressing Talent Management Opportunities

Activity Summary

A critical incident-based activity that provides a forum for supervising peers to explore talent management issues.

Goals

- To focus attention on a variety of situations that require talent management skills.

- To emphasize the importance of behavioral variables in dealing with talent management issues.

Group Size

Twelve to sixteen supervisors or managers.

Time Required

Approximately 2 hours.

Materials

- One Losses or Gains Incidents Worksheet for each participant.

- A flip chart and felt-tipped markers.

- Pen or pencil for each participant.

Physical Setting

A room with a U-shaped layout of tables and chairs.

Facilitating Risk Rating

Moderate.

Process

1. Begin by emphasizing how important the role of the supervisor/manager is in talent management. Explain that there are various opportunities each day to have an impact on company talent that will keep them energized or have the opposite effect. The right choice of supervisory/managerial behaviors will keep employees engaged because it will be clear that their talent is valued.

2. Tell a story from your own experience that highlights how you used the right behavior, or a time when you did not.
   (10 minutes.)

3. Distribute copies of the Losses and Gains Incidents Worksheet and pens or pencils.

4. Tell participants that they have 12 to 15 minutes to complete the worksheet. Let them know that you will answer any individual question that will help clarify the incident.
   (15 minutes.)

5. Call time after 15 minutes and ask two of the participants to share the responses they would make for Incident A. List their responses on a flip chart.

6. Invite other participants who have different responses to share them. Add these ideas to the flip chart.

7. Summarize and point out the importance of variation in "right" answers because of the diversity in personal awareness and style of talent in the organization.
   (10 minutes.)

8. Repeat Steps 5 through 7 for each of the other incidents.
   (75 minutes.)

9. Summarize the learning experience by pointing out that their role (supervisors/managers) is key to sound talent management. The actions they

choose to take can build stronger commitment from the talent or not build any commitment, so they need to reflect continuously on their behavior and its impact.

10. Debrief the activity by asking participants to share their lessons learned from the activity.
    (10 minutes.)

Submitted by Robert C. Preziosi.

Robert C. Preziosi, D.P.A., *is a professor of management in the Huizenga Business School at Nova Southeastern University and president of Preziosi Partners, Inc. He is the author of the new book,* The Leadership Zone. *He is also the editor of the* Pfeiffer Annual: Management Development. *He was recently chosen as one of fifty quintessential adult educators of the 21st Century. His areas of emphasis include leadership development and HRD. He teaches workshops on talent management.*

Copyright © 2009 by John Wiley & Sons, Inc. Reprinted by permission of Pfeiffer, an Imprint of Wiley. www.pfeiffer.com

Losses and Gains Incidents Worksheet

Instructions: List a few points for each of the following vignettes addressing how you would respond to the employee in each case.

Incident A

One of your employee stars has been working all morning on a new idea for process improvement that will impact all employees who work for you. Excitement has reached a high point, and your employee eagerly bangs on your office door. You are working day and night for your boss on a special project. You don't have any time to meet with the employee and probably won't have time until next week. What will you say to your star employee?

Key points of your response:

-
-
-
-

Incident B

You are meeting with an employee who has brought you an educational approval form. However, the degree program and its impact are not well-thought-out. Is the program really job-related? There is no consideration on how the employee's job might be affected by the employee needing more time to study. You need to discuss with the employee the need for more information about the degree's value. What will you say to the employee?

Key points of your response:

-
-
-
-

Incident C

You have a new high-potential employee who just came to you with some work experience from another company. The employee has an idea from the other company that sounds pretty good to you. You think it would work at your company. However, you don't want the new employee to become overconfident in his new job. Besides that . . . it wasn't your idea. You don't want anyone showing you up. You are going to suggest partnering with the employee to work together on the idea. What will you say?

Key points of your response:

-
-
-
-

Incident D

You have an employee who does exceptional work. The employee performs this job better than anyone else ever has. However, this employee is in constant conflict with other employees over small things. During a discussion with you, it becomes more obvious to you that the employee has poor interpersonal skills. You want the employee to go to training program on interpersonal skills, but you want the employee to self-nominate for the training. What will you do?

Key points of your response:

-
-
-
-

Incident E

You are meeting with two employees who have totally different perspectives on an idea they share. One of them is very technical. Every detail has a detail. The other associate has a very broad perspective. These two extremes are not working for you. Budget approval may hinge on a more clearly defined idea. You need both of them to alter their perspectives so that there is a middle ground between their extremes. What will you say to them?

Key points of your feedback:

-

-

-

-

Incident F

You have just discussed a project that might have wide organizational impact with a group of peers. As you walk back to your office, you begin to think that the idea was "cut off at the knees." No one seemed to want to risk presenting the total idea to management. You want to tell your peers that they need to take a risk. In addition, they all felt they were too busy to take on another project. You are sitting down at your computer to state your concerns in an email to all of them. What will you say?

Key points of your feedback:

-

-

-

The Key to Me
Understanding Work Style and Communication Preferences

Activity Summary

A follow-on activity to the Myers-Briggs Type Indicator (MBTI) to deepen understanding and apply individual communication and work style preferences in more practical and meaningful ways.

Goals

- To apply the Myers-Briggs theory to understanding individual work style and communication preferences on teams.

- To create open and honest discussion on a team through the sharing and validation of perceptions and true preferences.

- To build a sense of openness, trust and camaraderie on a team.

Group Size

Intact teams of 4 to 16 who have been working together for at least six months.

Time Required

2 to 3 hours after participants have completed the MBTI and received their individual reports.

Materials

Flip chart and pens or laptop computer with a projector.

Physical Setting

A room with tables arranged in a U shape. This activity can also be conducted by phone or VTC when the team is virtual and participants know one another.

Facilitating Risk Rating

Moderate.

Process

1. Begin with a brief review of the Myers-Briggs Type Indicator (MBTI) theory. Presumably, people have taken the MBTI and discussed their results in earlier meetings.
   (5 to 10 minutes.)

2. State that this session will focus on applying their MBTI information, with the goal of illuminating the best way to communicate with each individual on the team.

3. Ask for a volunteer to begin. Ask other team members, particularly those people who know this individual well, to share, based on their experience/perceptions, the best way to communicate with this person.

   > People will say things like: "I think Bob likes talking one-on-one or over the phone." Other examples include: "Bob likes you to get to the point early in your conversation and be credible backing up what you're saying with facts and logic" (ST preferences). "Marcia wants you to ask clearly for what you need. She doesn't like to reinvent the wheel and so will want to know what has worked in the past and therefore what some feasible solutions are." "Gerard likes to get to closure fast; he doesn't like endless discussion of possibilities or revisiting what has already been decided" (J preference). Each team member can contribute to the conversation, adding that has worked for them well in terms of communicating and interacting effectively with any given team member. Capture what they say, using one flip-chart sheet for each participant.

   (10 minutes.)

4. Once everyone has had a chance to say what they think about the volunteer's preferences, ask the volunteer to validate what has been said. The individual should say what is true for him or her and what works most effectively when communicating and interacting with him or her. If the

person isn't sure how to answer this question, ask, "Is voice mail, email, real-time conversation, or IM the best way of communicating with you? Does this differ by circumstance?" Such seemingly basic questions tend to evoke answers, like "To tell you the truth, if someone asks me anything big over email, it tends to be ignored." Because the range of individual differences is large, this question alone begins to open up new dialogue in areas that have only been matters of speculation or trial and error. (10 minutes.)

5. Repeat this process with each team member. (20 to 60 minutes.)

6. Say that you will now explore as a group how to get the best response out of each individual, particularly in a situation in which a request is involved. Ask each individual, "What is the KEY to communicating with you? In other words, if a team member wants you to respond most favorably to a particular request, how should he or she go about making the request?" (5 minutes.)

7. Ask this question of each team member in turn. This question often evokes out-of-the box (and priceless) responses such as, "If I were to tell you the most effective way of getting what you want from me, ask me about my dog first!" Or another example: "Anyone who approaches me on a bad day is not going to get far with anything. So if I look grumpy, don't even think about it!" Or still another: "My best advice is to have all of your evidence lined up before you get to me, because then I can fully evaluate what you have to say. Otherwise, I feel like I can't make a decision." (20 to 60 minutes.)

8. Ask the team discussion questions such as:

   • What was the most surprising thing you learned today about yourself/ perceptions of you, a colleague, or this team in general?

   • How will you use what you learned today to continue working together more effectively?

   • What needs to happen next on this team to ensure that you continue learning and performing at a high level?

   • What one key takeaway will you use as a result of this session today? (30 minutes.)

Facilitator's Note

This exercise raises the level of dialogue, motivation, openness, and the possibilities for collaboration as individuals begin learning critical information about each other that they can use in their daily work lives. Some individuals feel validated in their knowledge of a particular individual, and others are surprised that some of the assumptions they've been operating under regarding a particular individual, as well as some of the ways they have been working with a particular individual, may not be the most effective. Sharing of perceptions is often an eye-opener for the receivers as well, who are keen to hear how other people see them and what perceptions they have.

The facilitator's role during this Key to Me dialogue is (1) to create an open environment in which people feel safe and curious to learn more about themselves and each other, (2) to manage time, (3) to keep the agenda moving, (4) to keep the conversation on track, (5) to ask questions that draw out even more insights from the participants about what works for them, using the facilitator's knowledge of teams and MBTI as a basis for the questions, and (6) to track the information in some kind of document/table that will then be given back to the client team. This table can be shared with all team members and can become a living document edited as new members join or as other members leave the team. Team members can refer back to the document and use it in the future to ensure they are working together most effectively.

Variations

- If the team is large, the most effective way to do the activity is to group the participants together who have similar types. For example, ask the participants to share their perceptions regarding their colleagues who are ISTJs. Each ISTJ hears the group's perceptions and has an opportunity to respond. Because you are facilitating the activity by type, it avoids repetition. Most of the other ISTJs will say something like: "Similar to Bob, I like people to be efficient in their communication and to get to the point. One thing that's different for me is. . . ." This streamlines the conversation and allows participants to learn more deeply about each type, but without having the conversation become so long that people lose interest. This way of facilitating this activity in a larger group also allows you to drill down to individual communication and work style preferences, even within type, to demonstrate that, while there are many similarities in preferences, there can even be differences within type due to people's upbringing, values, and other aspects of what makes each individual unique. That helps people avoid the perception that they are being labeled as they begin to appreciate more the differences between different types and even within type.

- This activity can be used with a distributed or virtual team and conducted over the phone or using VTC provided the team members know one another. Team members do not have to know each other equally well, but they do need to know some team members really well in order to be able to contribute to deepening the conversation through their perceptions of what it takes to communicate and work with that team member most effectively.

Submitted by Sara Keenan Rohling and Sheryl D. Peck.

Sara Keenan Rohling *works as a senior consultant for Suntiva Executive Consulting (www.suntiva.com) partnering with organizations, teams, and individuals in a consulting and coaching capacity to discover the real factors affecting retention and engagement. She likes to create a safe space in which people experience trust, enabling them to open up and engage in deep meaningful discussions that transform the way they work. Rohling is certified in organization development and leadership coaching through Georgetown University.*

Sheryl D. Peck, Ph.D., *is an experienced clinical psychologist, executive coach, and leadership consultant. She is the director of leadership development for Suntiva Executive Consulting, a D.C.-based consulting firm. In that role, Dr. Peck drives Suntiva's strengths-based coaching methodology, coaches senior leaders in corporate and federal positions, and manages Suntiva's nationwide network of executive coaches. Dr. Peck earned her Ph.D. in clinical psychology from University of Virginia and her certificate in leadership coaching from Georgetown University.*

Speed Networking
Solving Problems Through Networking

Activity Summary

A fast-paced activity that demonstrates the value of networking by ensuring that group members meet a large number of people to identify potential leads to solve problems.

Goals

- To gather contacts who may be added to individuals' networks in order to help resolve selected business issues.

- To provide a forum for participants to experience the process of networking as an increasingly important skill for effective business leadership.

Group Size

15 to 30 people who are meeting for the first time to pursue a common goal such as a management workshop, planning meeting, business conference, etc.

Time Required

60 minutes or more, depending on group size.

Materials Required

- One Speed Networking Worksheet for each participant.

- One clipboard for each participant.

- One pen or pencil for each participant.

Physical Setting

A meeting room large enough so that participants can receive the initial briefing as a whole group, then stand and move around in order to network one-on-one before returning to the large group setting for a group discussion and debriefing.

Facilitating Risk Rating

Moderate.

Process

1. Introduce the activity by providing a short presentation on the increasing importance of networking as a skill for effective leaders and individual contributors in contemporary organisations.

2. Explain that the group will have the opportunity to engage in "speed networking" for the next half-hour (or proportionally more with larger groups), during which time each individual will identify a wide variety of resource people who may help in resolving specific business issues, while at the same time providing similar contacts to fellow group members. (5 minutes.)

3. Give participants copies of the Speed Networking Worksheet, pens or pencils, and clipboards. Ask them to fill in the two business problem areas of their worksheets and list the names of each of the other group members in the designated area. (5 minutes.)

4. Explain that each group of two will have 5 minutes (2½ minutes each) to pair up, explain their problems, and then gather resources or contact names of people who may be able to provide an insight into the problems. During the 5 minutes, *both* members will briefly present their problems and list suggested resources. (5 minutes.)

5. After 5 minutes, signal that the time is up and members are required to move into a conversation with another team member until all group members have paired with all other group members and engaged in conversation or until time is up. (5 minutes per pairing.)

6. After the procedure is completed, debrief with these questions:

- How many leads do you believe you may have gained for your selected issues?

- How will you make the most of those contacts?

- What do you believe is valuable about networking?

- What is the best way to go about it in the workplace?

- How might this activity change your behavior on the job in the future? (10 minutes.)

Variations

- The time for each conversation may be varied, giving more or less time.

- Much larger groups may be involved in the process but participants would contact only a specific number of new individuals, perhaps 10 to 15.

- The number of business problems may be increased to three or reduced to only one.

- Specific areas of focus may be assigned to the participants, such as improving quality, increasing sales, customer service, and so on.

- A prize may be given for the person who gained the most leads for a specific problem.

Submitted by Richard L. Bunning.

Richard L. Bunning, Ph.D., *is a European-based principal with Phoenix Associates, an American-based organization development consulting firm that specialises in change management and leadership development. He received his Ph.D. from Arizona State University and has published frequently, including a number of submissions through the Pfeiffer* Annuals. *In addition to consulting and teaching, Richard is a member of the editorial review boards for the* Journal of Management Development and Management Decisions and is listed in the current edition of Who's Who in the World.

Speed Networking Worksheet

Instructions: List below two important business issues or challenges in your area of responsibility that you consider to be difficult or ongoing but which have not lent themselves to easy solutions. These may include a range of issues such as levels of customer service, developing new business opportunities, infrastructure, staff issues, quality, or whatever is relevant to you.

Write the issue in terms of a satisfactory resolution or desired outcome, for example, achieving superior customer satisfaction or decreasing customer complaints.

1.

2.

Bridges
Building Teamwork

Activity Summary

A team-building activity that allows participants to examine communication, roles, leadership, competition, and cross-group teamwork.

Goals

- To examine team functioning, including communication, roles, and leadership.

- To explore competition versus collaboration among teams.

Group Size

Several groups of 5 to 7 persons each. One person per group will be designated as an observer.

Time Required

45 to 60 minutes (depending on the number of groups and the extent of debriefing).

Materials

- For the facilitator

  - One-pound box of sugar (any type) wrapped in gold paper.

  - Stopwatch.

- For each group

  - Bridges Instruction Sheet.

  - A piece of flip-chart paper with a river drawn on it.

- A zippered plastic bag with the following inside:
  - 13 marshmallows (standard size).
  - Approximately one-fourth pound of spaghetti.
- Bridges Observer Guidelines.
- Bridges Debriefing Sheet for each team.
- Paper and pens or pencils.
- Flip chart and felt-tipped markers.
- Masking tape.

Physical Setting

A room large enough for each group to build a bridge on a table.

Facilitating Risk Rating

Moderate.

Preparation

Draw a river on a piece of flip-chart paper for each group. The width of the river must be 14 inches. For fun you may want to draw alligators in the water.

Process

1. Introduce the session as a way to experience and learn about team dynamics. Form groups and have each group move to the table where they will be working. Read the situation on the Instruction Sheet to the participants and answer questions.

2. Give each team a flip-chart page with the river drawn on it. Give them each a bag of marshmallows and spaghetti. Explain that the only resources they may use to build the bridge are the marshmallows and the spaghetti.

3. Assign one observer to each group. Give the observers the Bridges Observer Guidelines and a pen or pencil for their responsibilities and to write notes. Announce the start, stating that they will have 20 minutes to complete the task. Announce intervals (15 minutes, 10 minutes, 5 minutes, and 1 minute to go).
(10 minutes.)

4. As teams finish, tell them that they may ask you to test their structure. Have a group member place the "1 ton gold brick" (1 pound box of sugar) on top of their bridge and then time it. If it holds for 15 seconds, they are successful, as long as all other criteria have been met.

5. Once all teams have finished and all bridges have been tested, or when 20 minutes have passed, stop the activity.
    (25 minutes.)

6. Hand out and ask participants to individually respond to the questions on the Bridges Debriefing Sheet. Ask the group observers to provide their observations. Provide time for each group to discuss their answers together.
    (10 minutes.)

7. Lead a large group discussion, using the debriefing questions as a guide.

8. Lead a concluding discussion based on the following questions:

    *   How can you relate the teamwork issues in this activity to teamwork in your own workplace?

    *   How can you relate collaboration and competition concerns to teamwork in your workplace?

    *   In what ways can you apply what you have learned to your work environment?
        (10 minutes.)

Variation

Do this activity after you teach specific teamwork skills or behaviors and have the observer look for those specific behaviors.

Submitted by Susan K. Gerke and Karon West.

Susan K. Gerke *is the president of Gerke Consulting & Development and helps people work better, together. Her focus is in designing, customizing, and implementing leadership and teamwork programs, meeting the needs of executives, managers, and employees in a wide number of companies and industries. She is the* *co-author of* The I in Team . . . Accelerating Performance of Remote and Co-Located Teams and Quick Guide to Interaction Styles and Working Remotely.

Karon West *is the president of West Consulting Group, a Canadian strategy and management consulting firm dedicated to organizations in planning, performance, and people development. Her focus is on strategic change, leadership, and partnerships in both public and private sectors. She holds a master's degree in organizational change from York University in Toronto, Canada.*

Bridges Instruction Sheet

You are members of an elite engineering firm, Konections, with a reputation for building quality bridges worldwide. Using state-of-the-art technology, you have the power to win over your competitors and consistently exceed customer expectations. In fact, you are the partner of choice for all major corporations needing bridges to somewhere.

You have recently been awarded a contract to construct a bridge over very troubled waters. These waters are known to be alligator-infested, and there is a rumor that any travel, foot or vehicular, is highly risky to life and limb of travelers. This is due to the insatiable hunger of the beastly alligators. Your client has discovered a land of riches on the other side of these dangerous waters and is scrambling to lay claim to the uncharted territory.

Your task in helping your client reach this new frontier is to build a bridge that will allow them to cross swiftly and safely to the other side.

The customer has specified the following key performance indicators:

- Length of bridge: 70 feet

- Height of bridge: Minimum of 10 feet

- Capacity of bridge: Carry 1 ton for 15 seconds

- Cost-effectiveness: May only use limited resources provided

- Timeliness: 20 minutes to delivery

The strength of Konections is people: Strategists, Problem Solvers, Communicators, and Implementers.

Assignment Guidelines:

1. Key for Bridge Construction

   - 5 feet = 1 inch

   - 1 ton = 1 pound

2. Assign team members to be:

   - Observer

   - Timekeeper

   - Reporter

3. Manage your time.

Bridges Observer Guidelines

What to look for:

1. Observe your group and record your observations of teamwork behaviors.

2. Observe other groups for ideas to share with your own group. These can be recorded as "best practices."

3. Observe behaviors that can be described as inter-group and intra-group cooperation and/or competition.

4. Jot down your observations in the space below in preparation to share what you observe with your group during the debriefing.

Bridges Debriefing Sheet

1. How successful was your group in accomplishing each of the key performance indicators? Why was this?

2. What were the different relationship and task roles group members took to help your group problem solve?

3. How did you communicate with each other in your group (verbal, non-verbal, interrupting each other, side conversations, everyone talking at once)? What was the impact of your communications on your problem-solving effectiveness?

4. In what ways did influence and leadership emerge in your group? What effect did this have on your group's effectiveness?

5. What was the impact of having an observer (your own and another group's) watching your group's problem-solving process?

6. Given your discussion on the above questions, on a scale of 1 (low) to 10 (high), how satisfied are you with the teamwork within your group?

7. How satisfied are you with the teamwork between the groups (level of sharing ideas, solutions, improvements to your bridge)? What got in the way of the cross-group cooperation? What action steps could you take to improve cross-group collaboration?

8. As a group, what are your collective learnings about group and cross-group teamwork? Be prepared to share two things you learned about teamwork with the larger group.

Conflict Resolve
Exploring Task and Relationship Conflict

Activity Summary

A team conflict activity that addresses task and relationship conflict.

Goals

- To learn about the differences between and impact of task and relationship conflict.

- To create an opportunity for team members to discuss what causes conflict within their teams.

- To develop plans for addressing conflict.

Group Size

At least 6 participants from an intact work group.

Time Required

Approximately 2 hours.

Materials

- One copy of the Conflict Resolve Lecturette for the facilitator.

- Post-it® Notes and pens for each participant.

Physical Setting

A large room with space that enables the participants to form small groups, varying in size from three to five persons per group.

Facilitating Risk Rating

Low.

Process

1. Introduce the objectives of the activity. Deliver the content in the lecturette. Form small groups of three to five persons and hand out Post-it Notes and pens.
   (5 minutes.)

2. Ask each participant to list several conflict examples, one per Post-it Note. The conflict examples could be based on past, current, or future experiences. Have participants share them within their small groups.
   (20 minutes.)

3. Tell team members to group their examples into categories by whether they are task or relationship conflicts. Tell them to assess and discuss that data, make assumptions and recommendations, and prepare a group presentation.
   (15 minutes.)

4. Have each group present its categories and the included conflicts.
   (15 minutes.)

5. As a large group, discuss and document similarities and differences. Ask the group to select the top two to four conflict areas to discuss.
   (15 minutes.)

6. Have participants move back into their same small groups to discuss the top three choices and make recommendations on how to more effectively manage each of the conflicts.
   (10 to 15 minutes.)

7. After 10 or 15 minutes, ask the small groups to make suggestions that may reduce or eliminate the conflicts in the three selected conflict areas.
   (10 minutes.)

8. Bring closure to the activity with these questions:

   - What did you learn about conflict?

   - What consistencies did you observe?

- How could our discussions contribute to future teamwork?

- What will you implement as a result of this activity?
(10 minutes.)

9. End the session by asking participants to choose a few suggestions to implement. Encourage them to create an action plan following the session. Lead the group in a rousing round of applause.
(10 minutes.)

Variation

Encourage participants to discuss their recent conflict experiences within their groups.

Suggested Reading

De Dreu, C., & Weingart, L. (2003). Task versus relationship conflict, team performance, and team member satisfaction: A meta analysis. *Journal of Applied Psychology, 88*(4), 741–749.

Submitted by Tim Buividas and Vera Litcheva.

Tim Buividas *is CEO of The Corporate Learning Institute. His passion is in change management consulting, training and development, coaching, and facilitation interventions. Through the delivery of his services, he has impacted the lives of over fifteen thousand participants from major corporations throughout the world. He is currently working on his doctorate in organizational leadership. Buividas is an adjunct professor for Benedictine University. In 2006, he co-authored* The A-Z Guide of Experiential Learning.

Vera Litcheva *is a graduate student in industrial and organizational psychology at The Chicago School of Professional Psychology. Her current passions include training and development, talent management, and survey development. She is currently working at The Corporate Learning Institute, a team-building organization in Lisle, Illinois.*

Conflict Resolve Lecturette

Conflicts may arise when team members have real or alleged differences. Conflict can reduce satisfaction, produce feelings of tension, and disrupt performance. However, conflict can also drive creativity, force people to learn and take on different views, and influence teams to make better decisions.

The two most common types of conflict seen in the workplace are *task conflict* and *relationship conflict*. Task conflict arises over differences of opinion or differing interpretations of facts, policies, and procedures. Low levels of task conflict can be beneficial to team effectiveness. But higher levels of task conflict can interfere with routine tasks or daily operations. Quite often with some level of task conflict, higher task performance is evident when a group is working on non-routine tasks that may be complex and not have definite solutions.

Relationship conflict arises out of differences in personal taste, political preferences, and interpersonal style and values. Relationship conflict reduces group focus on tasks while increasing focus on others. When task conflict is present, team members are generally more effective and innovative, whereas when relationship conflict is present it often interferes with team member satisfaction.

Find Your Team
Improving Teamwork with Diversity

Activity Summary

Two-part activity that explores diversity and inclusion in teams.

Goals

- To jolt people away from mindlessly teaming up with others on the basis of similarities.

- To experience the advantages of diversity in teams.

Group Size

Any number between 10 and 100. Best size is between 15 and 25.

Time Required

30 minutes.

Materials

- Index cards cut in half, each with one of the following letters: A, E, R, S, and T. Prepare enough cards for the estimated number of participants. Arrange the cards in sets of five in alphabetical order.

- One Find Your Team: Anagrams of AERST handout for each participant.

- One Find Your Team: Word List from the Champion Team for each participant.

- Timer.

- Whistle.

- Paper and pencils for participants.

- Flip chart and markers.

Physical Setting

Round tables for participants with sufficient space for them to walk around the room.

Facilitating Risk Rating

Low to Moderate.

Process

1. Distribute the letter cards, one card for each participant, and blank paper and pencils. Go through the cards in sequential order to ensure that equal numbers of cards with different letters are used.

2. Give these instructions to the participants:

    Hold up your letter cards so that other participants can see them. Work silently; do not talk to each other. Use the letters on the cards to group yourselves into teams. Do this as quickly as you can so that we can move on to the next phase of the activity.

3. Step aside and pause while the participants divide themselves into teams. It is very likely that participants will team up with others who have the same letter.
    (5 minutes.)

4. When participants have organized themselves into teams, blow the whistle to attract their attention. Congratulate them for getting themselves organized efficiently. Ask members of each team to work together and make up as many words as possible by arranging and rearranging the letters on the cards they have. The teams should write down the words they created on their sheets of paper.

5. It is very likely that the teams will not be able to make up any words because all members of a team have the same letter cards. In a playful manner, act surprised about the situation. Tell the participants that you thought they all knew the importance of diversity in teams.
    (5 minutes.)

6. Explain that you are going to try again. Remind participants that the task for the teams is to make up as many words as possible by arranging and rearranging the letter cards they have. Instruct the participants to display their letter cards and silently reorganize themselves into more effective teams. Step aside while the participants do this.
(5 minutes.)

7. When the new teams are ready, blow the whistle and repeat the previous instructions about making up as many different words as possible. Announce a 3-minute time limit.

8. At the end of 3 minutes, blow the whistle and ask each team to count the number of different words, making sure that no word uses any letter that is not found on a card. Identify and congratulate the team (or teams) with the longest list.
(5 minutes.)

9. Distribute copies of the anagram handout. Ask the teams to compare their lists of words with the list on the handout.

10. Distribute copies of the list of words from the Champion Team. Pause briefly to let the participants study the list and complain about duplicate letters. Explain that this team had eight members, giving them an extra E and S.

11. To go beyond merely playing a fun game, conduct a debriefing discussion to identify and share key learning points. Here are some suggested questions:

   • People generally tend to team up with others on the basis of similarities. Why does this happen? What are the advantages and disadvantages of this tendency?

   • What criteria did you use for forming teams during the second round? Why did you decide to do that?

   • Diversity among team members made it possible to better achieve the goal of making up different words. Can you think of some other goal that would be *hampered* by diversity?

   • The letter cards are visible indicators of diversity. In what other relevant ways could team members be different from one other? Which types of diversity would help you better achieve the team's goal?

- What made the Champion Team so productive? Why do most teams make the assumption that it may not have more than five members? What would have been an advantage of having members with duplicate letter cards in a team? What are potential disadvantages of having a large team?

- How does team behaviors in this game reflect team behaviors in your workplace?

- Thinking back on the insights from the play of the game, how would you change your behavior in real-world teams?

(10 minutes.)

Submitted by Sivasailam "Thiagi" Thiagarajan.

Sivasailam "Thiagi" Thiagarajan *is currently the Resident Mad Scientist at* The Thiagi Group, *an organization that is dedicated to improving human performance effectively and enjoyably. Thiagi's younger co-workers keep him supplied with food, books, and mortgage money and make him design a new training activity each day.*

Find Your Team: Anagrams of AERST

Here's a list of English words that can be generated by arranging the letters A, E, R, S, and T.

ARE	ERA	SET
ART	ERAS	STAR
ARTS	RAT	STARE
AS	RATE	TAR
ASTER	RATES	TARE
AT	RATS	TARES
ATE	REST	TARS
EAR	SAT	TEA
EARS	SATE	TEAR
EAST	SEA	TEARS
EAT	SEAR	TEAS
EATS	SEAT	TSAR

Find Your Team: Word List from the Champion Team

ARE	RESET	TART
ART	REST	TARTS
ARTS	RESTATE	TASTE
AS	RETEST	TASTER
ASTER	SAREE	TAT
AT	SAT	TATER
ATE	SATE	TATERS
EAR	SEA	TATS
EARS	SEAR	TEA
EASE	SEAT	TEAR
EAST	SEE	TEARS
EAT	SEER	TEAS
EATER	SERE	TEASE
EATERS	SET	TEASER
EATS	SETTER	TEAT
ERA	STAR	TEATS
ERAS	STARE	TEE
ERASE	START	TEES
ERE	STAT	TERSE
ESTATE	STATE	TEST
ESTER	STEER	TESTER
ETA	STET	TREAT
ETAS	STREET	TREATS
RAT	TAR	TREE
RATE	TARE	TREES
RATES	TARES	TSAR
RATS	TARS	

My Favorite Role
Exploring Team Roles

Activity Summary

A short activity that allows participants to learn about their common team behaviors and those of their teammates.

Goals

- To learn about common team behaviors and their function in team dynamics.

- To examine how individual preferences and styles impact roles played by various team members.

Group Size

7 to 12 members of the same work group.

Time Required

Approximately 70 minutes.

Materials

- One copy of the My Favorite Roles sheet for each participant.

- Paper and a pencil or pen for each participant.

- A flip chart and a felt-tipped marker.

- Masking tape for posting flip-chart sheets.

Physical Setting

A room large enough for the participants to move around. Writing surfaces should be provided and wall space should be available for posting.

Facilitating Risk Rating

Moderate.

Process

1. Introduce the session by explaining that, when people work in teams, they typically take on numerous roles throughout the team's interactions.

2. Distribute copies of the My Favorite Roles sheet and pens or pencils to all participants.

3. Ask participants to independently read all the descriptions on the handout. Allow approximately 8 to 10 minutes for reading, giving the participants a 2-minute warning before calling time.
(10 minutes.)

4. Ask participants to think about the five team behavior roles that they believe they tend to use frequently in team situations, and to record those in the space provided on their handouts. Allow approximately 5 minutes for this activity. Encourage silent, independent reflection and give participants a 1-minute warning before calling time.
(5 minutes.)

5. Tell participants to cross off one behavior type from their list that they are least likely to use of the five. Allow 30 to 60 seconds for this task.
(2 minutes.)

6. Instruct participants to cross off another role from their lists (reducing the list further, from four to three). Again, allow a few seconds to complete this task.

7. Repeat twice more, so that each participant ends up with *one* behavior role. Theoretically, it would be their most frequently used style. Expect some signs of discomfort or irritation at having to pare down to only one behavior. Assure participants that this is a natural part of the process; it is a forced prioritization.
(3 minutes.)

8. Ask the participants to form groups of three to five persons each, with members of their own work teams. Ask the group members to share their most frequently used team behavior roles and then to discuss similarities and differences among the various team members. Also instruct participants to consider benefits and blind spots each role brings to the team's interactions, decision-making process, and performance results. Finally, have participants discuss ways in which the work team can support each member's behavior style strengths as well as reduce the risks introduced by the potential blind spots. Allow approximately 15 minutes for the task, giving the participants a 2-minute warning before calling time.
(15 minutes.)

9. Ask a representative from each group to read aloud the styles selected by their group members. When all groups have finished reporting, ask the following questions, using flip-chart sheets to record significant learning points and/or issues and posting the sheets as necessary:

- How similar or different were the roles selected by the members of your group?

- What are some of the benefits of having diverse behavior roles preferred by various team members? What are some of the challenges this diversity poses?

- What were some of the specific behavior role benefits discussed? What were some ways that you suggested the team should support them to gain their full benefits?

- What were some of the blind spots you discussed? What are some ways you suggested to avoid them?

- What other learning points did you experience as a result of participating in this exercise?

- How will your discussions enhance teamwork in the future?
(30 minutes.)

Variation

Have the groups develop a list of actionable items that can be undertaken to improve the team dynamics of their work team.

References

Scholtes, P.R., Joiner, B.L., & Streibel, B.J. (2003). *The team handbook* (3rd ed.). Madison, WI: Oriel Incorporated.

Submitted by Halelly Azulay.

Halelly Azulay *is president of TalentGrow, a consulting company focused on improving the human side of work through services geared toward facilitating performance improvement. TalentGrow provides learning solutions, team building, performance improvement consulting, and coaching services. Halelly has worked with all organizational levels, from C-level and senior leaders to front-line managers and individual contributors, in corporate, government, non-profit, and educational settings. She specializes in team building, management and leadership, communication skills, coaching, and emotional intelligence.*

My Favorite Roles

Clarifier and elaborator: Gives examples, restates ideas in new ways, and interprets ideas and suggestions to clear up any confusion and to build on others' ideas and suggestions.

Consensus tester: Polls team to determine how close team members' positions are to each other.

Coordinator: Keeps records, organizes, provides structure, and plans future meetings.

Encourager: Welcomes others' ideas and opinions; is accepting of and responsive to others' perspectives; gives others an opportunity to contribute; and draws others in to achieve even participation.

Harmonizer: Emphasizes points of agreement and reconciles differences of opinion; reduces tension; uses humor appropriately; encourages group cohesion; admits errors.

Information or opinions giver: Shares relevant information, facts, data, ideas, and opinions.

Information or opinion seeker: Draws out relevant information, facts, data, ideas, and opinions from others.

Initiator: Proposes tasks and goals, suggests methods or strategies, and suggests steps to move the discussion forward.

Standards and norms setter: Establishes mutually acceptable ways of interacting within the team setting.

Summarizer: Organizes related ideas and integrates different ideas into cohesive statements; offers conclusions for the team to reflect on.

Team feelings monitor: Senses mood of team and reflects it back for discussion; shares own feelings about group processes; helps team be aware of significant shifts in tone.

My Top Five Most Common Team Behavior Roles

1.

2.

3.

4.

5.

Notes

What's Important?
Creating a Team Assessment

Activity Summary

Allows a group of people to create a team assessment tailored to the criteria they decide is most important to them.

Goals

- To provide members with an opportunity to reflect on what is most important to the team.

- To assess a team based on criteria chosen by the team members.

- To increase team ownership and likelihood of behavioral change as a result of an assessment.

Group Size

Any size team up to 20.

Time Required

Approximately 1 to 2 hours, depending on the size of the group.

Materials

- One copy of the What's Important? handout for each participant.

- Flip chart and markers.

- 3-by-3-inch Post-it® Notes.

- Pens or pencils for participants.

Physical Setting

Participants should be seated in small groups at tables to facilitate comfortable conversation (6 to 8 people per table).

Facilitating Risk Rating

Moderate.

Process

1. Introduce the activity and explain that its purpose is to assess the current state of the team by using criteria developed by the team members themselves. Distribute copies of the What's Important? handout to all participants.
   (5 minutes.)

2. Ask the participants to read the handout. Instruct them to imagine the ideal future vision of their team working well together and functioning at a very high level. Ask them to consider questions such as:

   • What would it look like?

   • How would it feel?

   • What would they accomplish?

   • How would they be viewed by their customers? By other departments in the organization?

     Ask them to take a few minutes to reflect on this image and answer the questions on the handout, paying particular attention to the third question.
   (5 to 10 minutes.)

3. If there are eight or fewer participants, do Step 4 as one group. If there are nine or more, do Step 4 in two or three smaller groups. Ideal group size is 5 to 7 people. In each group, ask people to go around and each briefly give answers to the questions. It is important to make sure all individuals have a chance to express their answers.
   (15 minutes.)

4. Have the group develop success criteria for their teams by focusing on the answers to Question 3. List "Success Criteria" at the top of a flip-chart page. Ask the group to brainstorm a list of the characteristics they think are most important in creating an ideal team. Write these on the flip chart. This step can be done by the whole group or be done in smaller groups. If you use the latter method, have the small groups create lists and then ask each group for their top three to five items. At the end of the brainstorming phase, be sure to ask whether there any critical ideas anyone has that have not made it onto the list.
(15 minutes.)

5. Consolidate the lists. Check for duplicates or overlapping ideas that can be combined. It is best to whittle the list down to the top seven to ten ideas. If necessary, use multivoting to aid in this selection. (Multivoting is a process whereby each team member has a certain number of votes [X], where X is one-third of the total number of ideas on the list. Ask all members to vote for their top X number of ideas and record their votes by putting check marks or sticky dots next to that idea on the flip chart to get a quick visual of the inclination of the whole group.) Highlight and number the success criteria selected by the team. At the end of this step, check with the group to ensure agreement on the list. Also check with the group to ensure that everyone is clear about the meaning of each success criterion. Write down the group's definitions of each if necessary.
(20 minutes.)

6. Distribute the Post-it Notes and pens or pencils to participants. Ask each person to rate the team's current performance on each of the final success criteria developed in Step 5. Use a rating scale of 1 to 10, with 1 being low and 10 being high. Have the team members write these scores on the Post-it Notes, rating only one criteria on one Post-it Note.
(10 minutes.)

7. While participants are doing Step 6, create a large table on flip-chart paper (several may be needed), with the Success Criteria on the left and a row of open boxes to the right. Have as many open boxes as there are team

members participating in the team assessment. An example could look like this:

Success Criterion	Ratings by Participants										
1. Open communication											
2. Excellent leadership											
3. Shared workload											
4. Clear direction											
5. Accounting support											
6. Respect between front and back office											
7. Good interface with the legal department											
8. High levels of trust											

In this example, there are eleven blank columns next to each Success Criterion to accommodate the rating scores of eleven participants. It is helpful to number the Success Criteria for clarity during the discussion. Tape the table to an open wall.
(10 minutes, concurrent with Step 6.)

8. Have participants go to the wall and place their rating scores (the Post-it Notes) on the table next to each criterion. This will give the group a quick visual of everyone's assessment of the team on each criteria.
(5 minutes.)

9. Ask the team for their reactions to the ratings.

- What do you notice?

- Are there discrepancies between the scores for any one item?

- What could be the cause of such discrepancies?

- Are there some criteria that are uniformly high and that need to be celebrated?

- Are there some criteria that are uniformly low and therefore need to be addressed?

10. Guide this discussion so that all participants can process their reactions and then move toward action planning. What agreements or commitments does the group want to make regarding this information? What next steps will be necessary after this meeting to ensure improvement?

Variation

If desired, the assessment can be conducted again in six to twelve months to see whether the agreed-on action steps made an improvement. In that case, the team would use the same Success Criteria developed at the first meeting and repeat only Steps 6 through 10.

Submitted by Steve Sphar.

Steve Sphar, J.D., *is an internal organization development consultant for Kaiser Permanente. He has counseled managers and employees in both the private and public sectors for over twenty years. He is a frequent contributor to professional publications, including the* Annuals *and the McGraw-Hill* Training and Performance Sourcebook.

What's Important?

It is helpful for every team to periodically take the time to reflect on how it is doing, recognize its strengths, and assess where it can improve. Please use this worksheet to reflect on your team.

Imagine the ideal future vision of your team working well together and functioning at a very high level of performance. Take a few minutes to reflect on what this would look like and answer the questions below.

1. What does your ideal team look like?

2. What makes it so successful?

3. What are its most important characteristics?

Communication Controversies
Clarifying Definitions for Improved Team Communication*

Activity Summary

A small group activity to improve team formation by encouraging individuals to share unique definitions of terms that may trigger misunderstanding.

Goals

- To be aware of various meanings of charged words in a way that improves team communication.

- To clarify meaning when having difficult conversations with others.

- To identify guidelines to avoid misunderstandings due to definitions.

Group Size

Groups of 3 to 5; easily scales to as many participants as you have.

Time Required

Approximately 60 to 75 minutes.

Materials

- Five blank index cards for each participant.

- Blank paper and writing utensils for participants.

---

*This activity is loosely based on the card game "Apples to Apples" www.otb-games.com/showcase/apples.html

- One set of five terms per team of three to five people (written on index cards or printed ahead of time).

- Small paper sacks for the sets of index cards (optional).

- Flip chart and markers.

Physical Setting

Participants will need a writing surface. Round tables for five participants work best.

Facilitating Risk Rating

Low.

Preparation

1. Depending on your topic, create a list of five words that are often used differently by different people or about which there has been controversy within the group with which you are working. This works best with words that are difficult to define and very personal. For example, if you are teaching a leadership class (see Variations for other topics), your words might be Integrity, Coaching, Feedback, Lead, and Manage.

2. Create five individual index cards, one for each of the words. (Each card should contain one word.) Build one set containing all five words for each team of three to five participants and place each set inside a paper sack.

Process

1. Divide participants into groups of three to five at tables. Distribute five blank index cards, some blank paper, and a writing utensil to each person. Give each group one sack containing the cards you have prepared.

2. Explain that they will be learning more about [topic you have chosen] through this experience. State that each person on a team will take turns being the Definer. Play begins with the person who is the oldest in that group and continues clockwise until everyone has taken a turn. Thus, if there are five team members, there will be five turns.

3. Tell the Definers to select one of the prepared word cards from the sack. The Definer should then read the word on the card out loud to the rest of his or her small group.
   (5 minutes.)

4. Next have each small group member privately write a definition for the word on a blank piece of paper. The definition must be between one and ten words and should take less than 30 seconds to write. Tell the Definers to collect the definitions and shuffle them.

5. Have Definers read each of the definitions out loud to their teams and recommend the definition he or she likes the best, explaining briefly why. Tell the groups to spend 4 to 6 minutes discussing how they felt about all the definitions and to reach agreement on a "team" definition. The Definer then should adjust the definition as the team agreed and write it on the work card drawn from the sack.
(10 minutes.)

6. Call time and have the person clockwise from the first Definer becomes the next Definer and play repeats until everyone has had a turn being the Definer.
(30 minutes.)

7. Debrief the activity by asking a spokesperson from each small group to read the definitions the team agreed on for each of its word to the whole group.

8. Continue this process with each of the other groups until all definitions have been presented.
(15 minutes.)

9. Ask the following questions about the terms:

   - How could the misunderstanding of words like these break down communication in a group?

   - Give an example of a time when someone used one of these terms and was misunderstood.

   - How did you feel when your definition was chosen? Was not chosen?

   - What occurred during the definition discussion for individual words? What was positive? What could have been handled better?

   - What guidelines can we list that would ensure we clarify meanings of words before misunderstandings occur? (Capture these on a flip-chart page.)

   - How might this be complicated when the conversation is emotionally charged? Would you have additional guidelines at these times? (Post these guidelines.)

- How can you incorporate what we have learned here into your future teamwork?

(20 minutes.)

Variations

- When teaching COMMUNICATION, consider the words Clarity, Concise, Clear, Influence, and Explain.

- When teaching SALES, consider the words Relationship, Question, Listen, Feature, and Benefit.

- When teaching TEAM BUILDING, consider the words Collaborate, Compete, Align, Empower, and Manage.

- When teaching COACHING, consider the words Reflect, Measurable, Specific, Understand, and Facts.

Submitted by Lou Russell.

Lou Russell *is president and CEO of Russell Martin & Associates, a consulting and training company focused on improving business results. Russell and her staff deliver learning experiences that are fun, flexible, fast. and measurable. She focuses on project management, leadership, and organizational learning problems. She is the author of six books on these subjects. She is a frequent contributor to many nationally recognized publications and also publishes the monthly* Learning Flash *electronic newsletter.*

Facilitime
Exploring Facilitation Techniques

Activity Summary

A role-play-based activity that allows participants to explore the concepts of effective and ineffective facilitation techniques.

Goals

- To practice effective facilitation techniques.

- To recognize and identify ineffective facilitation techniques.

- To explore the complexities and subtleties of facilitation.

Group Size

Up to four teams of three to five members each, made up of those who wish to practice facilitation skills.

Time Required

Approximately 90 minutes.

Materials

- One copy of the Facilitime: Components of Effective Facilitation for each participant.

- Blank index cards.

- A flip chart and felt-tipped markers for keeping score.

- A watch with a second hand.

- A pen or pencil for each participant.

Physical Setting

A room large enough for the groups to work without overhearing one another and enough wall space to post scores.

Facilitating Risk Rating

Moderate.

Process

1. Explain to the participants that the activity is a chance to not only demonstrate various facilitator characteristics, but also to observe others and to decide what is effective or ineffective.

2. Divide the group into small teams of three to five, then re-form the groups so that four teams are located together, but cannot overhear each other.

3. Tell the participants that each team will role play facilitation behaviors, some effective and some ineffective, and other teams within their groups will evaluate those role plays. List the following points on the flip chart and clarify them for everyone:

    - The team that is role playing will choose and demonstrate a facilitation characteristic, component, quality, or behavior at random.

    - Other teams will determine which type of behavior is being demonstrated.

    - Points will be awarded based on guessing correctly or incorrectly.

    - Each team has exactly 60 seconds to decide how they will role play the behavior or characteristic chosen, making sure the other teams cannot hear them during their planning phase.

    - When teams are ready, they will role play for the other teams in their groups.

    - At the end of each role play, each of the other teams has 30 seconds to decide whether the role play demonstrated an effective or ineffective characteristic, component, quality, or behavior and what that may be.

- Each team works independently to come up with an answer so that teams are scored separately.

  - The other teams present their answers and the role-playing team awards points as follows:

    - 1 point is awarded if a team correctly determines "effective" or "ineffective."

    - 1 point is awarded if the characteristic, component, quality, or behavior is identified correctly.
    (10 minutes.)

4. Before beginning, ask the participants whether they have any questions and review the rules and play of the game as needed.

5. Have each team take six blank index cards. As a team, they should choose three effective and three ineffective characteristics, components, qualities, or behaviors and write them on the cards, one per card. Have participants note whether the characteristic, component, quality, or behavior is effective or ineffective. *Note:* Many can be either effective or ineffective, depending on the situation.
   (10 minutes.)

6. When the cards are finished, one member of each team should collect the six cards and combine them as a draw pile face down.

7. Choose one team to begin. Play rotates clockwise after that until all four teams within a group have demonstrated two behaviors drawn at random from their card piles.

8. The winning team is the team to reach 10 points first or have the most points when 30 minutes have passed.
   (30 minutes.)

9. Lead a final processing discussion using the following questions:

   - What types of behavior was challenging during this activity? Are these a factor when you facilitate?

   - What was easy for you during this activity? When is facilitation easy for you?
   (10 minutes.)

10. Hand out the Facilitime: Components of Effective Facilitation and allow participants to read through it. Then ask the following questions:

- Which items do you resonate with and why?

- What did you learn about facilitation in general through the role plays?

- What did you learn about being an effective facilitator?

- Name one thing you will do differently the next time you facilitate based on this experience.
(20 minutes.)

Variation

Add various situations that the characteristic, component, quality, or behavior has to be applied to. For example, a situation may be: You have been asked to lead a discussion on a topic you know very little about. You would. . . .

Submitted by David Piltz.

David Piltz *is a managing partner of The Learning Key®, a company specializing in developing innovative learning solutions. He has been creating and offering programs in leadership, organizational and educational change, communication, teamwork, customer service, and personal and professional effectiveness for over thirteen years. He has developed* The House That Cards Built *and* Picture This.

Facilitime: Components of Effective Facilitation

- *Don't bring your agendas to the table.* Leave them at the door before you begin the facilitation. Remember that facilitators do not put their issues on a group.

- *It's not time to teach, but to listen.* Let the group talk. Be a facilitator who avoids taking the stage and who instead creates an environment for the group to discuss important issues.

- *Challenge and support each participant.* Instead of giving your expert advice, challenge and support the participants to develop answers themselves.

- *Ask questions from their frame of reference, not yours.* It is essential to check the assumptions you are making and realize the impact they may have on the group.

- *It's not about being the best facilitator.* Realize that your role as a facilitator is to be with the group when they need you. Facilitation is not the time to show your expertise or skills. Let the group be where they need to be, and challenge them when needed to be the best they can be.

Values Consensus
Clarifying Organizational Values

Activity Summary

A consensus-building activity designed to increase each individual's awareness and that of the entire group of the values of the organization.

Goals

- To provide group members an opportunity to clarify the values they believe are most important within the organization.

- To explore differences in values among the group members.

- To initiate the process of consensus-building within the group.

Group Size

10 to 15 members of an organization.

Time Required

Approximately 90 minutes.

Materials

- One copy of the Values Consensus Inventory for each group member.

- Pens or pencils for participants.

- A flip chart, paper, and a felt-tipped marker.

- Masking tape for posting newsprint.

Physical Setting

A room with a chair and a writing surface for each member of the planning group, plus space for group members to work in pairs or small groups. When the entire group is working together, members should be seated so that they can see each other, the facilitator, and the flip chart.

Facilitating Risk Rating

Moderate to High.

Process

1. Inform the participants that they will be exploring values held by their organization and that they will begin by working individually.

2. Give each participant a copy of the Values Consensus Inventory and a pen or pencil and ask that they each complete it individually. Inform them that they will have 5 minutes to complete this task.
   (8 minutes.)

3. After 5 minutes, tell the participants that they should pair up with someone else, share their lists, and agree on a list of the top five organizational values. State that each pair will have 5 minutes to reach consensus. Continue this process, merging pairs into quads, quads into eights, and so on, one or two more times as necessary until all participants are again in a single large group in order to come to a group consensus on the top five values of the organization. (Depending on the number of participants, you may have an odd number of people in some pairings.)
   (30 minutes.)

4. Debrief the experience with the following questions:

   - What values made it to your final list?

   - What was it like having to rank the organization's top five values?

   - How did you deal with organizational values you feel are important that were not in the top five?

   - What did you notice when you heard other participants' top-five lists? What similarities? What differences?

- What was it like gaining consensus as the group became larger?

- How can you utilize your learnings from this experience as you continue with strategic planning?
(30 minutes.)

Variation

Ask participants to select the top five values they want the organization to have in moving forward.

Submitted by Jeanette Goodstein and Leonard D. Goodstein.

Jeanette Goodstein, Ph.D., *a consultant and writer based in Washington, D.C., assists organizations in conducting a variety of research and analysis activities, focusing on needs assessment and program development and evaluation. She is co-author of* Who's Driving Your Bus?, *a book on codependency in the workplace, and developed accompanying instructional materials and assessment instruments. From 1997 through 2002, she chaired the board of directors of International Voluntary Services, a private non-profit organization dedicated to volunteer service in developing nations for nearly fifty years, and from 1997 to 2003 was a member of the board of the Washington, D.C., chapter of Young Audiences.*

Leonard D. Goodstein, Ph.D., *is an independent consulting psychologist based in Washington, D.C., with considerable experience in facilitating the Applied Strategic Planning process. His research interests are in the influence of values and culture on organizations and in psychological assessment. He formerly was CEO and executive vice president of the American Psychological Association and CEO of University Associates (now Pfeiffer). He previously held a variety of academic positions, including professorships at the Universities of Iowa, Cincinnati, and Arizona State, where he also served as department chair. He is a frequent contributor to the professional literature, including the Pfeiffer Annuals. His most recent book, co-authored with Erich P. Prien,* Individual Assessment in the Workplace: A Practical Guide for HR Professionals, Trainers, and Managers *was published by Pfeiffer in 2006.*

Values Consensus Inventory

Values are enduring beliefs about the proper course of behavior—about what is *right* and what is *wrong*. These beliefs are thus the basis for almost all of our important decisions and for the setting of our priorities. Values provide us with the rules of the game. And values exist on both the individual and organizational levels.

Organizational values develop from two sources: first, the values of the individual members of the organization, especially those involved early in the organization's history, and second, the history of the organization—both the challenges and problems encountered and how they were addressed or what is believed to account for the organization's success or lack of success.

Although organizational values play a critical role in the ongoing life of the organization and affect its choices and decisions, they are often covert and difficult for members of the organization to articulate. Given the importance of these values, deliberately identifying the central organizational values provides a basis for discussing them and evaluating their relevance in the current environment.

The following is a list of values that organizations hold. Your task is to select from the list the *five* values that you believe are the most important to *your* organization. Rank them 1 through 5, with 1 being the most important. Leave the others blank.

_____ ACCOUNTABILITY: Holding organizational members responsible for actions and results.

_____ ADVANCEMENT: Emphasizing moving upward, accepting increased responsibilities.

_____ BALANCE: Maintaining evenness of focus and priorities; balance of work and family.

_____ COMPETITION: Beating competitors; challenging competition.

_____ CITIZENSHIP: Intentionally helping to improve the community.

_____ COOPERATION: Working well with others, avoiding conflict, and compromising.

_____ CREATIVITY: Being imaginative, innovative, bringing new ideas to fruition.

_____ CUSTOMER SERVICE: Putting customers first.

_____ DIVERSITY: Working to achieve and valuing a diverse workforce.

_____ ECONOMIC SECURITY: Providing steady, adequate income; long-term financial support.

_____ EQUALITY: Believing that all people are created equal; ensuring fairness and equal opportunity.

_____ FUN: Intentionally providing for enjoyable experiences, having fun.

_____ HEALTH: Encouraging physical and mental fitness.

_____ HELPFULNESS: Providing guidance and assistance to those in need.

_____ IMAGE: Being well regarded; seen as a leading organization.

_____ INTEGRITY: Meeting high ethical standards; having integrity.

_____ LEADERSHIP: Taking the front position; expecting others will follow.

_____ LOYALTY: Demonstrating long-term support, trustworthiness, and obedience.

_____ PERSONAL DEVELOPMENT: Encouraging learning and development of new skills; expecting employees to improve.

_____ PROFIT: Focusing directly on the bottom line; continual focus on making money.

_____ QUALITY: Committing to zero defects and to doing it right the first time.

_____ RESPECT: Showing recognition and admiration for others.

_____ RESULTS: Meeting business expectations and targets.

_____ RISK TAKING: Rewarding experimentation and trying new things, new ventures.

_____ SAFETY: Assuring safety, providing protection.

_____ SPIRITUALITY: Emphasizing religious beliefs.

_____ TEAMWORK: Using a team approach and rewarding team players.

Please add any values below that you feel are missing and include them in your ranking.

Introduction
to the Editor's Choice Section

Unfortunately, in the past we have had to reject exceptional ideas that did not meet the criteria of one of the sections or did not fit into one of our categories. So we recently created an Editor's Choice Section that allows us to publish unique items that are useful to the profession rather than turn them down. This collection of contributions simply does not fit in one of the other three sections: Experiential Learning Activities; Inventories, Questionnaires, and Surveys; or Articles and Discussion Resources.

Based on the reason for creating this section, it is difficult to predict what you may find. You may anticipate a potpourri of topics, a variety of formats, and an assortment of categories. Some may be directly related to the training and consulting fields, and others may be related tangentially. Some may be obvious additions, and others may not. What you are sure to find is something you may not have expected but that will contribute to your growth and stretch your thinking. Suffice it to say that this section will provide you with a variety of useful ideas, practical strategies, and creative ways to look at the world. The material will add innovation to your training and consulting knowledge and skills. The contributions will challenge you to think differently, consider a new perspective, and add information you may not have considered before. The section will stretch your view of training and consulting topics.

The 2009 Pfeiffer Annual: Consulting includes two editor's choice selections. Keep in mind the purpose for this section—good ideas that don't fit in the other sections. The submissions by Audry Ellison and Kris Taylor are perfect examples of items that are valuable to the readers of the *Consulting Annual*, but simply do not fit in any of the other categories.

Article

Engineered Experiences and Their Influence on Customer Retention, by Audrey Ellison

Checklist

Organizational Change Checklist, by Kris Taylor

Engineered Experiences and Their Influence on Customer Retention

Audrey Ellison

Summary

Service quality is a critical area of marketing research; however, marketers continue to focus on mass marketing and do not consider the value of one customer. Customer relationship management (CRM) has become increasingly important in the service economy. CRM strategy can improve and manage customer relationships more efficiently by integrating technology and decision making. "Experience engineering" puts the customer experience at the core of doing business by creating a total experience and an emotional connection for the customer. The power and promise of customer experiences remains an abstract and untapped value for most companies (personal communication, Lewis Carbone, November 2, 2005). A strategic customer-centric approach can increase the profitability of an organization.

To participate in competitive marketplaces, organizations need to understand their customers and create value (Berry, Carbone, & Haeckel, 2002). Organizations must go beyond providing quality products and services to managing customer requirements systematically and to engineering customer experiences. This requires understanding customer needs (Haeckel, Carbone, & Berry, 2003). Loyalty is the fuel that drives financial success, especially in today's volatile economy, and can build a sustainable competitive advantage by creating enduring relationships, built on trust between employees and customers (Reichheld, 2001). The ability to build these relationships has become a differentiator for organizational success.

Experience engineering is less researched than CRM. The experience engineering construct explores CRM at a different level by using CRM data to create customer experiences. Designing and orchestrating customer experiences requires senior management commitment and a systematic approach (Berry, Wall, & Carbone, 2006). Service providers must be armed with customer experience clues in the areas of function (the quality of the service experience), mechanics (the sights, sounds, or sensory clues), and humanics (the behavior/appearance of service providers) (Haeckel, Carbone, & Berry, 2003). They need to understand these customer experience clues to effectively respond to customer needs and to create experiences based on these emotional and functional needs (Berry, Carbone, & Haeckel, 2002).

Services and products are dissimilar, as service is experienced and requires an opposite view of conventional product marketing practices (Shostack, 1977). In the 1980s, delivering quality services became a marketing priority for research and practitioner implementation. Service marketing faced different problems and required different strategies than goods marketing did (Zeithaml, Parasuraman, & Berry, 1985). The rationale for the separate treatment of services marketing is explained by the abstract characteristics of intangibility, inseparability of production and consumption, heterogeneity, and perishability (Zeithaml, Parasuraman, & Berry, 1985). The characteristics are defined as follows:

- Intangibility is service as performances rather than objects.

- Inseparability of production and consumption involves services being produced after being sold rather than before as with goods.

- Heterogeneity concerns the high variability in services.

- Perishability means services cannot be saved.

                                                    (Zeithaml, Parasuraman, & Berry, 1985)

These unique characteristics create the need for specific strategies. Despite the wealth of research conducted on consumer behavior, it is still difficult to capture the depth and meaning of consumers' thoughts, as they are not always aware of their thoughts (Zaltman, 2003). Most practitioners have no idea why customers behave as they do (Carbone, 2003).

Service Quality

As we have just discussed, service and product knowledge are inherently different and cannot be gained in the same way. The American Customer Satisfaction Index found a greater customer satisfaction for goods than for services and firms with a high ACSI such as Southwest Airlines and Wal-Mart developed difficult-to-imitate customer strategies (Fornell, Johnson, Anderson, Cha, & Bryant, 1996).

Delivering consistently good service quality is difficult because service firms may not always understand what high quality means to their customers, what attributes of service are needed to meet customer needs, and what levels of performance are necessary to delivery high-quality service. Consumers reach satisfaction decisions by comparing performance with different expectations for different products and services (Bitner, 1990). If expectations exceed performance, dissatisfaction occurs, and if performance exceeds expectations, satisfaction occurs. The implications of the study included the importance of managing and controlling every service encounter to enhance the perception of service quality. Customer service is an important component of the marketing mix.

Service quality relates to the retention of customers and the customers' behavioral responses at the aggregate level (Zeithaml, Berry, & Parasuraman, 1996). The research found customers being influenced by service quality and the decision to remain or defect, and it indicates that customer longevity has a direct impact on profitability. Research has also established a link between service quality and customer referrals. The overall findings indicate improving service quality can increase positive customer behavior and decrease unfavorable behavior. The findings demonstrate the importance of developing strategies to meet customers' desired level of service rather than performing at adequate levels (Zeithaml, Berry, & Parasuraman, 1996).

It is a holistic approach to gathering data and managing relationships. Marketing first wanted more data on customers to segment customers and markets, but as segmentation became a minimum required for doing business, organizations began to look more deeply into their customers' wants, needs, and preferences. Customer experiences have a powerful impact on positive or negative brand equity, and human performance plays the most critical role in brand building (Berry, 2002). Strong service brands reach customers on an emotional level. Service providers influence brand perception. Brand advertising influences employees; employees create the customer experience. For long-term brand success, the direct actions of employees, individualized to match customer expectations, serve to impact customer experience. Thus, organizations need to win not only the hearts and minds of customers but also of employees, and this is enhanced by the internal cultural experiences of employees (Leavy & Gannon, 1998). Relationship marketing has been explored as an alternative paradigm to service quality (Palmer, Lindgreen, & Vanhamme, 2005). The role of relationship marketing is to identify, establish, maintain, and enhance relationships with customers through a mutual exchange of promises (Palmer, Lindgreen, & Vanhamme, 2005). The integration of service quality and relationship marketing needs further exploration and research.

Studies have explored the link between service recovery, customer satisfaction and loyalty. When customers think they have been treated unfairly, their reactions tend to be immediate, emotional, and enduring (Seiders & Barry, 1990). Customer service recovery expectations increase based on the level of service failure. A poor service recovery effort will further damage the relationship with the customer. The recovery should be aligned with the severity of the failure; over-responding can be as detrimental to the relationship as under-responding (Hess, Ganesan, & Klein, 2003).

Customer Relationship Management (CRM)

Most organizations recognize the importance of developing good relationships with customers, but are not clear about how effective relationships can be developed or what the appropriate level of contact is (Bearden, Malhotra, & Uscategui, 1998). A CRM strategy can improve and manage customer relationships more efficiently by integrating technology and decision making. It is not a quick pill or magic bullet; rather, it helps organizations focus on a problem and deliver results based on customer needs. CRM helps tie together all of the organizational silos of data and integrate them into a common data source. CRM is important because, when an organization can turn data into information and knowledge, it can deliver customer value and realize bottom-line results. Customer information for decision making is the reason CRM has become a powerful tool in organizations. Employees are a powerful element in helping an organization differentiate, gain competitive advantage, and deliver value to customers (Judd, 2003). Judd posits the need to include "people power" in marketing. Knowledge about customers can help an organization sell more products and services more efficiently, and CRM creates an integration of technology and business processes to satisfy customer needs and improve results.

Mass customization has become more prevalent in the literature than mass marketing. Mass customization is possible because of CRM. Realizing the lifetime value of a customer has moved organizations to become more customer-centric. CRM is a systematic approach to a customer-centric strategy. Technology enables customer-centric environments, in which an individual customer's preferences are more important than the marketing mix. Transforming a business into a customer-centric enterprise requires an integrated process approach to drive revenue and profitability.

The Internet is a source for CRM data. Integrating the Internet and database marketing can improve CRM. Most organizations utilize active and passive customer data gathered on the Internet. However, actively supplied data provides a better understanding of customer needs and makes it easier for organizations to include permission-based email marketing in the strategy. However, it is critical for customers and prospects to know their data is private and secure. The organizational culture and commitment to Internet/database marketing enables marketers to target the most valued customers/prospects and to target offerings to identified needs. Internet/database marketing strategies can improve CRM through segmenting customers, cross-marketing, prospecting for new customers, retaining customers, one-to-one marketing, promoting or advertising, building customer loyalty, affiliate marketing and stealth marketing. Marketing strategies provide feedback, which allows the organization to fully incorporate customers into the value chain. Optimization technology continually adds new intelligent dimensions to CRM. The technology is emerging and evolving.

CRM and database management are not the same thing. CRM tends to be more externally driven, whereas DBM is more internally driven. Database management has become a business requirement, but merely collecting data can be a waste of resources, whereas CRM can be a differentiator (Cannon, 2002).

However, both CRM and DBM are designed to help organizations make better business decisions to impact profitability. Organizations invest in CRM in order to discriminate between profitable and unprofitable customers by providing customized services (Jaychandran, Sharma, Kaufman, & Raman, 2005). Relationship marketing is based on discovering and capitalizing on the shared interests of the customer and the organization. CRM provides a vehicle for sharing information. Creating a system guided by market intelligence that is accessible to relevant functions such as sales, customer service, and marketing require IT solutions (Jaychandran, Sharma, Kaufman, & Raman, 2005). The business applications for CRM communications with customers and prospects include cross-selling, upselling, retaining customers, and implementing service recovery.

The ultimate goal is to make CRM information available 24/7 to all organizational stakeholders with an interest in using CRM, to make it available on desktops, laptops, personal digital assistants (PDA), or cell phones. We want real-time solutions, quickly. In our high-tech, high-concept society, technology is no longer enough (Pink, 2005). Customers want high-touch marketing with high-tech approaches, which requires multiple touch points. Customers are motivated to buy more when kept informed. Customer interaction improves the relation and impact buyer behavior/purchasing intentions.

There are four steps to enabling CRM and building relationships to acquire, retain, and maximize customer value (O'Leary, Rao, & Perry, 2004).

1. Identifying customers, capturing and storing data, presenting it in a usable format and using technology effectively;

2. Differentiating between customers to build an understanding of similarities and differences. This requires a supportive organizational culture and a clear understanding of customers and data analysis;

3. Interacting with customers, which requires flexibility to store and respond to customer information, capability to handle customer relationships

individually, demonstration of benefits of sharing information, and ability to interact with customer data on a large scale; and

4. Customizing in order to meet the individual needs of customers and become customer-centric. It requires updating information continually, responding to customer needs, and creating tangible rewards for customers.

Their findings indicate that the Internet has not yet fulfilled its potential as a source of customer data for decision making.

Information processes and technology play a vital role in implementing CRM, however technology does not always deliver the desired results (Jayachandran, Sharma, Kaufman, & Raman, 2005). Organizations should use CRM technology to enhance the effectiveness of informational processes. While CRM is not a panacea, the technology can help to improve performance when a multi-stage approach is implemented. CRM can assist managers in making good decisions, even if it is not a replacement for traditional decision making. The challenge for organizations with CRM is that interpreting customer preference and market effectiveness data is sometimes considered "soft" data. CRM technology enables organizations to communicate better with customers and to help customers manage their own needs more effectively. Important goals for CRM are to allow decision-makers to discriminate between profitable and unprofitable customers, provide customized services, and improve customer retention. Decision-makers are motivated by the belief that information enables businesses to make better decisions and realize better returns.

CRM is a major investment for an organization, and it needs to be able to prove its worth by focusing on problem solving and delivering business results. CRM systems have to be able to achieve results better, faster, and cheaper. CRM should not be considered a tool or technology, but rather a business practice that utilizes technology and capitalizes on integrating human decision making with information. CRM means offering customers products and services with confidence. CRM is delivering marketing messages to customers efficiently and effectively.

Experience Engineering

In service environments, customers rely on clues to help evaluate the quality of the service (Bitner, 1990; Shostack, 1977). The physical environment impacts customers and employees in service organizations and influences their interactions. Customers "take away" an impression from each service encounter based on the barrage of clues that becomes the customer experience (Carbone & Haeckel, 1994). Customer responses to service designs are impacted by the length, nature, and quality of customers' prior experiences with the organization. Engineered experiences are a deliberate setting of the customer perception by systematically designing and orchestrating the signals customers receive (Carbone & Haeckel, 1994). It puts the customer experience at the core of doing business. It creates a total experience and emotional connection for the customer. Organizations systematically manage the customer experience by addressing the areas of function, mechanics, and humanics, as described earlier in this article (Haeckel, Carbone, & Berry, 2003). The total customer experience from before the experience to after experience needs to be managed and engineered for all customers to create superior value and improve business results.

Managing the total experience becomes a difficult to match competitive advantage (Berry, Carbone, & Haeckel, 2002). The difficulty is in distinguishing between fulfilling minimum requirements and providing value-enhancing services that will impact the bottom line. Creating value for customers means developing an emotional bond with customers by applying the tools of customer-experience management, which influence loyalty. Loyal customer are less likely to change suppliers and more likely to continue doing business with an organization (Berry, Carbone, & Haeckel, 2002). Experience engineering focuses on managing customer expectations by understanding customer clues and delivering total customer experiences to orchestrate stronger customer preferences. The customer experience becomes the service and the marketing strategy (Berry, Carbone, & Haeckel, 2002). Customers' experiences create emotional reactions to the service, such as pleasure, disappointment, frustration, or infuriation (Berry & Lampo, 2004).

Engineering the total customer experience requires focusing the entire organization on a common goal of creating an integrated and aligned customer feeling. It requires focusing on all of the customers' senses to create an emotional connection to the organization. The organization needs to understand what the customer is seeing and feeling. Rather than focusing on brand messages and images, experience engineering focuses on the brand as an experience (Haeckel, Carbone, & Barry, 2003). The first step is recognizing the clues being transmitted to customers and then building new competencies around the emotional components of the experience.

Much as organizations conduct financial or marketing audits, experience engineering needs an audit process. Engineering customer experiences may mean re-engineering business processes to focus on the customer experience to foster the emotional bond between the organization and the customer (Berry, Carbone, & Haeckel, 2002). The systematic and holistic approach of experience engineering makes it difficult for competitors to emulate.

While the area of experience engineering has been studied from a business perspective, it is relatively unstudied in empirical research. The area of "mechanic" clues provides an opportunity for additional research to help practitioners understand what changes will make a difference to customers and how they will influence retention behavior.

Examples of Engineered Experiences

Starbucks' third destination strategy (home, office, Starbucks) has an engineered component. Starbucks is more about the destination than the coffee. The comfortable couches, the music, the aromas, and the greeting are all engineered experiences. Disney knows where a car is parked based on arrival time (useful because so many people forget where they park). The view and the smells as you walk into the theme parks are engineered. The colors of fast-food restaurants are bright and lively to encourage faster eating, while the soft colors found in fine-dining restaurants slow down the pace. After the recent airplane restrictions on liquid carry-on items, car rental companies placed toiletries on the seats of the cars and hotels provided more toiletry items than in the past. The rental car companies that allow frequent customers to bypass the desk and go directly to the car are engineered experiences. The aisles in some stores are larger than in other stores and lighting can be different, which provides different "clues" to the customers.

It is important to understand the impact and influence of the clues on the customer experience and on customer retention. The physical environment needs to be designed and managed for optimal results. However, the humanic clues must be aligned with the mechanic clues to create positive customer experiences. The customer experience is the total sum of all the mechanic clues, which need to deliver a consistent message. The mechanic and humanic clues need to align with the marketing strategy to encourage customer loyalty behaviors.

Retention

The value a customer delivers to an organization over time is aligned with customer retention. Lowering customer defection rates and increasing longevity can positively impact profitability (Zeithaml, Barry, & Parasuraman, 1996). However, the links among quality, retention, and profits is not direct. The difficulty is distinguishing between fulfilling minimum requirements and providing value-enhancing services, which will impact the bottom line (Brandt, 1988). Creating value for customers can also mean developing an emotional bond with customers by applying the tools of customer-experience management, which influences loyalty. Loyal customer are less likely to change suppliers and more likely to continue doing business with an organization (Berry, Carbone, & Haeckel, 2002).

Studies have explored the relationship between customers and profitability. By tailoring services to a customer's profitability level, organizations can make their customer base more profitable. Customers leave organizations due to service failures; thus, organizations need to develop service systems to prevent customers from switching (Keveaney, 1995). Raising retention rates by 5 percent can increase customer value by 25 to 100 percent (Reichheld, 2001). The key to customer retention is customer satisfaction, and satisfied customers stay longer, talk favorably, pay less attention to the competition, are less price sensitive, offer new ideas, and cost less to service than do new customers.

Retention behaviors, including repeat business and referrals, impact long-term profitability. By maintaining loyal customers and providing extraordinary service, customer retention becomes more likely. Loyal customers equate to improved business performance and increased shareholder value. It is projected that, by engineering customer experiences, organizations can develop the loyalty behaviors that lead to increased retention and thereby increased profitability.

Delivering Customer Experiences

Business and academic literature support service quality as a significant differentiator and a powerful competitive weapon. Many leading organizations strive for superior service quality to attain customer loyalty. In approximately fifty years, the economy has moved from industrial to technology-based to knowledge-based, making service quality a prerequisite for business success and survival.

Long-term success in service marketing depends on how successfully customer expectations can be managed, satisfied, and exceeded. Because customer expectations evolve over time. Something that adds value today could become a minimum requirement tomorrow. Customer relationship management (CRM) has become increasingly important in a service economy. Delivering consistently good service quality is difficult because service firms may not always understand what high quality means to their customers, what attributes of service are needed to meet customer needs, and what levels of performance are necessary to delivery high-quality service.

Engineered customer experiences is an emerging set of principles and disciplines to manage customer value. Organizations create customer experiences, either intentionally or unintentionally. However, those that take a structured and disciplined approach to creating positive experiences will have a competitive advantage over those with a haphazard approach. The tangible attributes of a product or service have less influence on consumer preference than the unconscious sensory and emotional elements derived from the total experience. While practitioners continue to focus on building the brand to differentiate and build customer loyalty, managed experiences create a new paradigm for competitive advantage. Positive experiences make it more difficult for the competition to copy and commoditize services.

Organizations should look at what strategies and activities impact their customers and profitability. One of the ongoing challenges is establishing metrics for customer-focused performance. Better indicators and measures will help organizations to allocate resources for maximum impact on shareholder value. As organizations continue to cut budgets, they are going to want more value for their investments and more accountability from their people. Determining the right levers and selecting the right options to maximize resources and performance has to be further explored. Establishing long-term relationships with valued customers to increase profitability will differentiate the successful company from the unsuccessful company. It will require more of a return on activities and metrics for financial outcomes. This interrelationship among employee, customer, and shareholder value appears to be the unanswered paradox of the three.

Academics have researched and studied service quality and customer relationship management. Practitioners understand the importance of the customer relationship. However, organizations are not always obtaining desired results from their initiatives, so maximizing customer value continues to be a challenge. As customers continue to be more knowledgeable and demanding, it becomes more critical to find a way to create real value for customers and to differentiate based on services or engineered experiences.

Conclusion

Engineering the total customer experience creates superior value for the customer. A systematic approach is required to optimize customer value (Haeckel, Carbone, & Berry, 2003). It could involve things like special events or rewards to enhance brand loyalty by developing a synergistic approach to understanding customers' needs, wants, and expectations. Services and service quality can be customized. Flexibility and value-added services are often a component in engineering the experience. The experience is as branded as the products and services offered. At this level, customers are observed using the products and services to understand how and why they are used. Customers may become part of new product and service development teams. Customers may sit on advisory boards. Customers may be willing to recommend products and services to other high-level colleagues. When they are happy, customers have an emotional attachment to the relationship, making it harder for the competition to gain access. Every customer experience that is managed for maximum impact will lead to better results. Specially selected trained service providers can be made available at all times for customers. Service providers can be rewarded based on the entire customer experience. For good results, leadership, management, and employees must be in alignment on the organization's customer strategy, which will result in better business outcomes and increased customer retention.

References

Bearden, W.O., Malhotra, M.K., & Uscategui, K.H. (1998, December). Customer contact and the evaluation of service experiences: Propositions and implications for the design of service. *Psychology and Marketing, 15*, 783–809.

Berry, L.L. (2002). Cultivating service brand equity. *Journal of Marketing, 28*(1) 128–137.

Berry, L.L., Carbone, L.P., & Haeckel, S.H. (2002, Spring). Managing the total customer experience. *Sloan Management Review, 43*, 85–89.

Berry, L.L., & Lampo, S.S. (2004). Branding labor-intensive services. *Business Strategy Review, 15*(1), 18–25.

Bitner, M.J. (1990, April). Evaluating service encounters: The effects of physical surroundings and employee responses. *Journal of Marketing, 54*, 69–82.

Brandt, D.R. (1988, Summer). How service marketers can identify value-enhancing service elements. *Journal of Services Marketing, 2*, 35–41.

Cannon, D.A. (2002). The ethics of database management. *Information Management Journal, 36*(3), 42–44.

Carbone, L.P. (2003). What makes customers tick? *Marketing Management, 12*(4) 23–27.

Carbone, L.P., & Haeckel, S.H.(1994). Engineering customer experiences. *Marketing Management, 3*(3), 9–19.

Fornell, C., Johnson, M.D., Anderson, E.W., Cha, J. & Bryant, B.E. (1996, October). The American customer satisfaction index: Nature, purpose and findings. *Journal of Marketing, 60*, 7–18.

Haeckel, S.H., Carbone, L.P., & Berry, L.L. (2003, January/February). How to lead the customer experience. *Marketing Management, 12*, 18–23.

Hess, R., Jr., Ganesan, S., & Klein, N.M. (2003, Spring). Service failure and recovery: The impact of relationship factors on customer satisfaction. *Journal of Academy of Marketing Science, 31*.

Jayachandran, S., Sharma, S., Kaufman, P., & Raman, P. (2005, October). The role of rational information process and technology use in customer relationship management. *Journal of Marketing, 69*, 177–192.

Judd, V.C. (2003). Achieving a customer orientation using "people-power," the "5th P." *European Journal of Marketing, 37*(10), 1301–1313.

Keaveney, S.M. (1995, April). Customer switching behavior in service industries: An exploratory study. *Journal of Marketing, 59*, 71–83.

Leavy, B., & Gannon, M. (1998). Competing for hearts and minds: A corporate cultural perspective on marketing. *Irish Journal of Marketing, 11*(1), 39–48.

O'Leary, C., Rao, S., & Perry, C. (2004). Improving customer relationship management through database/Internet marketing: A theory-building action research project. *Journal of Database Marketing, 9*(2), 185–191.

Palmer, R., Lindgreen, A., & Vanhamme, J. (2005). Relationship marketing: Schools of thought and future research directions. *Marketing Intelligence & Planning, 23*(3), 313–330.

Pink, D. (2005). *A whole new mind: Moving from the information age to the conceptual age.* New York: Riverhead/Penguin.

Reichheld, F. (2001) *Loyalty rules!: How today's business leaders build lasting relationships.* Cambridge, MA: Harvard Business School Press.

Seiders, K., & Berry, L.L. (1990). Service fairness: What it is and why it matters. *Academy of Management Executive, 12*(2), 8–20.

Shostack, L.G. (1977, April). Breaking free of product marketing. *Journal of Marketing, 41*, 73–80.

Zaltman, G.(2003). *How customers think: Essential insights into the mind of the market.* Cambridge, MA: Harvard Business School Press.

Zeithaml, V.A., Berry, L.L., & Parasuraman, A. (1996, April). The behavioral consequences of service quality. *Journal of Marketing, 60*, 31–46.

Zeithaml, V.A., Parasuraman, A., & Berry, L.L. (1985, Spring). Problems and strategies in services marketing. *Journal of Marketing, 49*, 33–46.

Audrey Ellison *has twenty-five years of marketing and management experience working with organizations to develop and implement internal and external strategies. She teaches marketing and management courses at the University of Phoenix, West Florida University, and Nova Southeastern University, Tampa, Florida. She also teaches online and blended learning classes. She holds an MBA from Simmons College, a master's of library science and a B.S. in history from Southern Connecticut University. She is currently working on her DBA in marketing at Nova Southeastern University.*

Organizational Change Checklist

Kris Taylor

Summary

This article presents the use of an organizational change checklist that provides learning and performance professionals, HR professional, consultants, and organizational leaders with a tool to assess areas of strength and weakness in their existing change management approach. In addition to being used as a diagnostic tool, the checklist can be used as a planning tool in the early stages of a project or proposed organizational change to ensure a balanced and focused change effort.

Organizations have always had to change and adapt to remain viable and healthy. However, the pace of change experienced by organizations today is unprecedented. Organizations that are unable to change quickly in response to their environment fail. Yet, organizational change is difficult and organizations often find that the needed changes fail. Many times the failed effort is not due to the mechanics of the project. The software can work, the merger has been completed, the ERP is up and running, the new equipment is installed and working—yet efforts can fail due to lack of engagement, buy-in, and support from employees.

Failures can be absolute, in which case nothing changes after the expenditure of large amounts of time, money, and effort. Change efforts can also be stalled or take much longer than anticipated, resulting in more time, money, and effort than originally budgeted. And many times, the change can be implemented at a suboptimal level so that the desired results are evident, but in a lesser degree than anticipated. Too often, change efforts are planned and executed without heed to incorporating actions to build awareness, engagement, and buy-in of the people who are impacted by the change and ultimately must adopt and execute the change day-to-day. The projects or initiatives that require time for a thoughtful and purposeful approach experience a higher success rate for implementation and reduced time to adoption and are likely to more fully realize the benefits of the change.

An organization can take many steps to increase the likelihood of a successful change effort. Ideally, these are planned in the early stages of a project or initiative. The Organizational Change Checklist below provides a diagnostic tool to increase the likelihood of adaptation and success of a change effort.

Description of the Checklist

The Organizational Change Checklist provides a way to quickly diagnose the extent to which key actions for a change initiative are being planned for and executed with key stakeholders. The checklist has sixteen items, rated on a Likert scale from "not at all" to "very much." The sixteen items are organized into four groupings: Purpose, Plan, Picture, and Participation. Each area has four items describing key elements and actions that, if in place and executed, increase the likelihood of a successful change effort. The checklist can be used as a planning tool in the early stages of a change project or in the mid stages to identify areas in which additional effort and focus are needed. The tool is designed to be used with a specific change initiative in mind.

Theory Behind the Checklist

The organizational structure of the instrument (Purpose, Plan, Picture, and Participation) is adapted from William Bridges' (2003) *Managing Transitions: Making the Most of Change.* Bridges identifies four necessary categories for successful change efforts:

1. Clarity about the *purpose* of the change;

2. A well-defined *plan* for the change that helps stakeholders understand the timing of the change from their perspective and how and when they will be involved;

3. A *picture* in people's minds of what the change will look and feel like; and

4. Everyone having a role to play, which will build engagement and buy-in through *participation.*

The individual items under each category have been compiled from best practices in the field of change and transition management. The items are not meant to be an inclusive outline of the change management actions that are possible or may be needed, but provide an overview of many common and powerful actions organizational leaders can implement during a period of change.

Presenting the Checklist

The checklist is designed to be used with a specific change initiative in mind. Ideally, it will be completed by a group of people who are leading the change project or are ultimately responsible for seeing that the change project is successfully implemented. One person with change management expertise should be responsible for facilitating the session and guiding the use of the checklist. It should be administered in a group setting and followed by a discussion of individual results and agreement on areas of opportunity, as well as action planning based on the results. The checklist is best administered in the planning stages of a project, although it can also be used as a diagnostic tool later in a project to identify areas of strengths and challenges in the existing change management efforts.

In the meeting in which the instrument will be used, participants should be informed that they will be using a checklist to assess their overall approach to a specific change initiative. The facilitator should emphasize the following points:

- The purpose is to gain a realistic assessment of the current state of the organization, with the overall goal being a successful change effort.

- The instrument and consequent group discussion will help the group to identify the overall strength, depth, and breadth of their change management efforts.

- The accuracy of the results and their impact on the subsequent actions to be taken are dependent on truth and candor, even if the current state is less than desired.

- Each person brings a unique perspective to the questions. The group members must honor and respect one another's viewpoints.

Provide the group approximately ten minutes to complete the checklist independently. Be available to answer questions about specific terms and concepts.

Debriefing the Results

Once individuals have completed the checklist, debrief the findings and lead a group discussion to build deeper understanding of the current state, the desired next steps, and action items.

Begin by asking for general reactions and insights. Once the group has shared their initial reactions, begin to structure the feedback. Start by creating a list of the areas in which change management efforts were identified as in place and strong.

These will be the areas that individuals marked as "very much" or are to the right of the Likert scale. List these areas on a flip chart or whiteboard. Determine whether there is agreement on the items or whether anyone has a different perspective. If so, facilitate a group discussion on why there are varying perspectives. The goal of this discussion is not to come to agreement about what the scores say, but to uncover areas of the organization that have differing levels of change management focus. For example, one part of the organization may have key leaders who support the change in words and actions; others may not. By surfacing this difference, the organization may be able to reinforce and recognize the leaders who are supporting the change and coach and assist those who are not.

On a separate flip chart, list the areas that people scored lower or toward the "not at all" side. Again, discuss the areas in which there is varying feedback in order to come to a deeper understanding of the organizational dynamics, rather than consensus.

Next, ask the group to identify the critical actions they need to take for the specific change effort. Create a list of action steps the group would like to implement that will better position this particular change for success. It may be that some items are not being done at all. It also may be that some items are only marginally in place and need to be strengthened. For example, perhaps several key milestones were celebrated early in the change project, but lately milestones have been passed unnoticed. The group may decide that reviving the milestone celebrations is important.

Note that the degree of importance for each item is highly dependent on the specific organization and on the change it faces. In a leader-centric organization, having an engaged executive sponsor and key leaders who visibly support the change may be the most important element, and consequently be where the most time and focus should be. Some organizational changes are precipitated by a clearly obvious and highly visible need to change, and consequently, little effort has to be spent on helping stakeholders understand the need to change.

Once the list of specific change management actions is agreed on, help the group complete an action plan that lists action step and deliverable outcomes, the persons responsible, the resources needed to support the action, and either a date for completion or for a progress check-in date.

Interpreting the Results

The Organizational Change Checklist can be used as either a diagnostic or planning tool to facilitate awareness and discussion about key change management actions. Thus, there is neither a passing nor failing score. Ideally, a change effort would show activity in all four of the focus areas. Also ideally, that activity should be well planned and executed across all parts of the organization that are impacted by the change. Concern should be raised if there are no organizational change efforts at all—or only marginal efforts. Additionally, a clear lack of activity in any of the focus areas would highlight the need for additional action. For example, there may be strong scores in the participation area, but the checklist may indicate no activity in the planning area. Without a solid plan, the change effort will be fragmented and the direction unclear, leading to frustration, confusion, and a failed change effort. Conversely, an organization may have a painstakingly detailed project plan; but without widespread participation across stakeholder groups, the chances that the change will be realized are diminished.

By using the Organizational Change Checklist across the organization, one can determine whether there is disparate change management activity. One area of the organization may have solid participation and involvement, and another area may have much less. These discrepancies present opportunities to determine where to focus specific activities and actions. Areas in which change management is weak may require education, encouragement, support, and/or a person accountable.

Reliability and Validity

The Organizational Change Checklist is designed to aid organizational planning and provide a format for organizational leaders to examine their change management efforts. The results indicate only the perceptions of the respondents. Additionally, change efforts are very dynamic, and the data generated on the Organizational Change Checklist has applicability only for the time period in which it was filled out. This instrument was designed solely for planning, educational, and organizational development purposes. No correlation exists between items and a successful change outcome. It is reasonable to expect that organizational change efforts that are engaging stakeholders in all four areas of the checklist will be more likely to implement change more successfully; however, many other variables, both internal and external, impact the outcome.

Reference

Bridges, W. (2003). *Managing transitions: Making the most of changes.* Reading, MA: Addison–Wesley.

Kris Taylor, CPLP, SPHR, *is the president of K. Taylor & Associates, a consulting group that helps organizations successfully navigate the human side of strategically oriented change. She has twenty-seven years' experience in organizational change and development, learning, training, and human resources. K. Taylor & Associates provides change management services for large-scale organizational changes, including ERP and technology implementations, cultural changes, and enhancing the learning and development function.*

Organizational Change Checklist

Kris Taylor

Organization:

Description of change:

	Not At All		Very Much	
Purpose				
1. Is there a documented business case for change?	☐	☐	☐	☐
2. Is there leadership alignment on the need for change?	☐	☐	☐	☐
3. Has the implications of *not* changing been documented?	☐	☐	☐	☐
4. Does the change have an engaged executive sponsor?	☐	☐	☐	☐
Plan				
5. Is there an overall plan and roadmap for the change?	☐	☐	☐	☐
6. Are regular progress checks held with a leadership body?	☐	☐	☐	☐
7. Have potential risks to the project been identified? And are plans in place to mitigate them?	☐	☐	☐	☐
8. Are plans in place for the impact to people (training, communication, job changes, performance management, rewards, and retention)?	☐	☐	☐	☐
Picture				
9. Has a case for change message been developed?	☐	☐	☐	☐
10. Do leaders communicate the need for change with passion and conviction?	☐	☐	☐	☐
11. Have key milestones been identified, shared, and celebrated with a broad audience?	☐	☐	☐	☐
12. Has a clear picture of the end state been created?	☐	☐	☐	☐
Participation				
13. Do key leaders demonstrate in words and actions support for the change?	☐	☐	☐	☐
14. Have stakeholder groups been identified, and is a plan in place to build buy-in and support?	☐	☐	☐	☐
15. Are clear expectations established for leaders and other stakeholders?	☐	☐	☐	☐
16. Are there channels for two-way communication?	☐	☐	☐	☐

Introduction

to the Inventories, Questionnaires, and Surveys Section

Inventories, questionnaires, and surveys are valuable tools for the HRD professional. These feedback tools help respondents take an objective look at themselves and at their organizations. These tools also help to explain how a particular theory applies to them or to their situations.

Inventories, questionnaires, and surveys are useful in a number of training and consulting situations: privately for self-diagnosis; one-on-one to plan individual development; in a small group to open discussion; in a work team to help the team to focus on its highest priorities; or in an organization to gather data to achieve progress. You will find that the use of inventories, questionnaires, and surveys enriches, personalizes, and deepens training, development, and intervention designs. Many can be combined with other experiential learning activities or articles in this or other *Annuals* to design an exciting, involving, practical, and well-rounded intervention. Each instrument includes the background necessary for understanding, presenting, and using it. Interpretive information scales, and scoring sheets are also provided. In addition, we include the reliability and validity data contributed by the authors. If you wish additional information on any of these instruments, contact the authors directly. You will find their addresses and telephone numbers in the "Contributors" listing near the end of this volume.

The 2009 Pfeiffer Annual: Consulting includes three assessment tools in the following categories:

Groups and Teams

Spiritual Climate Inventory, by Ashish Pandey, Rajen K. Gupta, and A.P. Arora

Organizations

The New Empowerment Inventory, by K.S. Gupta

**Mind Aptitude Scale for Organizations (MASO), by James L. Moseley, Sacip Toker, and Ann T. Chow

---

**Talent Management topic

Spiritual Climate Inventory*

Ashish Pandey, Rajen K. Gupta, and A.P. Arora

Summary

Workplace spirituality provides a means for individuals to integrate their work and their spirituality, providing direction, connectedness, and wholeness at work. The Spiritual Climate Inventory is based on the variables derived from traditional wisdom, as well as contemporary thoughts of psychology and spirituality in workplace literature. The Inventory can be used by managers and/or consultants to gauge the level of spirituality in the workplace.

Theoretical and Conceptual Background for the Inventory

Spirituality is a reflection of one's search for meaning in life and place in the larger schema of existence. Search for meaning and sacred aspects of work are becoming increasingly prominent in academic as well as popular writings (Chakraborty, 1991; Gupta, 1996; Nicols, 1994; Pruzan, 2007; Sharma, 1996; Zohar, 2004). A recent upsurge in the area of spirituality in management has suggested the necessity for a validated instrument for practicing managers and consultants who wish to understand this phenomenon. The fundamental conceptualization of spirituality in contemporary literature indicates that it is a multi-dimensional multi-level phenomenon. It focuses on internal expression of being, quest for meaning, interconnectedness with self and others, and the transcendental aspect of being. A conceptual convergence can be traced in literature in the form of three dimensions: harmony with self, harmony in social and natural environment, and transcendence.

---

*The authors are thankful to Professor Naganand Kumar, Dr. N.C.B. Nath, Professor J.B.P. Sinha, Professor Subhash Sharma, Mr. Arun Wakhlu, and Professor Ashok Kapoor for their valuable suggestions and guidance.

Harmony with Self

Organizations are sites in which individuals find meaning for themselves and have their meaning shaped by others (Fineman, 1994). This aspect of spirituality in the workplace refers to the individual's alignment with the work. It is about finding meaning and purpose in work (Ashmosh & Duchon, 2000; Mitroff & Denton, 1999; Sheep, 2004). Variables like "quest for feeling good" (Morgan, 1993) and a profound feeling of well-being and joy (Kinjerski & Skrypnek, 2004) at work also indicate the theme "harmony with self" at work. Inner life at work, self-actualization (Ashforth & Pratt, 2003; Giacalone & Jurkiewicz, 2003; Pfeffer, 2003), or the development of one's full potential (Krishna Kumar & Neck, 2002), and becoming one with the activity (McCormick, 1994) form a part of this dimension of spirituality at the workplace.

Harmony in Work Environment

The second dimension of spirituality mentioned in literature is relational. Wilber (2000) suggests that spirituality manifests always and simultaneously as representing "I" and "we." It is manifest in relation to the social and natural environment in general, through respect for individuals and their diversity (Zohar & Marshal, 2002), community (Ashmos & Denton, 2000), being comfortable with the world (Morgan, 1993), workplace integration, connectedness (Ingersoll, 2004), compassion (McCormick, 1994), respect, humility, and courage (Heaton, Scmidt-Wilk, & Travis, 2004), and common purpose (Kinjerski & Skrypnek, 2004).

Transcendence: The Underlying Aspect

The third often-mentioned dimension of spirituality is transcendental. This is divine, mystical (Ingersoll, 2004) and an ability to reach into heightened spiritual states of consciousness (Emmons, 2000). This is a glimpse of unitary awareness and the direct experience of connectedness in existence. Connection to something greater than oneself (transcendence of self) is a firmly embedded component of this aspect of spirituality in management (Ashforth & Pratt, 2003; Dehler & Welsh, 2003; Sheep, 2004). Ashforth and Pratt (2003) explain that this "something" can be "other people, cause, nature, or a belief in a higher power."

Spiritual Climate at the Workplace

The prevailing perceptions about work and immediate work group that have spiritual content constitute the spiritual climate of the workplace. Based on a broad definition of spirituality and the concept of spiritual climate, a "spiritually prosperous" workplace is defined as a workplace that facilitates harmony among its members as well as harmony with the natural and social environment through meaningful work that takes place in the context of a work community.

The contemporary understanding of spirituality in management is in line with traditional Vedic literature, in which "truth" has two meaning; *Dharma* and *Rta* (pronounced rit) (Bhattacharyya, 1995). *Dharma* is that which sustains all beings, according to their own nature and in harmony with each other. *Bhagwad Gita* teaches that to discover and follow the self dharma (*Swadharma*) is the ideal of human life. One never becomes tired of one's Swadharma. One's Swadharma gives one maximum satisfaction and joy and finally leads to making the mind quiet and still. Work, which leads to agitation, is not Swadharma.

The second meaning for "truth" in the *Vedic* literature is *Rta*. This aspect is termed as the "unseen order of things." It is the eternal path of divine righteousness for all beings, both humans and deities. The order must be followed to maintain the world order. Experience of Rta is termed as ego transcendence or expansion of awareness. According to *Bhagawata Gita*, in the ordinary vocations of life Rta may manifest as *Loksangrah*, that is, "working for world maintenance" or performing one's job with intent of welfare of the larger social and natural environment. Thus, *Swadharma* and *Loksangrah* are the two constructs to contemporary thoughts about spirituality. We have tried to capture their presence through the Inventory.

The positive impact of different aspects of spirituality in organizations is reported in the form of heightened motivation, commitment, learning, creativity (Jurkiewicz & Giacalone, 2004), and quality orientation (Gupta, 1995; Marques, Dhiman, & King, 2005; Wagner-Marsh & Conley, 1999). Figure 1 summarizes the ideas presented so far.

Development of the Inventory

Based on the variables identified from traditional and contemporary literature, a battery of questions was developed. After gauging face and content validity through experts' opinions, two pilot tests were conducted. The final version of the Inventory was tested on two different samples in India. The first sample was of 162 managerial-level employees in the manufacturing sector, and second sample was of 225 employees of different levels of service-sector corporations. The results showed more than 70 percent variance being explained in factor analysis, showing internal consistency (Cronbach alpha) of more than 0.85 and KMO sherecity of more than 0.55 in both the samples. Discriminant validity of the sub-constructs was largely established through factor analysis. The construct validity was ascertained by examining the correlation of the "spiritual climate" construct with similar constructs such as engagement, internal locus of control, and so forth. Significant positive correlations were observed between these constructs and the construct of spiritual

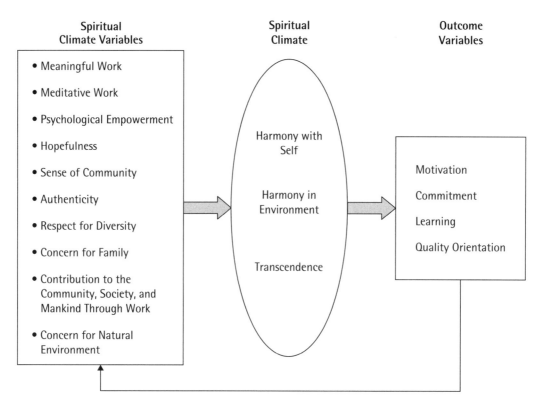

Figure 1. Spirituality in the Workplace

climate at the workplace. Marques (2005) suggested that the opposites of the spirituality in the workplace are excessive individualism, over-protectionism, paternalism, and authoritarianism. Items related to these variables showed high negative correlation with spiritual climate questions.

Limitations of the Inventory

The items of the inventory are designed in such a way that they reflect the perception of employees about their work and their immediate work groups. The nature of data is such that it can be combined to reach the collective level (group or organizational level) outcome. Before reaching any conclusion about the organizational level, some factual information should also be considered, such as investment of the organization in larger social and natural causes, holistic human development, initiatives and policies for community building, and the well-being of the employees' families.

Administration and Scoring of the Inventory

The Inventory should be duplicated and distributed to the respondents with an explanation of how the items should be scored. For example, scores of reverse questions should be inversed before the final total is calculated and a letter score should be chosen for items 12 and 18. Individual scores should be combined and a mean score for each item should be calculated. Mean scores give representative scores of the group or organization on a particular item or aspect of spiritual climate. Group/department/organization mean scores represent the level of perception about a particular item. Differences between current perception and desired level can also be calculated to gain insights about strong and weak areas of spiritual climate in an organization. Based on the group scores, a discussion should be initiated about strengths and weaknesses of the various dimensions of spiritual climate for the particular group or organization. The mean score of a particular item will be affected by exceptionally high or low values assigned by some respondents. Thus, items given very high or very low values by the group of respondents or by individual respondents should be discussed specifically to explore the reasons behind the response.

References

Ashforth, B.E., & Pratt, M.G. (2003). Institutionalized spirituality: An oxymoron? In R.A. Giacalone & C.L. Jurkiewicz (Eds.), *Handbook of workplace spirituality and organizational performance* (pp. 93–107). New York: M.E. Sharpe.

Ashmos, D.P., & Duchon, D. (2000). Spirituality at work: A conceptualization and measure. *Journal of Management Inquiry, 9*(2), 134–146.

Bhattacharyya, K. (1995). Vedanta as philosophy of spiritual life. In K. Sivaraman (Ed.), *Hindu spirituality: Vedas through Vedanta.* New Delhi: Motilal Banarsidass.

Chakraborty, S.K. (1991). *Management by values: Towards cultural congruence.* New Delhi: Oxford University Press.

Dehler, G.E., & Welsh, M.A. (1994). Spirituality and organizational transformation. *Journal of Managerial Psychology, 9*(6), 17–24.

Emmons, R.A. (2000). Is spirituality intelligence? Motivation, cognition, and the psychology of ultimate concern. *International Journal for the Psychology of Religion, 10*(1), 3–26.

Fineman, S., (1993). Organizations as emotional arenas. In S. Fineman (Ed.), *Emotion in organizations.* Newbury Park, CA: Sage.

Giacalone, R.A., & Jurkiewicz, C.L. (2003). Right from wrong: The influence of spirituality on perceptions of unethical business activities. *Journal of Business Ethics, 46*(1), 85–97.

Gupta, R.K. (1996). Is there a place for the sacred in organizations and their development. *Journal of Human Values, 2*(2), 149–158.

Gupta, R.K. (1995). Conflict and congruence between Vedantic wisdom and modern management. In S.K. Chakraborty (Ed.), *Human values for managers.* New Delhi: Wheeler Publishing.

Heaton, D., Schmidt-Wilk, J., & Travis, F. (2004). Construct, method, and measures for researching spirituality in organizations. *Journal of Organizational Change Management, 17*(1), 62–82.

Ingersoll, R.E. (2004). Spiritual wellness in the workplace. In R.A. Giacalone & C.L. Jurkiewicz (Eds.), *Handbook of workplace spirituality and organizational performance.* New York: M.E. Sharpe.

Jurkiewicz, C.L., & Giacalone, R.A. (2004). A values framework for measuring the impact of workplace spirituality on organizational performance. *Journal of Business Ethics, 49*(2), 129–142.

Kinjerski, V.M., & Skrypnek, B.J. (2004). Defining spirit at work: Finding common ground. *Journal of Organizational Change Management,17*(1), 26–42.

Krishnakumar, S., & Neck, C.P. (2002). The "what," "why," and "how" of spirituality in the workplace. *Journal of Managerial Psychology, 17*(3), 153–164.

Marcqus, J. Dhiman, S., & King, R. (2005, September). Spirituality in the workplace: Developing an integral model and a comprehensive definition. *Journal of the American Academy of Business, 7*(1), 81–92.

Marques, J. (2005). Redefining the bottom line. *The Journal of the American Academy of Business, 7*(1), 283–287.

McCormick, D.W. (1994), Spirituality and management. *Journal of Management Psychology, 9*(6), 5–8.

Mitroff, I.I., & Denton, E.A. (1999). *A spiritual audit of corporate America: A hard look at spirituality, religion, and values in the workplace.* San Francisco, CA: Jossey-Bass.

Morgan, J.D. (1993). The existential quest for meaning. In K.J. Doka & J.D. Morga (Eds.), *Death and spirituality* (pp. 3–9). Amityville, NY: Baywood.

Puzan P., & Mikkelsen, K.P. (2007). *Leading with wisdom: Spiritual based leadership in business.* New Delhi: Sage.

Sheep, M.L. (2004). Nailing down gossamer: A valid measure of the person-organization fit of workplace spirituality. Academy of Management, Best Conference Paper MSR.

Sharma, S. (1996). *Western windows, Easter doors.* New Delhi: New Age Publishing.

Zohar, D., & Marshall, I. (2004). *Spiritual capital: Wealth we can live by.* London: Bloomsbury.

Ashish Pandey *is leading the Research and Development function at Pragati Leadership Institute Pvt. Ltd., a leadership and organization development consulting firm. He is a Fellow of the Management Development Institute (M.D.I.), Gurgaon, India. This inventory was developed and validated as part of his doctoral-level research work at M.D.I. His main interest area in research and consulting work is spirituality in leadership and organizational development. His research has appeared in the* Journal of Business Ethics, Journal of European Industrial Training, *and* Global Business Review, *among others.*

Rajen K. Gupta *is professor of organization development at M.D.I., Sukhrali, Gurgaon, Haryana, India. He is an alumnus of the Indian Institute of Technology (Kanpur) and Fellow of the Indian Institute of*

Management (Ahmedabad). His main research and consulting interests are HRD, organization design and development, coaching and mentoring, and organizational culture. He sits on the editorial boards of several management research journals and has published more than seventy articles and research papers in reputed journals of social sciences and management.

A.P. Arora *is professor of market research at M.D.I., Sukharali, Gurgaon, Haryana, India. He is also a Fellow of the Indian Institute of Management (Ahmedabad). His main interests in consulting and research are in the areas of marketing research, consumer behavior, marketing strategy and brand management, and cyber marketing. He has consulted with more than thirty organizations in India and abroad.*

Spiritual Climate Inventory

Ashish Pandey, Rajen K. Gupta, and A.P. Arora

Team/Group/Department:

Date:

Name of respondent:

Instructions: Taking this Inventory will help you to assess the climate of the unit or work group where you work. The questions represent different dimensions of the organizational climate. There are no "right" or "wrong" answers. Please read each statement and fill in the blank space how you feel about that statement, using the following key:

  5   The statement truly represents your experience about your work or work group.

  4   The statement is usually true.

  3   the statement is sometimes true.

  2   The statement is not representative of the work group most of the time.

  1   The statement is not at all true.

Harmony with Self at Work

_____ 1. My job helps me to understand my life's purpose.

_____ 2. Working here makes my life meaningful.

_____ 3. Working here is a means for realizing my real self.

_____ 4. Work itself is enjoyable for me.

_____ 5. I am deeply involved in my work here.

_____ 6. I feel frustrated after working here (reverse).

_____ 7. People here feel that they are in charge of their own destinies.

_____ 8. People here are able to use their talents at work.

_____ 9. People in the group/department are able to apply their creativity at work.

_____ 10. People generally believe that business targets of the group/department can be achieved.

_____ 11. People doubt the success of any new plan for business growth (reverse).

Harmony in Work Environment

_____ 12. When. stuck with a problem, people feel free to ask for (choose a number for each one):

     a. advice from colleagues

     b. advice from a superior

     c. help from their colleagues

     d. help from a superior

_____ 13. Peoples' actions here are aligned with their words.

_____ 14. People own up to mistakes with others in the group.

_____ 15. Manipulation is the way people perform their jobs here (reverse).

_____ 16. Diversity of views is accepted in my group/department.

_____ 17. People here are concerned about each other's family responsibilities.

Transcendence

_____ 18. People here perform their duties as if they contribute to (choose a number for one):

     a. the community

     b. the larger society

     c. mankind in general

_____ 19. People here try to avoid wastage of any kind (paper, electricity, etc.).

_____ 20. People are concerned about the natural environment while working here.

Spiritual Climate Inventory Scoring Sheet

Variables	Question	Aggregated Mean Scores
Meaningful work	1, 2, 3	
Meditative work	4, 5, 6	
Psychological empowerment and expression of talents and creativity	7, 8, 9	
Hopefulness	10, 11	
Harmony with Self	Total of Mean scores divided by 4	
Sense of community	12 a, b, c, d, 15	
Authenticity	13, 14	
Respect for diversity	16	
Concern for family	17	
Harmony in social environment	Total Mean scores divided by 9	
Contribution of the work to community	18 a, b, c	
Concern for natural environment	19, 20	
Transcendence	Total Mean scores divided by 4	

Diagnostic Questions

In which aspect of spirituality the group/organization score highest?

How can this strength be leveraged to meet group/departmental/organization objectives?

What are the items on which the scores are low and the company should give urgent attention?

How can the climate of the workplace be made more spiritual?

The New Empowerment Inventory

K.S. Gupta

Summary

Due to the globalization of businesses, competition has grown rapidly. The management of global organizations has looked for approaches to make organizations self-sufficient. The concept of empowerment has gained momentum as it has been seen to produce desired results in many organizations. Highly empowered employees create an empowered organization, which ultimately performs well. The first version of the Empowerment Inventory was published in the *2002 Annual: Volume 1, Training* and was intended to be used for measuring the level of individual empowerment and thus the mean of a group in an organization. At this time, the author found the need to reconstruct and revalidate the inventory.

Development of the New Empowerment Inventory

While administering the original Empowerment Inventory during training programs, I found that respondents had a need for clarification, and thus I decided to study and revalidate the Inventory. I found that there were some errors in the statements, such as connecting two issues with the word "and," which led to less clarity in capturing the responses.

I modified and tested the Inventory for content and face validity by administering it to an expert group and also determining the value of Cronbach alpha.

Empowering Framework

The empowerment framework was published earlier (Gupta, 2002). In it the factors were grouped into *empowering* variables and *outcome* variables (consequences).

Empowering variables contribute directly to level of empowerment, whereas outcome variables affect empowerment indirectly through feedback in a closed loop process. The details are explained in the earlier paper (Gupta, 2002).

Out of thirty-seven items on the Inventory, twenty-nine were found to be error-free. The other eight items were found to have errors, such as two issues connected with "and," ambiguity of meaning, lower span of coverage for a particular parameter, and negative framing. Therefore, the following modifications were made to the Inventory:

- Five items were split and reframed to avoid confusion in prioritizing the response.

- Three items were modified to improve clarity and focus.

- Five items were newly framed and expanded to improve the capturing of parameters.

- One item was positively framed.

The original framework is presented in Figure 1. The details of the items in the New Empowerment Inventory are given in Table 1.

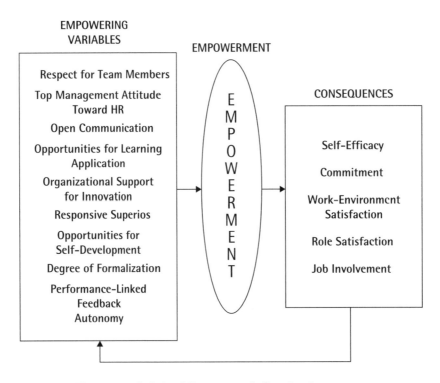

Figure 1. Original Framework for the Inventory

Table 1. Items in the New Empowerment Inventory

SI Number	Items	Source
1.	1, 2, 6 (3 items)	
	9 to 19 (11 items)	
	22 to 26 (5 items)	
	28 to 37 (10 items)	
	Total 29 items	29 items from the Empowerment Inventory (Gupta, 2002)
2.	5, 7, 8, 21, 27 (5 items)	
	39 to 42 and 48 (5 items)	Ten items split and reframed to avoid confusion in prioritizing the response
3.	3, 4, 20 (3 items)	Three items modified to improve clarity and focus
4.	43 to 47 (5 items)	Five items newly framed and added to improve the capturing of parameters
5.	38	Positively framed

Reliability and Validity of the New Empowerment Inventory

Reliability was measured for *repeatability* and *internal consistency.* Repeatability was measured by the test-retest method, and internal consistency was measured by Cronbach's alpha. The greater the correlation is to a score of 1, the higher the internal consistency; a score of 0.60 or less indicates that the items measure different characteristics.

Reliability was measured through Cronbach's coefficient alpha, a measure of internal consistency that quantifies the degree of homogeneity of items within an inventory.

The reliability coefficient for forty-eight items on the modified scale is 0.9121, and the sensitivity of Cronbach alpha to exclusion of an item ranges from 0.9069 to 0.9145. Thus, the range of variation of alpha is 0.007 (Gupta, 2002).

Construct validity of the scales was assessed by a confirmatory factor analysis of the empowerment scale. Content validity was ascertained by asking experts on the test topic to assess the inventory for its content. The appropriate modifications suggested by the experts were made.

Additionally, the validity of the inventory was determined by *internal consistency,* an estimation based on the correlation among the variables comprising the set called Cronbach's alpha, the most common form of internal consistency reliability coefficient. By convention, a lenient cutoff of .60 is common in exploratory research; alpha should be at least .70 or higher to retain an item in an "adequate" scale; and many researchers require a cutoff of .80 for a "good scale."

In the New Empowerment Inventory, the value of Cronbach alpha is .9382. Isolated-item value of Cronbach alpha range from .9350 to .9413 (see Table 2). The range is .0063, which is very narrow. Therefore, the item homogeneity is quite high. Since each alpha is larger than 0.80, it is considered significant. This indicates high consistency or internal agreement between an item and the entire set of items in the inventory. From this, it can be concluded that the internal consistency of the new inventory is acceptable for all the items in the questionnaire.

The reliability of the Inventory has increased. A scale (or subscale) is internally consistent to the degree that its items are highly correlated. High correlations imply that items are all measuring or manifestations of the same underlying construct. Having more reliable scales increases the statistical power for a given sample size.

Administering the Inventory

This inventory is useful to find out the individual, team, and organizational level of empowerment. It also gives the level of consequences. The administrator must explain the purpose and utility of the Inventory before administering it. Respondents must be given ten minutes to respond to the Inventory.

Table 2. Reliability Coefficient

Item	Alpha	Item	Alpha	Item	Alpha
1	.9372	17	.9353	33	.9360
2	.9360	18	.9355	34	.9362
3	.9380	19	.9356	35	.9352
4	.9368	20	.9375	36	.9376
5	.9371	21	.9372	37	.9350
6	.9376	22	.9388	38	.9356
7	.9357	23	.9379	39	.9352
8	.9380	24	.9369	40	.9371
9	.9359	25	.9381	41	.9389
10	.9351	26	.9351	42	.9413
11	.9381	27	.9375	43	.9371
12	.9362	28	.9377	44	.9370
13	.9357	29	.9376	45	.9357
14	.9357	30	.9366	46	.9371
15	.9350	31	.9411	47	.9372
16	.9373	32	.9382	48	.9369

Results: **.9350** to **.9413**
Number of Cases = 227   Number of items = 48

Scoring and Interpretation

After ten minutes, or when all have completed the Inventory, the Scoring Sheet should be handed out for respondents to transfer their ratings. Then average scores should be computed. The administrator should lead a discussion on the different factors to help respondents understand their scores and to help them focus their efforts to enhance areas on which they scored low. Some scoring interpretations include:

- A score above 4.5 is excellent and the individual or group having this score is highly empowered.

- A score of 3.5 to 4.5 is very good, but there is some room for improvement. Respondents should analyze the items on which their scores were low and find ways to improve.

- A score from 2.5 to 3.5 is good, but there is quite a bit of room for improvement. Again, respondents should analyze which items they scored low on and find ways to bring their scores up in the future.

- A score below 2.5 is alarming, and groups must take immediate action to work on the parameters that were scored low, using suitable interventions to improve. It is recommended that the facilitator work with the group on one issue at a time over a period of weeks and then measure the empowerment level again after a gap of five or six months.

Conclusion

The Empowerment Inventory has been modified to remove the ambiguities of the scale and also to enhance its reliability. It is now more useful to measure the empowerment level of individuals, teams, and organizations. At an individual level, taking and scoring the Inventory creates awareness of the respondent's level of empowerment and need for improvement. At a later time, taking the Inventory again can allow the respondent to see improvement.

Teams can improve their effectiveness by enhancing the sense of empowerment of individual team members, and finally, at the organization level, working with the Inventory helps the organization to understand what is causing low scores and to take steps required to improve.

References

American Psychological Association. (1954). Technical recommendations for psychological tests and diagnostic techniques. *Psychological Bulletin, 51*(2), 201–238.

American Psychological Association. (1966). *Standards for educational and psychological tests and manuals.* Washington, DC: Author.

Cronbach, L.J., & Meehl, P.E. (1955). Construct validity in psychological tests. *Psychological Bulletin, 52,* 281–302.

Dijkstra, A., Buist, G., & Dassen, T. (1998). A criterion-related validity study of the nursing care dependency. *International Journal of Nursing Studies, 35,* 163–170.

Gupta, K.S. (2002). Empowerment inventory. In *The 2002 annual, volume I: Training.* San Francisco, CA: Pfeiffer.

Dr. K.S. Gupta *is the associate dean at Icfai Business School, Bangalore, India. He holds a doctorate in management, a master's in business administration (specializing in HRM and marketing), and a master's in electronics engineering. Dr. Gupta has thirty-seven years of experience covering different areas of the aerospace industry and as a faculty member in various management disciplines. He has presented and published over forty papers, including ten inventories. His interest area are human potential development, research in organizational behavior, organization development, restructuring and empowerment, knowledge sharing and transfer, training, and counseling for children, parents, and married couples.*

The New Empowerment Inventory

K.S. Gupta

Instructions: The following inventory consists of 48 items reflecting the level of empowerment in your organization. Circle the rating you feel is appropriate for each of the items using the following scale:

1 = Never

2 = Sometimes

3 = Moderately Often

4 = Often

5 = Very Often

1.	My organization is flexible enough to adopt to any change quickly.	1	2	3	4	5	
2.	My organization encourages innovation.	1	2	3	4	5	
3.	Top management encourages risk taking.	1	2	3	4	5	
4.	Most of the people in this organization are receptive to new ideas.	1	2	3	4	5	
5.	This organization provides opportunities for individuals to do creative work.	1	2	3	4	5	
6.	Top management treats people as a vital resource for gaining competitive advantage.	1	2	3	4	5	
7.	The top management of this organization believes that human resources are extremely important.	1	2	3	4	5	
8.	Problems between departments are generally resolved through mutual understanding.	1	2	3	4	5	
9.	Everyone has a chance to express opinions on how to do the work.	1	2	3	4	5	
10.	Communication within this organization is very open.	1	2	3	4	5	
11.	It is easy to ask for advice from anyone in my organization.	1	2	3	4	5	
12.	People in my organization solve their work-related problems with mutual discussions.	1	2	3	4	5	
13.	I am satisfied with my career progress in this organization.	1	2	3	4	5	
14.	I receive necessary information in time to carry out my work efficiently.	1	2	3	4	5	
15.	I receive regular feedback on my work performance.	1	2	3	4	5	
16.	Any weaknesses are communicated to employees in a non-threatening way.	1	2	3	4	5	
17.	Employees are sponsored for training on the basis of genuine training needs.	1	2	3	4	5	
18.	People here have an opportunity to develop their job skills further.	1	2	3	4	5	
19.	My organization facilitates employee self-improvement.	1	2	3	4	5	
20.	Generally, buck passing is avoided for taking important decisions.	1	2	3	4	5	
21.	I make most of the decisions regarding my own work.	1	2	3	4	5	

1 = Never

2 = Sometimes

3 = Moderately Often

4 = Often

5 = Very Often

22.	I allow my subordinates to make their own decisions while carrying out their work.	1	2	3	4	5
23.	My boss asks for my views before making decisions about my work.	1	2	3	4	5
24.	Superiors invite their subordinates for informal discussions about their work.	1	2	3	4	5
25.	My colleagues share their views before any decisions are made on work issues.	1	2	3	4	5
26.	Employees returning from training programs are given opportunities to try out what they learned.	1	2	3	4	5
27.	Operating procedures are used as guidelines.	1	2	3	4	5
28.	Here people are able to do their jobs without much help from their supervisors.	1	2	3	4	5
29.	I feel that I am responsible for whatever happens to my organization, whether good or bad.	1	2	3	4	5
30.	I care about the growth of this organization.	1	2	3	4	5
31.	While away from the job, I often worry that my work is suffering.	1	2	3	4	5
32.	I am willing to devote my free time to work.	1	2	3	4	5
33.	I am satisfied with the people in my work group.	1	2	3	4	5
34.	I am satisfied with my superior.	1	2	3	4	5
35.	I am satisfied with my job.	1	2	3	4	5
36.	I am satisfied with my organization, compared to most other organizations I have heard about or worked for.	1	2	3	4	5
37.	I am satisfied with my role in this organization.	1	2	3	4	5
38.	Bosses encourage new ideas.	1	2	3	4	5
39.	This organization facilitates individuals to do creative work.	1	2	3	4	5
40.	The top management of this organization practices treating people humanely.	1	2	3	4	5
41.	I make most of the decisions in my area of responsibility.	1	2	3	4	5
42.	Operating procedures are followed flexibly.	1	2	3	4	5
43.	My role enhances my image.	1	2	3	4	5
44.	My strengths are utilized in my role.	1	2	3	4	5
45.	The requirements of my role are in line with my values.	1	2	3	4	5
46.	My role fulfills my needs.	1	2	3	4	5
47.	Superiors respond to the needs of subordinates on priority.	1	2	3	4	5
48.	Problems between departments are generally resolved through mutual efforts.	1	2	3	4	5

The New Empowerment Inventory Scoring Sheet

Instructions: Use the grid below to calculate your scores for each variable. First, look at each item number and write the score you assigned to that item in the score box. Add the numbers in each score box together and divide by the number of items. The total is the points you assigned for each of the variables and consequences.

Empowering Variable	Item Numbers	Average Score
Respect for Team Members (RTM)	23, 24, 25	
Top-Management Attitude Toward Human Resources (TMA)	6, 7, 40	
Open Communication (OC)	8, 9, 10, 11, 12	
Opportunities for Learning Application (OLA)	26	
Organizational Support for Innovation (OSI)	1, 2, 3, 4, 5, 38, 39	
Responsive Superiors (RSR)	20, 47	
Opportunities for Self-Development (OSD)	18, 19	
Degree of Formalization (DF)	27, 42, 48	
Performance-Linked Feedback (PLF)	13, 14, 15, 16, 17	
Autonomy (AMY)	21, 22, 41	
Consequences	**Item Numbers**	**Average Score**
Self-Efficacy (SE)	28	
Commitment (CMT)	29, 30	
Work Environment Satisfaction (WES)	33, 34, 35, 36	
Role Satisfaction (RS)	37, 43, 44, 45, 46	
Job Involvement (JI)	31, 32	

Mind Aptitude Scale for Organizations (MASO)

James L. Moseley, Sacip Toker*, and Ann T. Chow

Summary

The Mind Aptitude Scale for Organizations (MASO) is a diagnostic tool to use as an initial and probing discussion into organizational mindset. It is intended for use by work groups and teams to gauge their sense of what is important in the organization, what makes the organization run efficiently and effectively, and what the organizational impact is. It suggests strategies, interventions, and actions that organizations can use to make a difference in bottom-line results. It may also be used as an evaluation tool.

The human mind is a complex aggregate of conscious and unconscious processes. When we think of how the mind develops and how it is organized, we recall words like consciousness, disposition, intellect, reason, senses, soul, thought, and others. The basis of the Mind Aptitude Scale for Organizations (MASO) is Howard Gardner's *Five Minds for the Future* (2006). Gardner identifies five "minds" that individuals must possess in order to function in the future. To his primary mindset, he suggests seven complementary minds that strengthen the primary minds. Individuals who collectively possess these minds are positioned for success. One need only think of the many religious, historical, social, and cultural individuals whose names can be appended to each of the twelve minds. Picture the human brain. Figure 1 shows Gardner's minds superimposed on the human brain.

Figure 1 depicts the interlocking relationships of Gardner's minds. On this Brain Net, the primary minds are the inner circles (solid lines) and the complementary minds are the outer circles (dotted lines). The net shows that the minds are

---

*The author would like to express special thanks to The Scientific and Technological Research Council of Turkey for the support they provided to pursue his doctoral studies.

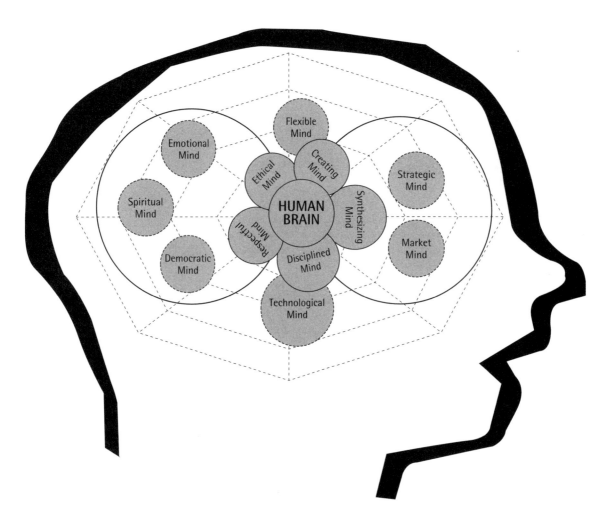

Figure 1. Gardner's Brain Net

interrelated and influenced by each other. Two large circles describe the close association between and among the mindsets. For example, a realistic and implementable strategic and marketing plan of an organization is created by the employees who possess a sound Strategic Mind and a Market Mind grounded on the excellence of the Creating Mind, Synthesizing Mind, and Disciplined Mind.

The authors of this diagnostic instrument have taken liberty with Gardner's work and applied it to organizations and their leadership personnel. We contend that if organizations are going to survive and maintain their competitive edge in the future, they must possess structural dimensions (formalization, specialization, hierarchy of authority, centralization, professionalism, and personnel ratios) and contextual dimensions (size, organizational technology, environment, goals and strategy, and culture). The synergy generated by these two dimensions when combined produces high-performing organizations that add value to the bottom line.

The MASO provides a systematic and systemic approach to determining how organizations and their leadership use the twelve mindsets to capture their internal voices and position themselves for future impact. It is possible that organizations that lack one or more mindsets may still be profitable and gain market share. Market share is dependent on many factors, including mindset. It is the authors' opinion that organizations that possess and exhibit greater diversification in mindsets add substantial value to the bottom line. Each of the mindsets, adapted from Gardner's work, is defined in Table 1.

The shell of the MASO instrument is based on the Organizational Readiness Inventory (ORI): Diagnosing Your Organization's Ability to Adapt to the Future (Moseley & Swiatkowski, 2000). It uses a 5-point scale and is meant to be used for judging future organizational success. The seventy-two statements (six for each of the twelve categories) were developed through literature and Internet searches from the behavioral, social, and natural sciences. Statements were formed based on common themes and threads that constitute the fabric of the searches. The instrument has been piloted for clarity and integrity of purpose.

Table 1. Mindsets from the MASO

Creating Mind (CRM): Capacity to think outside the box and uncover and process new phenomena.

Democratic Mind (DEM): Emphasizes the importance of making everyone's voice heard and protecting individual, group, and organizational rights.

Disciplined Mind (DIM): Mastery of major disciplines and fields of study, capacity to think independently, and ability to analyze, synthesize, and evaluate simple and complex life problems.

Emotional Mind (EMM): Utilizing one's abilities to apply knowledge from emotions and the emotions of others in order to make on-the-spot prudent decisions and choices that impact organizational success.

Ethical Mind (ETM): Being true to self by fulfilling responsibilities at work, at home, in community, and globally.

Flexible Mind (FLM): Ability to adjust, adapt, and modify situations when needed.

Market Mind (MAM): Ability to communicate and deliver values and bottom-line results to stakeholders, clients, sponsors, and audiences.

Respectful Mind (REM): Appreciation and tolerance for diversity in individuals and groups.

Spiritual Mind (SPM): Emphasizes community and societal responsibility, bringing out the best in each employee for the common good of the organization.

Strategic Mind (STM): Emphasizes long-range thinking and planning at the individual, group, and societal levels.

Synthesizing Mind (SYM): Integration and connectivity between ideas and the ability to communicate and integrate them with broad audiences.

Technological Mind (TEM): Capitalizes on application of both soft and hard technologies to make daily life and work comfortable and pleasurable.

Description of the Instrument

The Mind Aptitude Scale for Organizations (MASO) consists of seventy-two statements, six for each mind, a Scoring Sheet, a Profile Chart, and a Diagnostic Sheet. The intended audience of the MASO is a work group, a team, or an organization. Each employee in a work group or team is asked to complete the inventory carefully, reflecting on the current workplace and organization, and choosing the response that best describes the organization's application, implementation, or belief. See Table 2 for a list of the responses and their corresponding meanings and numeric values.

Administration of the Instrument

It is best to designate an individual in a team to collect, tally, and compute scores. Each member completes the survey, adds the scores given for each mind, and then transposes the scores of each mind to the MASO Scoring Sheet. The designated individual collects the Scoring Sheets, follows the direction on the MASO Profile Chart, and places numbers on the chart representing the team members' minds.

Members of the team review the results collectively. The interpretations on the MASO Diagnostic Sheet serve as the basis for discussion and possible further action plans. A work group applies the results of each mind selection to their own environment and draw their own conclusions.

Presentation of Theory

Since the introduction of the Multiple Intelligence concept more than twenty years ago, Howard Gardner's *Five Minds for the Future* challenges our thoughts and

Table 2. Responses and Corresponding Values

5	Your organization **strongly agrees** with the statement. Your organization believes, practices, applies, or implements the statement **all of the time**.
4	Your organization **agrees** with the statement. Your organization believes in, practices, applies, or implements the statement **most of the time**.
3	Your organization **somewhat agrees** with the statement. Your organization believes in, practices, applies, or implements the statement **some of the time**.
2	Your organization **disagrees** with the statement. Your organization **rarely** believes in, practices, applies, or implements the statement.
1	Your organization **strongly disagrees** with the statement. Your organization **does not** believe in, practice, apply, or implement the statement.

aptitudes. In his approach to intelligences and minds, Gardner pictures *intelligence* as a technical mechanism. In other words, *intelligences* are the cognitive capacities termed by psychology, whereas *minds* are the practical actions that can be fostered and developed in schools and in the workplace. Minds use various types of intelligences; minds can be deepened by continuous nurturing.

Suggested Uses for the Instrument

The MASO is intended to be used to collect and compile the opinions of employees in a work group on what is important, the efficiency, effectiveness, and impact of group actions and how the organization's mindsets influence bottom-line results. For effective results, employees must be open-minded, take a critical look at their organization, and answer each statement truthfully. Since the mindsets overlap and interrelate, it is entirely possible that certain mindset statements can be placed in more than one category. This is okay given that the instrument can also be used as a discussion-generating tool. The MASO is designed for use by organizations in the United States. Adapting the MASO to an international and more global workforce would require further research.

Validity and Reliability

There are no available data for content and construct validity. Validity is a matter of degree. It is the authors' intuitive sense that the instrument has moderate validity.

There are also no data to demonstrate reliability. However, reliability measures are highly associated with the total number of items. In other words, the more items that are included in the instrument, the higher the level of reliability. MASO has seventy-two items and thus has remarkable potential for high reliability.

References

Blanchard, K., Robinson, D., & Robinson, J. (2002). *Zap the gaps! Target higher performance and achieve it!* New York: HarperCollins.

Bryan, L.L., & Joyce, C.I. (2007). *Mobilizing minds: Creating wealth from talent in the 21st century organization.* New York: McGraw-Hill.

Gardner, H. (2006). *Five minds for the future.* Boston, MA: Harvard Business School Press.

Kaufman, R., Oakley-Browne, H., Watkins, R., & Leigh, D. (2003). *Strategic planning for success: Aligning people, performance, and payoffs.* San Francisco, CA: Jossey-Bass/Pfeiffer.

Moseley, J.L., & Swiatkowski, D.J. (2000). The organizational readiness inventory (ORI): Diagnosing your organization's ability to adapt to the future. In E. Biech (Ed.), *The 2000 annual: Volume 2, consulting* (pp. 117–136). San Francisco, CA: Pfeiffer.

James L. Moseley, Ed.D., LPC, CHES, CPT, *is an associate professor of instructional technology in the College of Education at Wayne State University, Detroit, Michigan. He teaches performance technology and program evaluation courses and directs dissertations and projects. He consults with all levels of management. Moseley is the recipient of teaching awards and service awards and the co-author of five books, numerous articles, and book chapters. He is a member of both ISPI and ASTD.*

Sacip Toker, BSc, MSc, *is an instructional technology doctoral applicant and graduate research assistant in the College of Education at Wayne State University, Detroit, Michigan. In Turkey, he was involved in several online training programs and provided instructional technology support to the faculties at Middle East Technical University. He also taught information technology and instructional planning courses at Suleyman Demirel University.*

Ann T. Chow, BA, MS, *is an instructional technology full-time doctoral applicant in the College of Education at Wayne State University, Detroit, Michigan. Ann received her education in Taiwan, Vietnam, Italy, and America. Her business and managerial experiences are as diverse as her academic credentials. She has worked as manager and consultant in companies in Asia and corporations in the United States. Currently, she is the associate director of The Metro Bureau Inc.*

Mind Aptitude Scale for Organizations (MASO)

James L. Moseley, Sacip Toker, and Ann T. Chow

Instructions: Read each numbered statement in the instrument and place a check mark in the box that best describes your response to that statement. Your immediate response is usually the most accurate:

5 Your organization *strongly agrees* with the statement. Your organization believes practices, applies, or implements the statement *all of the time*.

4 Your organization *agrees* with the statement. Your organization believes in, practices, applies, or implements the statement *most of the time*.

3 Your organization *somewhat agrees* with the statement. Your organization believes in, practices, applies, or implements the statement *some of the time*.

2 Your organization *disagrees* with the statement. Your organization *rarely* believes in, practices, applies, or implements the statement.

1 Your organization *strongly disagrees* with the statement. Your organization *does not* believe in, practice, apply, or implement the statement.

Statement	5	4	3	2	1
1. The organization makes a concerted effort to organize and build teams with workers of multicultural and diverse backgrounds.					
2. The organization has a bottom-up and top-down management infrastructure.					
3. Workers are encouraged to acquire, develop, and diversify their skills and knowledge bases.					
4. When the organization's mission and values are aligned with the employee's sense of what is important in the organization, work productivity, and energy increase.					
5. When employees go that extra mile to succeed, when they work collaboratively as team members, and when they are professionally and personally accountable for their actions, their organization becomes healthy and mature.					
6. When the market changes, the organization forms and regroups projects and teams quickly.					
7. The organization's website is well-designed, user-friendly, and, where appropriate, is targeted to a global audience.					
8. The organization views competitors as a positive and an integral part of the market.					
9. The organization rewards employees who voluntarily choose to tutor at the youth center, clean up local parks and rivers, and grocery shop for seniors.					
10. The organization adapts new and unconventional methods in planning and implementing its actions.					

Statement	5	4	3	2	1
11. The organization moderates dialogues and ideas of cross-disciplinary and multi-functional work groups.					
12. The organization responds quickly to the needs of its clients and the market with various information technologies.					
13. The new workplace calls for continuous learners who are totally in touch with their peers and who possess the self-confidence, initiative, integrity, and achievement orientation necessary for organizational health.					
14. The organization takes pride in its product and services.					
15. The organization forms teams that have a balance of people, education, specialties, and experiences.					
16. The organization has a centralized information-management infrastructure that reduces workplace uncertainty for members.					
17. When individuals from multi-cultural backgrounds and status are employed, the organization adapts formal and informal personal and professional rules that generate admiration toward them.					
18. The organization provides the infrastructure that allows workers to manage their own time and resources, such as telecommuting and virtual private networking.					
19. The organization trains and refines selling skills of its salesforce and provides sales professionals with up-to-date materials, products, and services.					
20. The organization values and rewards self-reliant workers.					
21. The organization's decision-making process includes discussions, debates, and consensus-based activities.					
22. The organizational climate provides opportunities for employees to reflect on their jobs and roles.					
23. When learners create a hospitable space for reflection within which employees can discuss and discover their connections to one another, the organization becomes revitalized.					
24. Workers feel safe to contribute innovative ideas and to suggest better and effective ways to accomplish tasks.					
25. Workers and management exchange ideas, sharing knowledge and business information.					
26. When leaders gather ideas from co-workers to help generate an atmosphere of truth throughout the workplace, the organization transforms itself into a catalyst of change.					
27. The organization provides a variety of training programs to upgrade and broaden the professional knowledge of workers.					
28. The organization partners with other communities in practices that enhance the greater good of society.					
29. One way of adding value to the organization is by understanding different multi-cultural backgrounds and status.					
30. The organization invests consistently in the research and development of innovative and profitable products and/or services.					

Statement	5	4	3	2	1
31. The organization encourages workers to use its products and services and solicits feedback and comments from its workers.					
32. The organization delegates authority and responsibility to managers and workers so that they can make the best decisions and accomplish tasks promptly.					
33. The organization aligns its short- and long-range plans with its mission and vision.					
34. The organization aligns the demands of work, worker, and workplace to the technological resources available.					
35. Employees can criticize the management constructively without fear of losing their jobs.					
36. Establishing an emphatic organizational culture creates awareness of employee feelings, needs, wants, and concerns.					
37. The workers have access to a company-wide knowledge bank (which can be as simple as email distribution to a complex electronic knowledge management system) that captures and stores employees' explicit and tacit knowledge.					
38. The organization sponsors enrollment in motivational training programs for employees to find balance between personal and professional demands.					
39. The organization promotes a global environment that fosters lifelong learning.					
40. The organization listens and rewards customers for their comments and feedback.					
41. The organization encourages its workers to think outside the box and rewards them for their efforts.					
42. The organization manages employee relations by setting positive cooperative and collaborative tones, honoring boundaries and establishing trust.					
43. The organization continuously and systematically improves and evaluates the performance of workers and its policies, procedures, and practices.					
44. The organization aims to serve the common good of society.					
45. The management removes obstacles and supports the workers to complete their tasks freely.					
46. The impact of technological resources on both procedural and social dimensions of the organization is measured and evaluated in terms of effectiveness and efficiency.					
47. The HRD department selects potential candidates for employment who are confident about who they are and who model through their actions all that is good and beneficial to the organization.					
48. The organization values ideas and opinions of all groups of people.					
49. An organization that reflectively monitors the emotions of its stakeholders builds bonds of trust and acts as a change catalyst.					
50. It is critical for the organization to facilitate and encourage employees who do not follow the American-centric procedure or think like Americans.					
51. When the workplace becomes an essential arena for connection to a larger world, the personality of the organization transforms from self-interest to common good.					
52. Organizations that encourage their employees to volunteer in the community by mentoring children and adolescents, by serving as role models, and by other forms of service learning significantly add value to both the community and the organization.					

Statement	5	4	3	2	1
53. The organization has robust management information systems that link information and data to support human decision making.					
54. The organization has a decentralized and flat management structure.					
55. The management of the organization knows how to manage freelance workers and full-timers.					
56. The management of the organization knows when and how to form interdisciplinary projects and integrated teams.					
57. The multicultural workplace can enhance productivity and influence the organization's bottom line.					
58. The organization analyzes its current strengths and weaknesses based on its future needs and wants.					
59. The organization encourages and rewards workers who broaden their professional knowledge and are discreet in applying their knowledge.					
60. The organization is fully aware of the power of mass collaboration and crowd sourcing and is communicating with its clients via a variety of virtual platforms such as Second Life, multi-language Wikipedia, and Google.					
61. Innovation and creativity can be defined as ideas and interventions that add value such as monetary gain and human performance improvement.					
62. All members of the organization are listened to and acknowledged when they want to propose suggestions or ideas.					
63. Management considers cultural diversity, professional knowledge, and educational background when forming project and program teams.					
64. An employee who exhibits self-awareness, self-motivation, and self-regulation can positively influence organizational health and add to the organization's service-profit chain.					
65. Employees speak out when policies, procedures, and practices are contrary to the organization's mission, culture, mores, and beliefs.					
66. Communication and ideas flow smoothly and dialogue stimulates cross-pollination among workers, work teams, and management.					
67. Employees can access, understand, and follow the organization's strategic and marketing plans.					
68. Understanding individuals from different background and status is an important strength of the organization.					
69. By building work relationships on a foundation of trust at all organizational levels, leaders can bring joy, purpose, and fulfillment to their organization.					
70. The organization aligns its workers and work groups with its mission, vision, and goals.					
71. Management knows when and how to form inter-disciplinary workers and projects.					
72. Technological resources are one part of tools and methods used for change in organizational structure, skill enhancement, deskilling of employees, and/or change in employment opportunities such as web-based training, knowledge management, or electronic performance support systems.					

MASO Scoring Sheet

Instructions: In each of the mindset charts below, find the question numbers from the survey and place your letter score for that item in the box beneath the item number. Once you have done this for all twelve mindsets, assign the appropriate numerical value to each letter using the following scale:

   5 = All of the time

   4 = Most of the time

   3 = Some of the time

   2 = Rarely

   1 = Does not believe

Finally, add the values for each mindset and place the number you obtain in the box below the chart. See the example below:

Questions	3	54	71	73	77	78
Value	3	2	2	3	3	2
					Score	15

Creating Mind

Questions	1	24	30	41	50	61
Value					Score	

Democratic Mind

Questions	2	21	35	48	54	62
Value					Score	

Disciplined Mind

Questions	3	20	27	39	59	63
Value					Score	

Emotional Mind

Questions	4	13	36	42	49	64
Value					Score	

Ethical Mind

Questions	5	22	28	47	52	65
Value					Score	

Flexible Mind

Questions	6	18	32	45	55	66
Value					Score	

Respectful Mind

Questions	8	17	29	44	57	68
Value					Score	

Market Mind

Questions	7	19	31	40	60	67
Value					Score	

Spiritual Mind

Questions	9	23	26	38	51	69
Value					Score	

Strategic Mind

Questions	10	14	33	43	58	70
Value					Score	

Synthesizing Mind

Questions	11	15	25	37	56	71
Value					Score	

Technological Mind

Questions	12	16	34	46	53	72
Value					Score	

MASO Profile Chart

Instructions:

- *Step 1:* Add the scores of the participants for each mind, divide the sum by the number of participants (rounding applies), then circle the quotient of each mind on the chart. For example, in a workgroup of ten participants, add the scores of the Disciplined Mind for each of the ten participants, divide the sum by 10 (rounding applies), and circle the numbers on the chart. Complete all twelve minds on the chart.

- *Step 2:* Next, calculate the placement number by adding all the circled numbers on the chart, then divide the sum by 12 (rounding applies). When you obtain the placement number, then go to the MASO Diagnostic Sheet and read the section that is pertinent to your score.

	Strongly Agree/ All of the Time	Agree/Most of the Time	Somewhat Agree/ Some of the Time	Disagree/ Rarely	Strongly Disagree/ Does Not believe
Creating Mind	30 29 28 27 26 25	24 23 22 21 20 19	18 17 16 15 14 13	12 11 10 9 8 7	6 5 4 3 2 1
Democratic Mind	30 29 28 27 26 25	24 23 22 21 20 19	18 17 16 15 14 13	12 11 10 9 8 7	6 5 4 3 2 1
Disciplined Mind	30 29 28 27 26 25	24 23 22 21 20 19	18 17 16 15 14 13	12 11 10 9 8 7	6 5 4 3 2 1
Emotional Mind	30 29 28 27 26 25	24 23 22 21 20 19	18 17 16 15 14 13	12 11 10 9 8 7	6 5 4 3 2 1
Ethical Mind	30 29 28 27 26 25	24 23 22 21 20 19	18 17 16 15 14 13	12 11 10 9 8 7	6 5 4 3 2 1
Flexible Mind	30 29 28 27 26 25	24 23 22 21 20 19	18 17 16 15 14 13	12 11 10 9 8 7	6 5 4 3 2 1
Market Mind	30 29 28 27 26 25	24 23 22 21 20 19	18 17 16 15 14 13	12 11 10 9 8 7	6 5 4 3 2 1
Respectful Mind	30 29 28 27 26 25	24 23 22 21 20 19	18 17 16 15 14 13	12 11 10 9 8 7	6 5 4 3 2 1
Spiritual Mind	30 29 28 27 26 25	24 23 22 21 20 19	18 17 16 15 14 13	12 11 10 9 8 7	6 5 4 3 2 1
Strategic Mind	30 29 28 27 26 25	24 23 22 21 20 19	18 17 16 15 14 13	12 11 10 9 8 7	6 5 4 3 2 1
Synthesizing Mind	30 29 28 27 26 25	24 23 22 21 20 19	18 17 16 15 14 13	12 11 10 9 8 7	6 5 4 3 2 1
Technological Mind	30 29 28 27 26 25	24 23 22 21 20 19	18 17 16 15 14 13	12 11 10 9 8 7	6 5 4 3 2 1
MASO Placement:					

MASO Diagnostic Sheet

The following descriptions are short interpretations of what each placement may mean for your organization. There is no one perfect system or one perfect organization. These interpretations are intended to help you understand the collective minds of your organization. As mentioned previously, there is no right or wrong. The placement represents a position on the chart. The participants are to apply their results of each mind and the placement of all minds of their work group, team, or organization within the context and environment in which they work. They draw their own conclusions.

If the number is between 25 to 30 then	This means that 90 to 100 percent of employees in the organization might possess all minds individually and collectively. The organization perhaps has a superior position in the industry. The organization must be producing quality products and services as a result of excellent employees and management teams. The organization should continue to form project and program teams with workers who complement each other with their strong minds to attain the best results they are charged to accomplish. The organization should be actively nurturing the growth of all minds of the employees, encouraging and supporting the development of minds so that the organization continuously grows and maintains its position in the market.
If the number is between 19 and 24, then	This placement means the organization is in tune with balancing the minds of employees and work teams. From 80 to 89 percent of the employees in the organization possess most of the mindsets individually and collectively. The organization might have a strong presence in its industry. The organization is producing high-quality products and services as a result of fine employees and management teams. The organization should be actively nurturing the growth of all minds of the employees, encouraging and supporting the development of minds to not only maintain its market position but also to continuously gain market share. The organization might be forming project and program teams who complement each other with their strong mindsets.

If the number is between 13 and 18, then	The organization might be complacent and is comfortable maintaining the status quo. Perhaps 60 to 79 percent of the workers in the organization are not aware of and not interested in developing their minds. The employees and management are saying and using the right words, yet act indifferently. The organization might be profitable. However, to sustain and grow the business, repositioning of the organization's strategic plan might be necessary.
If the number is between 7 and 12 then	The organization should think critically about its future. Perhaps 40 to 59 percent—over half of the employees in the organization—might not have plans to develop their minds. Both the employees and organization might be just "going through the motions." The organization might be doing quite well; however, the real question is whether its market position could be diminishing in the future. Its products and services might not be viewed as competitively as the organization might think.
If the number is between 1 and 6, then	The organization might want to rethink its future vision and strategies. Perhaps only 20 to 39 percent of the employees in the organization possess only a few minds or the mix of minds is unbalanced. The majority of the employees and the organization are probably not willing to plan and develop their minds. The organization might be profitable for now, but the real question is for how long. Conversely, the organization might be experiencing difficult times in attracting talented and hardworking employees. In this case, the organization might desire to overhaul its workforce and reengineer its workplace.

Introduction

to the Articles and Discussion
Resources Section

The Articles and Discussion Resources Section is a collection of materials useful to every facilitator. The theories, background information, models, and methods will challenge facilitators' thinking, enrich their professional development, and assist their internal and external clients with productive change. These articles may be used as a basis for lecturettes, as handouts in training sessions, or as background reading material. This section will provide you with a variety of useful ideas, theoretical opinions, teachable models, practical strategies, and proven intervention methods. The articles will add richness and depth to your training and consulting knowledge and skills. They will challenge you to think differently, explore new concepts, and experiment with new interventions. The articles will continue to add a fresh perspective to your work.

The 2009 Pfeiffer Annual: Consulting includes twelve articles, in the following categories:

Individual Development: Developing Awareness and Understanding

**Setting Standards for Organizational Diversity Work: It's a Lot More Than Culture Fairs and Ethnic Food, by Julie O'Mara and Alan Richter

Individual Development: Life/Career Planning

What's Your Networking Quotient (NQ) and How Can You Improve It? by Michael Dulworth

Communication: Coaching and Encouraging

Coaching for Respectful Leadership, by Jan C. Salisbury

**Talent Management Topics

Communication: Communication in Organizations

Exploring the Compromise of Trust When Using Email, by William J. Shirey

Groups and Teams: Behavior and Roles in Groups

**Managing Free Agents, by Mohandas Nair

Consulting/Training: OD Theory and Practice

**Managing Talent Management Takes Talent: A Guide to Setting Up the Process, by Andy Beaulieu

Consulting/Training: Strategies and Techniques

Looking on the Bright Side: Conceptual Frameworks for Positive Performance, by Martha C. Yopp and Michael Kroth

Coaching for Behavioral Change, by Marshall Goldsmith

Facilitating: Techniques and Strategies

The Seven Habits of Highly Effective Facilitators (with Thanks to Stephen R. Covey), by Judith R. Holt

Facilitating: Evaluation

**New Accountabilities: Non-Financial Measures of Performance, by Ajay M. Pangarkar and Teresa Kirkwood

Leadership: Theories and Models

Leadership and Idiosyncrasy Credit: The IC Model and Its Implications for Leadership Practice, by Ingo Winkler

Leadership: Top-Management Issues and Concerns

**Job Analysis: Its Critical Role in Human Capital Management, by Leonard D. Goodstein and Erich P. Prien

As with previous *Annuals*, this volume covers a wide variety of topics. The range of articles presented encourages thought-provoking discussion about the present and future of HRD. We have done our best to categorize the articles for easy reference; however, many of the articles encompass a range of topics, disciplines, and

---

**Talent Management Topics

applications. If you do not find what you are looking for under one category, check a related category. In some cases we may place an article in the "Training" *Annual* that also has implications for "Consulting" and vice versa. As the field of HRD continues to grow and develop, there is more and more crossover between training and consulting. Explore all the contents of both volumes of the *Annual* in order to realize the full potential for learning and development that each offers.

Setting Standards for Organizational Diversity Work
It's a Lot More Than Culture Fairs and Ethnic Food

Julie O'Mara and Alan Richter, Ph.D.

Summary

One of the best strategic organizational tools for measuring "How are we doing?" in the diversity and inclusion arena is benchmarking against current global best practices. The recently published *Global Diversity & Inclusion Benchmarks* (O'Mara & Richter, 2006) provides fourteen categories of best practice and provides a useful way of rating an organization on any or all of these benchmarks.

Some organizations around the world excel at approaching diversity and inclusion in a way that helps meet their organizational goals. However, some organizations aren't sure what to do and flounder.

Some put the majority of their efforts into events such as culture fairs, ethnic lunches, and cultural performances at meetings and assuring that the gender and race of their employees mirror their marketplace. While there's nothing wrong with the above activities, especially if they are part of a strategy to meet organizational goals, these activities are not the essence of quality diversity and inclusion work.

The field of diversity, like the fields of training and organization development, is often criticized for being weak on measuring results. But that criticism is not only about the process of measuring, it's about having the right goals and having standards of achievement. Before measurements can be determined, realistic, meaningful goals must be set. This is where having a set of standards based on best practices can be very useful. Knowing what constitutes excellent work as opposed to substandard work helps organizations set and achieve meaningful diversity and inclusion goals.

Once meaningful goals are set, measuring their achievement becomes less mysterious. It becomes a relatively simple matter of determining how you will know when the goal is achieved and then putting measurement processes in place. The key is having the right goals based on the organization's business or service needs and challenges.

Exhibit 1. Defining Diversity and Inclusion

"Diversity" and "inclusion" are defined broadly. "Diversity" refers to the variety of differences and similarities among people, such as gender, race/ethnicity/tribe, age, religion, language, nationality, disability, sexual orientation, work style, work experience, job role and function, thinking style, personality type, socio-economic status, and so forth. "Inclusion" refers to how these differences and similarities are respected and create an equitable, healthy, and high-performing organization or community in which all individuals and their contributions are valued.

By "global," we simply mean that these benchmarks are universally applicable, not specific to a country or culture. However, cultural and country differences will greatly impact which categories you select and prioritize.

Examples of Diversity and Inclusion Standards

Examples of high-level standards, which are also referred to as benchmarks, include the following:

- Diversity has become part of the fabric of the organization. It is ingrained in the business and is not seen as an isolated program, but rather as a key to growth and success.

- Senior managers are seen as change agents and role models. They routinely discuss the importance of diversity as a core organizational strategy, and they provide consistent, visible leadership.

- The organization lives its diversity values as it supports the raising of issues and concerns, and encourages ideas from all employees.

- The organization accepts diversity in language, dress, physical expression, non-traditional schedules and leave, including parental leave, as fully legitimate.

- Reward and compensation systems have been designed specifically to reduce bias in retention and development of high-performing talent.

The above five examples are from standards at the top level in five of the fourteen benchmarking categories in *Global Diversity and Inclusion Benchmarks* by Julie O'Mara and Alan Richter (see Exhibit 2). The GDI Benchmarks tool is available at no charge on the authors' websites: www.omaraassoc.com and www.qedconsulting.com. Anyone can use this tool provided they credit the authors and agree to keep them posted on how GDI Benchmarks is being used.

Exhibit 2. The Fourteen Global Diversity and Inclusion Categories

1. *Vision, Goals, and Policies.* Covers the organization's overall concept of and approach to diversity, including its formal articulation of the value of diversity, the requirements of managing diversity, and how diversity is embedded in the fabric of the organization.

2. *Leadership and Accountability.* Covers the responsibilities of the organization's leadership in shaping, guiding, and supporting the organization's diversity initiatives. It also covers the accountability methods for leadership and for the organization as a whole.

3. *Infrastructure and Implementation.* Explores the way the organization structures or organizes its diversity function so that it can carry out its diversity goals effectively. This covers diversity staffing, diversity councils, and diversity networks.

4. *Work Schedules and Rules/Flexibility.* Describes the way work is organized and the extent to which there are flexible work arrangements for employees, including rules about taking leave.

5. *Job Design, Classification, and Compensation.* Explores the way jobs are designed, classified, compensated, and assigned. It includes assessment of reward and recognition systems and the degree to which an organization is healthy and equitable.

6. *Employee Benefits and Services.* Gauges the benefits and services provided to employees to meet their specific needs and concerns.

7. *Measurement, Research, and Assessment.* Evaluates the way diversity and inclusion are measured, whether the organization does the research to support diversity strategies, and the organization's assessment processes around diversity, inclusion, and organizational culture.

8. *Recruitment, Staffing, and Advancement.* Describes how the organization ensures diversity and inclusion in the hiring and selection process, and whether it creates an inclusive culture that enhances professional excellence and supports a healthy rate of retention.

9. *Diversity Training and Education.* Explores diversity and inclusion awareness, skill-building training and education, and the integration of such training in the overall training and development of all employees.

10. *Diversity Communications.* Describes how diversity is articulated and promoted, both internally and externally.

11. *Performance Improvement, Training, and Career Development.* Explores the extent to which performance improvement, training, and career development are equitably provided to enable all employees to succeed in their careers.

12. *Community and Government Relations.* Covers the organization's efforts to establish links with and invest in the communities it interacts with. This category also covers government relations and social responsibility.

13. *Products, Services, and Supplier Relations.* Gauges the organization's recognition of the diversity of its customer base and its effectiveness in designing and delivering appropriate products and services to current and future customers. This includes the processes of selecting, contracting, and interacting with the organization's suppliers and vendors.

14. *Marketing and Customer Service.* Surveys the organization's recognition of the diversity of its customer base and its sensitivity to the nuances of language, symbols, and images used in its marketing strategy, thereby attracting and satisfying its prospective and current customers.

(O'Mara & Richter, 2006)

Overview of Global Diversity and Inclusion Benchmarks

Wanting to help organizations improve the quality of the diversity work they do, O'Mara and Richter worked with an expert panel of forty-seven persons from around the world to build on an original set of benchmarks created by The Tennessee Valley Authority in the early 1990s. This original work was limited by being U.S.-focused and in great need of updating. O'Mara and Richter set out to update those standards, make them global in scope, and applicable across all kinds of organizations.

The fourteen categories cover a wide range of topics. In using the benchmarks, one can select from the fourteen categories offered—not all need apply, nor are they to be weighted equally. Different organizations will choose different categories and weightings for those categories, which recognizes and respects the diversity of interests and approaches globally.

Benchmarks usually incorporate best practices (or those perceived to be best practices at the time, although these can change). Organizations that do benchmarking may look upon these benchmarks as prescriptive for success or simply as descriptive of current best practices. The descriptive approach is safest, as the context is usually critical in assessing importance and relevance of the benchmarks. In one context one might ignore a best practice, while in another context it may be a critically sought factor. From a global perspective, therefore, it is imperative not to blindly follow these benchmarks, but to first evaluate the relevance and importance of them to your organization.

The best practices in each category are shown in the descriptors at 100 percent. For each category, the benchmarks are divided into five levels that indicate progress toward the best practices in that category—from 0 percent (where no work has begun) to 25 percent to 50 percent to 75 percent and then on to the best practices at 100 percent. For example, if your organization's practices generally match the 50 percent level in a category, you can consider your organization to be at the 50 percent level of the best practice in that category. It is important to stress that the 100 percent level is not an end-point, but rather the current best practice. To become a pioneer, an organization will go beyond the 100 percent descriptors and will then, hopefully, be benchmarked in the next update with those pioneering ideas set at 100 percent.

Exhibit 3 shows an example of the five levels of benchmarks in the Leadership and Accountability category.

Exhibit 3. Benchmarks for the Leadership and Accountability Category

0% ___ There is little or no leadership, involvement, or accountability regarding diversity.

___ Leaders strive to treat everyone the same and express that no diversity issues exist.

25% ___ The organization views diversity as a staff function.

___ Managers and supervisors accept some responsibility for diversity, especially as it relates to equal opportunity.

___ Leaders require scripts to discuss diversity.

___ Reactive measures are taken to deal with difficult diversity situations.

50% ___ Managers and supervisors view managing diversity as one of their responsibilities. Some employees and managers take individual responsibility for diversity.

___ Some leaders in the organization are active in diversity initiatives.

___ Senior management willingly makes speeches and public statements, but these are usually limited to diversity-specific functions and groups.

___ Senior management actively sponsors diversity networks.

___ Leaders understand that diversity is about treating people fairly rather than the same (equally) and strive to accommodate differences.

75% ___ Many managers, supervisors, and employees are involved in diversity issues and rewards and recognition are given to diversity champions or advocates.

___ Leaders support employee involvement in diversity networks.

___ Leaders often make internal and external scripted and extemporaneous speeches or statements relating to diversity to a variety of groups.

___ The board of directors is diverse, engaged in diversity issues, and holds the leadership team accountable for achieving the diversity vision.

___ Most managers receive some coaching in diversity and provide coaching to others.

___ Diversity is automatically incorporated into talent management processes.

100% ___ Management pay, bonuses, and promotions are tied to a variety of diversity indicators. Leaders are accountable for a balanced workforce, business performance, and providing tools and resources.

___ Managing diversity is considered an essential leadership competency.

___ Senior managers are seen as change agents and role models. They routinely discuss the importance of diversity as a core organizational strategy, and they provide consistent, visible leadership.

___ Leaders and board members publicly support diversity-related initiatives, even if they are perceived to be controversial.

___ Leaders and board members understand that the work of diversity is systemic and designed to change the organization's culture. They see themselves as owners, not just sponsors, of the organization's diversity work.

How the GDI Benchmarks are Being Used

Jason Mak, diversity and equity manager for the City of Eugene, Oregon, United States, used GDI benchmarks as a tool to help set a new vision for diversity work in the city. Eighty employees representing six departments and multiple levels in the organization met and used all fourteen categories of the GDI benchmarks to rate the results of their diversity and inclusion work to date. "When they started working with these GDI benchmarks, many of the raters realized that what we thought was good work, wasn't yet at the standard we now realized it needed to be. We were setting our goals too low with too much focus on activities that weren't going to make that much of a difference," Jason explained. The next step in their process was to imagine that it was five years in the future and they had reached the highest standards at the 100 percent level. The question they responded to next was: "What was done in years 1, 2, 3, 4, and 5 to reach the 100 percent level?" That reflection and projection process helped define their diversity and inclusion strategy for the next five years.

Nolitha Fakude, executive Director of SASOL and head of its human resources worldwide, based in Johannesburg, South Africa, was responsible for organizing a global diversity workshop for the Group Executive Committee of around a dozen global leaders. In the course of this workshop, five benchmarks, previously selected, were presented to participants who worked in three separate teams. Each team's objective was to rate SASOL from their perspective on these five benchmarks and see whether there was consensus on the scores as well as to comment on the level of satisfaction with those scores. Although the scores on all five categories were relatively high, reflecting the company's strong ongoing commitment to diversity, what did emerge was the gap between the rating for the South African-focused business versus the international arm of SASOL, which had significantly lower comparative scores. This immediately set the stage for SASOL to pay closer attention to its diversity strategy outside of South Africa, especially as the company grew internationally.

Helena Traschel, head of diversity management and consulting at Swiss Reinsurance Company, headquartered in Zurich, used just one benchmark, Leadership and Accountability, at a large leadership meeting to obtain feedback from this large group of leaders at the company on how they perceived themselves against best practices in this area. Although there were variations in the rating, the outcome was the strong realization that SwissRe was not at 100 percent and had room for improvement in this area of diversity. The exercise served as a useful catalyst to further strategy and action planning for leaders at the company.

As the above three examples show, the specific way these GDI benchmarks can be used varies. Generally, uses fall into these areas:

- To set and stretch standards

- To engage employees and promote accountability for progress

- To determine short-term and long-term diversity goals

- To develop or align organizational competency models and capabilities to maximize diversity efforts

When using these benchmarks, keep in mind that they are based on relatively limited experience—those of the authors and the forty-seven-member expert panel. Use these benchmarks only to guide your organization. Avoid making individual compensation decisions or judging the effectiveness of an individual based on them.

Conclusion

Using a researched set of standards for diversity and inclusion, such as the *Global Diversity and Inclusion Benchmarks*, can help organizations around the world meet their organizational goals. It also helps assure that, when measurements are put in place, the organization is measuring the strategies and activities that help achieve meaningful business or service goals. These strategies and activities need to be reviewed and updated from a global perspective to serve as effective benchmarks encapsulating current best practices.

Reference

O'Mara, J., & Richter, A. (2006). *Global diversity and inclusion benchmarks*. www.omaraassoc
.com and www.qedconsulting.com

Julie O'Mara, *president of O'Mara and Associates, an organization development consulting firm, specializes in leadership and managing diversity. A former national president of ASTD, she is currently writing a book on diversity best practices around the world to be published in 2009 by Pfeiffer. She is co-author of* Managing Workforce 2000: Gaining the Diversity Advantage, *a best-seller published by Jossey-Bass, and author of* Diversity Activities and Training Designs, *published by Pfeiffer.*

Alan Richter, Ph.D., *president of QED Consulting, specializes in consulting and training in the areas of leadership, values, culture, and change. He has designed innovative curricula for global diversity and intercultural effectiveness. He is author of the* Global Diversity Game *and the* Global Diversity Survey *and presents at conferences around the world. He has an M.A. and a B.A.B.Sc. from the University of Cape Town and a Ph.D. in philosophy from Birkbeck College, London University.*

What's Your Networking Quotient (NQ) and How Can You Improve It?

Michael Dulworth

Summary

People are finding that strong personal, professional, and virtual networks are an increasingly essential element in their development, effectiveness, and well-being. Just look at the popularity of virtual networks like MySpace®, Flickr™, LinkedIn®, and Ryze. A strong network can help you navigate rapid change in a number of ways, including broadening your exposure to information and your access to expertise. Networking is something that we all do naturally every day, even if we don't call it that. The people who are most successful in life do it purposefully. The purpose of this article is to help you do what you already do naturally, more consciously, more systematically, and more effectively. You will learn how to create new relationships and cultivate existing ones, and increase the size and quality of your current network.

Equation for Success

Below, you will have an opportunity to assess your NQ, or networking quotient. By having a single measure of your ability to develop strong networks—your Networking Quotient (NQ)—you'll understand the strength of your network and where you can improve.

Before we get to the assessment of your NQ, let me share with you my equation for success:

IQ + EQ + NQ = Success

IQ is the capacity to learn and understand and can be measured by standardized tests. EQ is an acronym for Emotional Intelligence Quotient. In his best-selling book, *Emotional Intelligence*, Daniel Goleman asserts that emotional intelligence (EQ) describes an ability, capacity, or skill to perceive, assess, and manage the emotions of one's self, of others, and of groups.

IQ, as the capacity to learn and understand, is pretty much a fixed capability in all of us. You may be pretty smart, but probably don't have the IQ of Stephen Hawking, the theoretical physicist. If we can't change our IQ and want to be more successful, what can we do?

We have some control over our EQ, so that can be a place to spend some time. It's an excellent idea for all of us to better understand ourselves and others from this perspective. But, like IQ, this can only take us so far. We all seem to be wired in certain ways, and it's unlikely that personal understanding, psychotherapy, or self-development are going to change these innate traits or behaviors.

It probably won't surprise you, then, that I think our NQ is where we have the greatest potential for exponential change. *We have almost 100 percent control over our ability to build, nurture, and leverage our networks.* Some might argue that being an extrovert or an introvert can greatly affect, if not determine, one's NQ score, but my experience tells me that this is not the case. Some of the best networkers I've ever met are introverts—and that includes me!

So, *IQ + EQ + NQ = Success*—and the best way to improve this equation is by improving your NQ. Before you can improve it, however, you need to know what your NQ is. Before we turn to assessing your NQ, it helps to take a look at exactly what we are assessing by taking a look at what makes a strong network to begin with.

The Qualities of Strong Networks

A number of years ago, Rob Cross, a University of Virginia researcher, wrote, "What really distinguishes high performers from the rest of the pack is their ability to maintain and leverage personal networks. The most effective create and tap large, diversified networks that are rich in experience and span all organizational boundaries."

Quantity

Size matters—you never know when an important connection will lead to a positive outcome. Virtually everyone I talked to in researching this topic stressed that larger networks are better networks. John Zapolski, partner, Management Innovation Group, says, "I am constantly looking to expand my network, especially people on the periphery of my network." The more people you have in your network, the more opportunities you have open to you, the more knowledge you can access, the more talent you can tap.

Relationships

Vibrant networks are more than a collection of business cards or email addresses: They are built on relationships. When you have strong relationships with people, they are more willing to spend time with you, share information with you, and open doors for you. You have to build those relationships, and you do that by showing a genuine interest in other people. IDEO's John Foster believes that a critical success factor in building a strong network is "making sure that you're dealing in a reciprocal relationship. You must give back to the relationship in some meaningful way, and there has to be a real exchange of value for a network relationship to be worthwhile."

Diversity

As Cross indicates, the best networks are diverse and span organizational boundaries. If everyone in your network looks like you, acts like you, and has your interests, how are you ever going to learn new things, discover new opportunities, or move in new directions? Let's hear from John Zapolski again: "I pretty actively look for opportunities to go to new events that are really outside of the typical domain of events that I would normally go to. For example, I met a woman recently who works in innovation, but she has a science background, so in talking with her I asked her a lot of questions about her background in bioengineering and genetics and I learned a lot. Inevitably, I'll find out what groups people like this belong to or events that they go to, and maybe I'll try to attend just so I can meet people outside of my core network. I look for those new events where I can get pulled into a direction of a deeper interest." Meeting diverse people with very different interests is the best way to keep expanding your horizons.

Quality

While quantity is important, quality is perhaps even more important. What does quality mean here? As Rob Cross indicated, a network should be "rich in experience." Quality refers to people who are experienced, who have strong networks of their own, who have authority, who can open doors, who command respect in their fields. Scott Saslow, executive director of The Institute of Executive Development, believes, "There is too much focus on the quantity of one's network right now ('I have eight billion colleagues from Linked-In'), and eventually the focus will shift to quality." In today's egalitarian world, we may try to treat everyone the same. But when it comes to networking, that idea makes little sense.

Now that we understand what makes for strong, vibrant networks, we can turn to measuring your NQ.

What's Your NQ?

Before you answer the questions below, take some time to list all the people in your network universe. Your networking universe consists of three primary types: (1) personal network, (2) professional network, and (3) virtual network. Each plays a role in determining your NQ. Your personal network is made up of your family, extended family, school friends and contacts, lifelong friends, and so on. It is also made up of your active friends (people you see face-to-face at least once a month) and people from your church, clubs, activities, neighborhood, and community.

Your professional network includes contacts from previous jobs, colleagues from other firms, and contacts in your current organization.

Your virtual network is comprised of people you know only through online interactions or other non-face-to-face connections.

Obviously, these networks overlap. You may be close friends with a business associate—or a family member may help you make a professional connection. And more and more networking is being done online. But they can serve as useful groupings in determining your NQ.

Two components go into your NQ: Part A focuses the scope and strength of your existing network, and Part B focuses on how active you are in building and maintaining your network.

With these components in mind, assess your NQ by honestly answering the following questions using the scales provided:

Part A: Network Scope and Strength

1. How many total people are in your personal, professional, and virtual networks? Add them all together and then score according to the following scale:

   0 = Under 10

   1 = 11 − 100

   2 = 101 − 200

   3 = 201 − 400

   4 = more than 400

2. How strong are your relationships with your network? Is someone just a *business card trader* (you traded cards but can hardly remember where or when), an *acquaintance* (she knows who you are and will probably return

a call); a *personal contact* (he'll do a favor if asked); or a *close friend* (you can count on him or her when the chips are down)?

0 = Everyone is a card trader

1 = Mostly acquaintances

2 = Lots of personal contacts

3 = A mix of personal contacts and close friends

4 = Mostly close friends with a few personal contacts and acquaintances

3. How diverse is your network? If everyone you know is the same age and gender as you, shares your cultural background, and works in the same area, your network is not diverse at all. On the other hand, if you network with everyone from eight to eighty, of both genders and a variety of cultural backgrounds, in different kinds of jobs in different industries, you have a very diverse network.

0 = Looking at my network is like looking in a mirror.

1 = My network is mostly people like me, but there is some diversity.

2 = There is a good amount of diversity.

3 = My network includes people from a wide variety of backgrounds and industries.

4 = My network includes many people from a wide variety of backgrounds, interests, and industries.

4. What's the overall quality of your network contacts? Are the people in your network experienced, with significant accomplishments? Do they have strong networks of their own? Are they well-known within a professional sphere? Can they open doors for you?

0 = I like them, but they aren't movers and shakers by any means.

1 = There are a few people with some connections.

2 = Some people in my network really command attention.

3 = Many people in my network are at the top of their fields and very well connected.

4 = I can contact almost anyone on earth through the people in my network.

Part B: Networking Activities

1. To what extent do you actively work on building your network relationships? Do you follow up after the first meeting? Do you make sure to periodically connect with people? Do you return phone calls and answer emails promptly? Do you try to meet face-to-face regularly?

   0 = I don't have time for that.

   1 = I try to reach out if I can find the time.

   2 = I try to make time, but it's hit or miss.

   3 = I consistently make time to connect with people.

   4 = I make connecting with people my top priority every day.

2. How actively do you recruit new members to your network?

   0 = do nothing

   1 = hardly at all

   2 = sometimes

   3 = often

   4 = all the time

3. How often do you help others in your network (both when asked for help and unsolicited)?

   0 = never

   1 = rarely

   2 = sometimes

   3 = often

   4 = very often

4. To what extent do you leverage the Internet to build and maintain your networks?

   0 = never

   1 = rarely

   2 = sometimes

   3 = often

   4 = all the time

Add your scores together and multiply the total by 5. You'll end up with an NQ between 0 and 160. The following chart can be used to interpret your score.

Score	Rating	Action
0–80	Below Average—Networking has not been on your radar screen	You need to be much more active in establishing and maintaining connections.
81–110	Average—nothing to brag about	You could benefit from being much more proactive
111–140	Above Average—a natural networker	You are doing well, but a more systematic effort could help
141–160	Networking genius!	You know it takes ongoing effort to maintain your network.

So how did you do? Are you a networking neophyte or a world-class contender? Does this self-assessment point to some areas for improvement? Remember, no matter what your score, you can always improve. That's the point.

Analyzing Your NQ

Let's examine your answers to the NQ survey. Add your answers for Part A and Part B separately. Because Part A assesses the strength of your current network and Part B assesses the time and effort you put into networking, the scores should be somewhat similar. We would expect, after all, that there is a direct correlation between the amount of time and effort we put into networking and the results we achieve.

If your results are out of whack (you score much higher on one part of the assessment than the other), you should take a few minutes to consider why. If your score on Part A indicates that you have a strong and vibrant network, while your score on Part B indicates you do not put much time and effort into networking, you're in a highly unusual situation. You've received something for nothing. Perhaps you inherited your network and interested family members are doing all the work to include you. Perhaps your spouse or a close associate is a genius networker and you are just going along for the ride. This could be dangerous; you might wake up one day and find no one bothers to return your calls. Remember, it is your responsibility to build and maintain your network, no one else's.

The more likely situation, if your scores for Part A and B are significantly different, is that your Part B score is higher that your Part A score. In other words your networking activities are not producing much in the way of results. Also take a moment to look at your lowest scores for both parts, which can show you where you should invest the most effort. You may have a large network with strong relationships, for example, but lack diversity and quality. As you work to build your network, you can directly address those issues. Or you may discover that you rarely give back to people in your network. Over time, this can lead to people labeling you as a "user"—and cause them to distance themselves from you.

Building and Improving Your Network

Most people are not very good networkers. I've come to this conclusion by talking with and watching the thousands of people I've come into contact with over the past twenty-five years. I also know that people can become better networkers by following a few simple steps. And these guidelines are not what you read about in most books on networking, for example, "the five steps to working a room" or "get out there and join a lot of groups." My advice and guidance, I hope, are much more practical and straightforward and can be weaved into your daily life without becoming too time-consuming. Becoming a better networker is not rocket science, but it does require that you learn some different behaviors.

As discussed above, strong, powerful networks have four key qualities: (1) quantity, (2) relationships, (3) diversity, and (4) quality. What do you get when you have a network with all these qualities? The tag line I use for my networking business sums it up:

The right people, the right conversations, the right time

This phrase encapsulates so much about having an effective network and being an effective networker. Having the right people in a network should be everyone's first priority. The *quality* of one's network trumps the *quantity* every time. Does your network have high-quality individuals in it? Is it a diverse group of people in terms of age, race, nationality, gender, occupation, and so on? One of the best ways to tell whether you have a high-quality network is if positive, unexpected things occur because of it.

Knowing the right people won't get you very far if you can't have the right conversations with them. You need to move beyond idle chatter. If you have a personal challenge, can you have a conversation with a trusted friend or mentor? If you have a business challenge, can you tap into the expertise of a knowledgeable peer? Probably the best way to get a feel for this issue is by evaluating past conversations with your network members. Were you able to have the right types of conversations with your network members, whether via an email, on the phone, or in person? If you've been frustrated by the quality of the advice and guidance you've received from your network, your network is not as good as it might be.

Finally, timing is everything, so "the right time" is the last critical component to a successful network. If it takes more than twenty-four hours to hear back from someone in your network, you haven't established the right type of relationship with that person. Let's consider guidelines for developing your network so that you can have the right conversations with the right people, at the right time.

Understanding Your Network

Your current network, no matter how large or small, is a key tool for you to use in growing the connections you have. And to use it effectively, you must understand who is in it, who is closest to you, who is more peripheral, who needs more attention, who needs your help, and who you owe favors to. So the first thing to do is to map your network, using one of the approaches discussed in the Mapping Your Network box below. Once you've mapped your network, you can start appreciating it, analyzing it, and assessing it—and then move on to building it, not as a one-time event, but as a lifelong journey.

Mapping Your Network

There isn't one set way to map your network. You can take a few different approaches.

1. Personal Networking Journey: This approach asks you to write out your networking history from birth to the present in a chronological timeline in the form of a narrative.
   - Start with parents (the first two nodes of your network).
   - List your immediate family and your extended family.
   - Recall your family friends and the friends you've made, starting as far back as you can remember.
   - List classmates and teachers from grade school, high school, college, and graduate school.
   - Write down colleagues and bosses from the jobs you've held.
   - Describe people you've met at church, through clubs, and any other groups you belong to.
   - List people you've met along the way, whether on airplanes, the bus, or on the street.

   I like this particular approach to mapping your network because it puts all of your network members into a context, that is, where you met them, how important they've been to you life and career, etc. This method also shows you how networks build over time and build organically. You'll probably also realize that your network is larger than you thought.

2. Address Book: This approach asks you to fill out an address book (whether online or on paper) with all of your network members. Most likely, you already have an address book of one type or another, but it probably does not have all of your network members listed. So start at A and go to Z and see how many people you actually know.

(Continued)

---

3. Tree Diagram: This approach starts with the first two nodes of your network (again, your parents) and lists your network in a tree diagram format. The powerful thing about using this method is that it'll show you who is connected to whom. Did you meet someone in your network through a friend, a colleague, or a casual acquaintance? Remembering these connections can be valuable when you want to tap into the power of your network because you'll understand the origin of the connection and be able to refer back to it. This visual depiction of your network will also help you to quickly identify a critical person in your network, especially if you properly label the various branches of the tree diagram. You might consider using one of the many software programs available for creating tree diagrams.

4. Spreadsheet: This approach allows you to create categories of information on your network members and to easily expand the information stored in these fields over time. For each name in a row, you can make column names (or fields) for information, such as a network member's contact information, where and when you met him or her, when you've contacted the person, area of expertise, personal information such as birth date, children's names, etc. The obvious limitation to this approach is that you need to continually update this information manually, which takes a lot of discipline and time.

5. Software Database: This approach is very similar to using a spreadsheet, but the organization of the information can be much more flexible and, if properly constructed, the database can be automatically updated with information from other sources. Many services exist on the web that are essentially database tools for building and maintaining your network contacts. Some, of course, go further and link your database of contacts to others so that you can leverage the networks of others.

6. Automated Web Tools: A new breed of networking tools is emerging that uses software agents to gather information on people in your network via your Outlook contacts, your email messages, your cell phone directory, and other sources. These tools automatically compile this information and help you organize and maintain it. Some also provide some intelligence on your network, such as the last time you contacted a network member or the strength of your relationship, or alert you to an upcoming birthday of a network member. These tools will improve a great deal over the next few years and will help us more easily build, maintain, and leverage our networks.

If you have taken the time to map your network, you have a pretty good idea who's who. That's a good start, but if you want to grow your network, it helps to go a little further.

First, go through your network and identify everyone as a *business card trader* (you traded cards but can hardly remember where or when); an *acquaintance* (knows who you are and will probably return a call); a *personal contact* (will do a favor if asked); or a *close friend* (you can count on the person when the chips are down).

Next, identify your top contacts, not in terms of their relationships with you, but in terms of their quality, their experience, their accomplishments, and their own networks. Who are the stars who can open lots of doors? Who has the ability to confer credibility?

Finally, figure out who you want to upgrade. In other words, for those who are not (yet) personal friends, who do you want to become more close to? Some business card trader may have made an impression and you neglected to follow up. Do you want to upgrade the person to an acquaintance? Are there acquaintances who deserve to become personal contacts or friends? Make a list of all these people. If you have a lot, you may want to prioritize them and focus just on the top five or so. Later on, we'll look at ways to upgrade people, which just amounts to strengthening your relationships with them.

Plan for Networking

You don't have to be outgoing or a social butterfly to network. In fact, social butterflies are not necessarily good networkers (they often don't make meaningful connections, and may not follow up). As I said, building your network is not rocket science.

You need to plan to build your network and follow it on a regular basis. Networks don't happen by accident. Don't tell yourself that you are too busy. A little forethought can go a long way. Make plans to attend a meeting or conference. Make time to reach out to people. Listen to what Barbara Howes (vice president of learning and development at Walt Disney and a member of Executive Networks' Chief Learning Officer Forum) has to say: "I think you actually have to plan for it. I think you have to want to network and want to nurture that network. I think those are things people forget about. They might have cast a wide net of acquaintances, but they're not truly networking. One isn't leading them to another; they've just got a lot of business cards in their wallets. The key is that you have to want to network, and you have to want to be in somebody else's network as well. So be open to the idea of sharing or introducing folks to others they may find interesting or valuable to know. You have to make time for it. You have to actually plan this and take the effort to send a personal note or an email, or just to stay current on the contact information."

You need to have your network in place before you really need it, Michael Drapkin emphasizes that you need to plan to make that happen. Michael and I have kept in touch over for ten years, ever since we were introduced by a mutual friend. As a musician and head of his own technology firm, he networks in two different spheres. Michael says, "You should always set aside a certain amount of time every week for networking, because you need to have the network going before you actually need it. Your network has to be active. If you wait to activate a network after you have some specific need, it's going to be much more difficult."

Sometimes people say they just don't have the time to network, that they are too busy. I think that is just an excuse when the actual problem is poor planning.

Being busy is never a good reason not to network, according to Joanne Black, author of the book *No More Cold Calling*. She is an excellent networker and, although she is extremely busy, she made time to talk to me. "I know everyone is super busy," she told me, "but like anything else, just put it on the calendar." Joanne adds, "One of the things I do when I want to attend something is to pay for it, because then I know I'm going to show up. If I say, 'Oh, I'll think about it and maybe do it later,' it rarely happens because it's not on the calendar." John Zapolski thinks people can make too big a deal out of being busy: "A lot of times we get into our routines and we get busy and we forget that there are small investments that need to be made to just maintain your ties."

Tammy Erickson, who was my boss when I worked at The Concours Group, offers the following advice to people who find it difficult to network. "One tip I would offer if it's difficult for you to network is to put yourself in a process where networking will occur by definition of the process. I think one of the great advantages, for example, of a program such as the ones that Concours runs is that it's virtually impossible not to network. You're there, and the events are carefully constructed so that there are opportunities to get to know other people both on a professional and on a social level. They're relaxed so that those kinds of relationships can form. They're provocative so that new ideas can be discussed." And of course, you have to intentionally join such groups and place their meetings on your calendar.

Take a look at your calendar for the next several weeks. Do you have any events scheduled primarily for networking? Have you set aside at least a few blocks of time for feeding your existing connections through phone calls, writing notes, or meetings? Your calendar can be very revealing of your actual priorities, as opposed to your good intentions.

Take Care of Your Network

Taking care of your network isn't complicated or difficult. It involves four key ingredients:

- Building relationships

- Recruiting new people

- Giving back or giving first

- Being sensitive

There is nothing magic about having a strong, vibrant network. It's all about how you treat people. Let's look at each of these key ingredients in turn.

Building Relationships

There's nothing mysterious about building networks, as Joanne Black told me, "It's about building relationships and getting to know people." Jim Kouzes, author of *The Leadership Challenge,* agrees: "It's all about relationships." And good relationships depend on trust. He adds, "The underlying factor like any relationship for me is trust. For example, take The Learning Network, which is organized by Marshall Goldsmith. People have become, over time, very self-disclosing in that group about not only professional, but personal stuff that's going on in their lives, whether it's health issues or business issues." And talking to people on a deeply personal level can only occur if there is a bond of trust. Trust means being discreet; you keep confidences and don't pass on gossip. It means keeping your word. It means being responsive. It means being honorable and not taking unfair advantage of information others share with you. "Trust can't be taken for granted," Jim says. "It always has to be nurtured."

You can't build relationships with people if you never connect with them. I've known Jim for over fifteen years. I make it a point to stay in touch with him. We try to get together for lunch at least once a year. You've got to stay in touch with people. As Bill Morin, the chairman of WJM Associates, says, "Networking is keeping your network alive and well and fresh and current. We recommend that you drop little notes to people from time to time, that you let them know things are going well, or that you're available to chat with them, or just constantly thinking of it as your mailing list, your contact list. And you've got to work at it all the time. Every day I call five or six people on our contact list, just call them out of the blue. I have been doing that for years, because I'm aware you can lose position and lose recognition so quickly." If you have trouble staying in touch with people, follow Joanne Black's advice above and set aside time on your calendar.

This does not mean that you can build relationships by "sending two-sentence emails or constantly updating your Rolodex," says Rob Cross. "I think the problem with so much advice about networking is that it is treated as a surface-level activity, creating a massive network of loose relationships as opposed to a well-invested one." Rob thinks it is much better to have a smaller network of close relationships than a large one of tangential connections. "What the smaller, better-invested network is good for is that it tends to bring you opportunities and it tends to be there when things aren't going well." The message is clear: Focus on building quality relationships, not quantities of relationships.

Recruiting New People

How do you keep yourself fresh and interested (and interesting) year after year? How do you continue to grow and develop long after you've mastered the basics of your professional role? The answer is to expose yourself to new situations and new opportunities. And the best way to do that is to refresh your network with new people who bring new dimensions to your network. Rob Cross puts it this way: "At points where leaders or others need better connectivity or new insights, innovative thinking, new opportunities, things that keep them fresh and making good decisions, a lot of time they're hearing the same voices over and over again. We know that people who fight that tendency and continue to bridge out, even when they don't see the immediate opportunity, tend to do much better. Over their careers, they're paid more, they are more mobile, and they advance more rapidly. My work shows they're more likely to be in the top 20 percent."

One way to meet new people is to ask people in your network to make introductions for you. Introductions are the most natural way to meet. Michael Drapkin reminded me: "How do you make the contacts that go into your network? Let's take the example of how you and I met. You and I met because I used to work at Lehman Brothers. We had a common friend in Andy Bergen, and Andy thought, 'Gee, you two guys should meet.' He made an introduction, you and I met at some bar in Manhattan, and we established a relationship. And we stayed in touch, so there's that personal introduction acquisition mode."

Joanne Black says that, to meet new people, you should "take a look at people you already know and know well. There are hundreds of different categories of people who could be sources of referrals and we're just not asking." People you have done business with, for example, are great resources for new business opportunities. "The most underleveraged, overlooked, source of referrals are current clients. . . . We just assume, 'We've done great work so of course they'll refer us.' Well, yeah, sometimes they do. But I only count on what I bring about. I don't wait for the phone to ring."

But it's not only clients who can refer us to new people. Joanne says, "Let's not forget all the other categories of people who could be referrals: our peers, our colleagues, our vendors, the associations we belong to, our neighbors, people we meet on airplanes. It is not just about who these people are . . . it's about who they know."

According to Joanne, meetings, associations, and other network accelerators are also effective ways to meet new people. Unfortunately, people often do not use these accelerators very effectively. And they are often too impatient.

Sometimes, if you have identified someone you want to meet, you can bypass introductions and meetings and go for the direct approach. Often, just picking up the phone works. Jeff Rosenthal, a search consultant with Russell Reynolds, and I meet every six months or so to trade possible contacts. He told me, "Sometimes I've called people just to say 'I respect what you do.' I clearly say up-front 'Here's why I'd like to meet with you.'" The point is to be clear about why you want to meet. Bill Morin told me that meeting new people is not about chatting. It's about "being specific, being open and straightforward when requesting information or ideas, [and] realizing it's not a cathartic experience when you meet with someone or chat with him or her on the phone, it's specific. Ask, 'Who do you know at Acme? Who do you know at XX business?' Don't say, 'Gee, can you help me?' That's too general, too wide open. Most of us just don't have the time to think for the other person."

People really appreciate the direct approach. They're often willing to help, but only if they know what it's about. If you want to meet someone, you need to have a well-defined reason. Nothing turns busy people off more than pointless networking. "I can't tell you how often people come up and give me a card as if I should want it," Richard Leider, the CEO of the Inventure Group, stated with considerable heat, "and it's not that they're not nice people. What am I supposed to do with it? What is your request or what is your offer when you're networking? More than half the time, I don't know what they're asking of me. I know they want me to either send them business or endorse their work, or do something. But they don't say. And so I think it's more honest and it works more effectively if one is transparent. What is it you want, or what is it you're offering?" To repeat the point: When trading business cards with someone new, be clear about what you want or what you are offering.

Of course, meeting new people is only the starting point. If you really want to build a relationship with someone, you have to follow up. Quality trumps quantity every time. When you meet a new person, "The initial handshake is the beginning of what could be a very durable long-term relationship," Patricia Franklin told me. "But it relies on excellent follow-up." Patricia is the chief learning officer for Vistage International, a professional networking company that has 13,500 members in fifteen countries. She says: "Let's say you go to a fantastic networking function and you walk away with a fistful of business cards, but you don't do anything with them. And weeks go by, and suddenly you really feel like you might need to follow up, but you can't because you have lost the context. You can't remember what you spoke to somebody about. Methodical, logical, follow-up is key." When people give you cards, she says, "write down on the back of the card what it is that you're going to be doing for the person, or what the person is going to be doing for you."

In addition to following up, you need to be patient. Relationships take time to develop. You are not going to go from a business-card-trading relationship to personal friendship overnight.

Giving Back or Giving First

As a skilled networker, your job is to see that all the people in your network achieve success. As Marshall Goldsmith explains: "To me a key to networking is not focusing on what you can get—the key to networking is focusing on what you can give. My general philosophy is very simple. Find great people, give them things, and work on a relationship where they try to give me as much as I give them."

The idea of giving back or reciprocity came up again and again in my interviews.

Jim Kouzes states, "If you're going to be in a relationship, add value rather than always asking for something. A lot of networking is one-way, which [is] sort of the hot button for me. There needs to be reciprocity first of all."

Richard Leider adds: "I don't approach networking with an expectation that I'm going to get something out of this personally. It's really more of an opportunity to participate and be generous in sharing your own contacts with other people or [sharing] your own expertise. Expect to give more than you get."

John Foster believes: "The key to reciprocity is having a level of self-awareness about how you behave with other people." We've all come across people who are so focused on themselves they really can't see how others react to them—and they don't realize how self-centered they seem. If you find yourself constantly asking for favors—instead of offering help—it is time to do a little soul searching.

"Probably the most important thing," Disney's Barbara Howes says, "is you have to be a good network member yourself. You have to be available for people when *they* need help in opening doors."

Part of being available to people is to be open about yourself. Let others know about your background and interests. When people know about you—what you are good at and what connections you have—then they know how you might be able to help them. If you are always pumping others for information, but not disclosing much about yourself, you aren't creating balanced relationships. Here is how IDEO's John Foster put it: "I think it's important to have a point of view and some sense of self-awareness and aspiration so that others know how to connect to you. If people know what I'm interested in, they may have more of a desire to stay connected to me, so I become 'sticky.'"

Be open about who you are, what interests you, and what your goals are. The more people know about you, the more they are able to help.

Being Sensitive

Finally, effective networkers are sensitive to other people's busy schedules. "Be very, very sensitive to another person's time," Bill Morin advises. "Get to the point." Don't think you should be taking up time chatting about families with people unless they're personal friends. "I would recommend not [taking more than five to ten minutes for] a networking interview or a chat. I'm talking about a telephone contact. Now, if the person says, 'Come on in,' I would still plan for twenty minutes, a half-hour max. You can always stay longer, but from an expectation point of view, I'd actually [advise] the person going for the interview to say, 'I'm only going to need twenty minutes, maybe half and hour of your time.' Give me a framework, rather than the fear I would have that someone's going to come in and chat for two hours."

Conclusion

Building your network doesn't have to be hard work, but as we have seen, it does take planning, attention to detail, and sensitivity to the needs of others. The most effective tool you have at your disposal is the network you already have. If you pay attention to the care and nurture of your existing network, and use it to meet new people, build reciprocal relationships, and maintain a business-like approach that is sensitive to the time constraints of others, your network will blossom over time.

References

Goleman (1995). *Emotional intelligence: Why it can matter more than IQ.* New York: Bantam Books.

Michael Dulworth *is the chairman and CEO of Executive Networks, Inc. (www.executivenetworks.com), a leading provider of peer-to-peer network for HR professionals in large organizations worldwide. Before acquiring Executive Networks in 2003, he was vice president of Learning Services at The Concours Group. Prior to that, Dulworth was a founder and CEO of Learning Technologies Group, Inc. Dulworth has also held positions at The Conference Board, Sirota & Alper Associates, and the U.S. General Accounting Office. He is the author, co-author, or a contributor to seven books on executive development, learning, and high-performance organizations. His most recent books are* Corporate Learning: Proven and Practical Guidelines for Building a Sustainable Learning Strategy *(Pfeiffer, 2005),* Strategic Executive Development: The Five Essential Investments *(Pfeiffer, 2005), and* The Connect Effect: Building Strong Personal, Professional and Virtual Networks *(Berrett-Koehler, 2008). Dulworth has a BA from the University of Michigan and an MPA, with a concentration in organizational behavior, from the University of Southern California.*

Coaching for Respectful Leadership

Jan C. Salisbury

Summary

Executive coaching and leadership development is in high gear these days as organizations understand that leaders at every level make the difference in accomplishing the mission. In addition, leadership experts tend to agree with the common wisdom that "most good leaders are made, not born." Yet there is little in the coaching or leadership literature that addresses a frequent challenge in leadership development: How do you transform leaders who behave in ways that are perceived as disrespectful? Regardless of how technically competent and bright a leader may be, intimidating, emotionally negative, or biased behaviors seriously undermine a leader's credibility and effectiveness. "Coaching for Respectful Leadership" is a model for addressing and improving these leadership behaviors. The goal of this approach is not only to extinguish disrespectful and inappropriate behaviors, but also to increase a leader's capacity to lead. This article describes five stages, strategies, and themes coaches can apply when faced with leaders who misbehave.

At its heart, coaching for respectful leadership is about emotional intelligence and understanding diversity. Emotional intelligence or the ability to feel, understand, articulate and effectively apply the power of emotions in our work is essential to why leaders behave disrespectfully in the workplace (Goleman, Boyatzis, & McKee, 2002). EI competencies, such as conflict resolution, working on diverse teams, and coping with ambiguity, change, and stress, are rarely taught in traditional higher education. Leaders often advance because they are technically superior, not because of their emotional intelligence. However, EI accounts for an astounding 85 to 90 percent of the difference between outstanding leaders and their average peers (Cherniss & Goleman, 2001; Goleman, Boyatzis, & McKee, 2002; Kellerman, 2004). Why does it matter so much? High-potential employees will not stay or excel in an atmosphere in which they feel mistreated or unfairly treated. Furthermore, employees are diverse in their backgrounds and cultural influences. Unless leaders can create an atmosphere that brings out the best in *each* employee, organizations risk losing a critical competitive advantage (Druskat & Wolff, 2001). From an emotional intelligence perspective, the leadership coach who addresses disrespectful behavior should be prepared to explore: (1) the emotional reasons for behaving disrespectfully, (2) the impact of the behavior on the workplace, and (3) the role of diversity and bias.

I define disrespectful leadership as any leader behavior that violates professional, cultural, and/or organizational standards of treating others and has the impact of offending, intimidating, or fundamentally disrupting the emotional trust between a leader and follower. Degrees of disrespectful behavior range from episodic, subtle and unintentional behavior to harassing, bullying and intimidation (Vardi & Weitz, 2004). Intentional harassment or bullying that creates a risk to the health and safety of employees is not the focus of coaching for respectful leadership (Salisbury & Dominick, 2004). More often than not, these behaviors result in termination and are not likely to change through a coaching process. However, any type of disrespect or incivility can affect an employee's satisfaction levels and commitment to work (Cortina, Magley, Williams, & Langout, 2001). Unintentional disrespect is more difficult to precisely define because it is often highly contextual. Respect reflects on integrity and trust. Furthermore, while we tend to believe respect is universally understood, our ideas of respect are deeply felt, disparately formed, and rarely articulated or shared directly. The adage, "We know it when we feel or see it" often rings true when we speak of someone who is respectful or disrespectful.

A leader's power exacerbates the impact of disrespect and challenges the organization to promptly correct the breach of trust. "Coaching for Respectful Leadership" is one method for doing so. By targeting disrespectful behavior, this coaching model can help motivated leaders transform a serious deficit into an opportunity for growth.

Coaching Prerequisites

There are three basic prerequisites for engaging in respectful leadership coaching: (1) the organization should deliver a clear message to the leader about what is and is not acceptable behavior, (2) the leader must be committed to engaging in coaching to change the problematic behavior, and (3) the leadership coach must have the background for understanding and addressing disrespectful behavior.

The Organization

It is unusual for a leader to proactively seek coaching for disrespectful behavior. Organizations usually confront a leader with feedback that his behavior offends employees and will not be allowed to continue. Although the feedback is often given under an "anonymous" umbrella (because of the fear of retaliation), it should be as specific as possible, both in terms of the behaviors and of the impact on people. The organization must also feel and communicate that the leader is valued and worth the investment of individual coaching. These conversations are emotionally laden. The leader may not always "hear" all the information. The organization may need several meetings and a period of reflection to assess whether the leader is open to change.

The Leader

Leaders commonly respond to feedback regarding disrespectful behavior with a mixture of disbelief and defensiveness. How does the organization or the coach know, then, whether the leader is willing to use coaching to address his or her behavior? I explore several questions with the organization including: Is the leader ethical and generally competent? Do employees and the organization feel the leader adds value to the organization? Has the leader expressed an authentic desire to change and does he or she show signs of "owning" the feedback? Is the leader's ego capable of absorbing the feedback and not inclined to retaliate against those who gave the feedback? Is he or she willing to spend the time and resources to change? The coach can also question the leader during the first few meetings. The answers to these questions before and during the coaching should help gauge a leader's readiness and potential for success. At the very least, these questions can help all parties involved understand that the coaching process is a serious commitment.

The Coach

Coaches who undertake coaching for respectful leadership should be experienced in the following general areas: First, they should understand the psychological dynamics of disrespectful behavior in the workplace, including why individuals misbehave and the impact they have on employees and organizations. Second, they should have a background in leadership theory, communication, and interpersonal dynamics. If the behavior is perceived as biased, coaches should be able to explore the role diversity plays in the situations described. Third, they should be comfortable confronting as well as supporting leaders as they work through defensive, angry, and frustrating feelings. The ability to both help leaders see the truth in others' perceptions and advocate strongly for their ability to change is essential.

When the organization, leader, and coach agree that the coaching is appropriate, the leader and coach can meet directly to discuss in greater detail the background of the concerns and the process of coaching. Experienced coaches understand the importance of establishing a relationship of trust and support during these first meetings. The following stages describe the process and special concerns of coaching for respectful leadership.

Stage I: Holding Up the Mirror: Understanding the Basis of Disrespect

Data describing disrespectful behavior comes from many sources: performance reviews, 360-degree feedback assessments, and complaints to human resources, etc. Usually, disrespectful behavior merits coaching when its impact is significant and/ or there is a pattern of behavior. The leader and the coach must first understand what is wrong and why before defining the goals.

Collecting Data

The coach must begin with clear, behavioral data of what has felt disrespectful and understand the impact on those targeted. Sometimes the organizational feedback for the leader is insufficient. The examples are too broad and the leader does not clearly understand the extent of the problem. The leadership coach may recommend additional conversations with the organizational representative. The following example is representative of how a coach may proceed when the coach or leader decides additional feedback is warranted.

> Joleen was an experienced IT director for a municipality. She had been lauded by her superiors for her quick wit, her innovative vision, and her drive. Yet, there was also a pattern of capable managers leaving her team, reports of angry outbursts, and sporadic micromanaging. Joleen's annual review picked up a growing chorus of peers and superiors who felt Joleen's career would be stifled unless these behaviors changed. Joleen was incredulous about her feedback. Although she acknowledged a few lapses in communication, she did not understand why these behaviors were career stoppers. She worried that a few malcontents had skewed the feedback. She requested that the coach collect additional data.
>
> Joleen e-mailed fifteen members of her staff, management peers, and others with the news that she was working with a coach to further develop her leadership, and that she needed their help. She encouraged them to be honest with the coach and assured them that the feedback would be anonymous. Using phone interviews, the coach gathered the data by asking generic leadership development questions about style, strengths and weaknesses, accessibility, what they looked for in a leader, and what they would like the leader to do more of and less of. The coach also specifically asked whether the interviewees felt respected and treated fairly. The interview data was summarized in terms of themes and helped in two ways: It greatly clarified what others experienced

as disrespectful and it supported Joleen's strengths as a leader. Joleen's resistance dissipated. She accepted the validity of the feedback and moved forward, toward defining the leader she wanted to become.

Leaders may feel challenged and even threatened when they initially hear critical feedback. However, most people don't mind confrontation as long as they feel supported and there is a way to "fix" the problem. By holding up a mirror for the leader, coaches can teach leaders to see and accept how others perceive them. This is key emotional intelligence ability for leaders.

Personality Versus Behavioral Change

Leaders also need to hear that coaching for respectful leadership is not focused on changing the leader's personality, because that is not possible or appropriate. Communication styles and values, however, may be very relevant, particularly when factored into diversity issues. For example, a leader's direct style of communicating may greatly conflict with cultural and individual norms that prefer indirect styles. While communicating the data, coaches should check carefully with the leader's perceptions and emotions. How do they feel, and what do they think about the new information? What is surprising or confusing, what is not? These open-ended questions serve two purposes: They teach the leader tools for reflecting on feedback and they help the leaders understand how their emotions work.

Accurate data collecting is vital for initiating the next stage of coaching for respectful leadership, identifying what factors contribute to the leader's behavior and understanding the impact of the behavior on others.

Stage II: Understanding the Roots of Disrespectful Behavior

Understanding the reasons why someone will choose to behave disrespectfully is central to a successful coaching process. From an emotional intelligence perspective, exploring the basis for any kind of behavior helps leaders become conscious of their behavior on a deeper level. Their awareness can then lead to addressing what is misunderstood or unresolved and to modifying their reactions. The goal is to enable leaders to employ respectful leadership practices. While the causes of a leader's behavior are diverse, there are several common themes underlying most disrespectful behavior.

Defining the Blind Spot

The primary reason a leader has continued to behave in ways that are counter to organizational values is that he or she does not see the impact of his or her behavior on others and on the ability to lead. Leaders have failed to perceive others and themselves as they truly are. Perhaps they are so focused on their own needs that others aren't in the picture at all, or perhaps they don't have the knowledge to complete the picture. Using the Johari Window (a psychological tool created by Joseph Luft and Harry Ingham in 1955) as a model for effective communication, the coach can demonstrate the importance of increasing self-knowledge in the leader's development plan. The larger the blind spot, the longer it may take to see what is. In the case of Joleen, her blind spot was in her valuing the outcome and not *how* she reached her goal.

Intent Versus Impact

Leaders' initial defensive reaction to feedback is often focused on their intent. They argue that that their intentions were reasonable and that the recipients are equally or more responsible for their reactions. Coaches should help leaders clearly distinguish between their intent and the impact, each a product of an individual's background and cultural filters. Detailing the emotional impact (intimidation, anger, fear, etc.) of specific behaviors underscores why impact is more important than intent. The key learning here is that successful and respectful leadership aligns intention with the impact on others. Once leaders accept and understand this concept, they are ready to look at alternative ways to behave.

Lack of Appreciation and Understanding of Power

Many leaders don't acknowledge or understand the power that they wield. A leader's need to be liked or to be perfect may undermine his or her ability to understand the power of disrespectful communication. By focusing on how others and the organization define their power, leaders are more likely to see why others have reacted so strongly to their actions. They can also better understand why others don't confront them directly (a common frustration of leaders). Acknowledging one's power can be daunting, but it can motivate leaders to reflect before they act!

Focusing on the Task and Not the Relationship

Many leaders are promoted because they "know how to get things done." They are "experts" in the technical aspects of their jobs and consummate problem-solvers. They may believe in the adage, "If you want something done right, do it yourself." However, their drive for performance is focused strictly on outcome, not process. As a result, they are prone to impatience, critical communication, micromanaging, shutting people off, and other hyper-task-focused leadership. Education about concepts such as Situational Leadership and factors that spur great performance in others can enable leaders to focus on building relationships and increasing their ability to engage in connective leadership (Lipmman-Blumen, 1996).

The Psychology of Unmet Needs

Anxiety, depression, obsessive-compulsive disorders, workaholic tendencies, lack of work-life balance, and other, long-lasting psychological issues can also undermine respectful leadership. Leaders who are so afraid of failure that their anxiety triggers angry outbursts or who have little empathy for others because they received little support from others in their own development may not be able to change their behavior until they receive help from a mental health professional. The role of the coach is to help the leader identify these issues and then to encourage him or her to seek additional resources immediately. In some cases, failure to address these psychological issues will greatly impede or undermine the coaching process.

The Role of Bias, Prejudice, and Culture

Leaders who have made remarks or comments that show bias toward ethnic groups, women, or other groups protected under law are under the greatest pressure to change. The organization must show that, in addition to sanctioning the leader in some way, it has done something that deters that sort of behavior from happening again (Salisbury & Dominic, 2004). While rarely intended to do harm, low-level "harassing" behavior by a leader can be destructive to individuals and workplaces (Salisbury & Dominick, 2004). Unfortunately, most harassment training does little to help leaders understand their own cultural biases. Coaches who choose to address these behaviors should be well versed in the dynamics of stereotyping, sexism, racism, and other systems of bias. In addition, they may have to be prepared to help the leader recognize and adapt to cultural differences. For specific guidelines, consult *Individual Training for Harassers* (Salisbury & Jaffey, 1995).

The Dynamics of the Organizational Climate

Organizational cultures sometimes play an important role in eliciting disrespectful behavior. Too often, other leaders are engaging in similar behavior, or else the stress level is overwhelming. The leader may be frustrated and thwarted from meeting unreasonable expectations and aggressive, even hostile behavior may result (Vardi & Weitz, 2004). The leader may not have direct control over these factors. However, recognizing how their environment affects them can help leaders detach themselves and cope more effectively with the pressures of the environment.

Leadership Development and Role Models

Unfortunately, many leaders have never experienced formal leadership education. They model their styles after a parent or other leaders in and outside the workplace. Traditional supervision training may expose them to supervising tasks but not to the added role of a leader whose role is to encourage, inspire, and motivate (among other things). Furthermore, they do not have the advantage of formal training that can provide a template for effective leadership. Depending on the learning style of the leader and the resources available, coaches should help the leader explore outside training and mentoring resources for increasing their leadership knowledge. They should also be ready to help leaders understand the sources of their passion and values about leadership and provide articles, videos, and other resources (George, 2007).

Leaders who understand their disrespectful behavior from both their own and others' perspectives are then ready to identify their goals for the coaching process.

Stage III: Defining the Goals and a Plan for Change

As the themes from the feedback emerge, the coaching sessions should focus on definable goals and strategies. Goals create accountability for the coach and the leader. Generally, the goals focus primarily on respectful and effective leadership behavior. However, it's important once again not to avoid articulating the types of behavior that must stop or decrease. From a staff perspective, any reoccurrence of the "disrespectful" behaviors will wipe away gains made by appropriate behavior.

The coach and leader can work together on the goals; each summarizing what the leader believes will make the most difference. The leader can decide to share his goals with his boss or direct reports. Sharing goals communicates transparency and enlists the support of others. As goals are achieved, new goals can emerge until the leader and the organization see that the original behavior has been corrected and new practices are in place.

The goals below are for Joleen, the IT manager.

Goal I: Learn to Listen and Coach

- Refrain from giving advice and being critical.

- Practice active listening skills.

- Enroll in a leader coaching course.

Goal II: Communicate Respectfully at All Times

- Decrease the use of email and impersonal communications, especially about emotional issues.

- When aware of frustration or anger, choose to delay responding to situations until decided on the best response for the situation.

- Do not act on the urge to micromanage. Plan how to approach the solution by enabling and coaching others.

- Take a communication style assessment and become aware of different communication styles.

Goal III: Create a Collaborative, Inclusive Atmosphere for the Team

- Explore opportunities for building relationships and understanding differences between members of the team.

- Facilitate a team-wide process of developing behavioral norms that will increase our productivity, trust, and creativity.

- Observe and meet with a leader/mentor who can model the behaviors targeted in the goals.

The coach should also discuss how the leader will measure his or her success in reaching these goals, including periodic feedback with a significant boss, human resources manager, or other objective sources. As the coaching moves into the fourth stage, the coach can also elicit specific examples that illustrate what is going well and what continues to be a challenge for the leader.

Stage IV: Exploring and Experimenting

The fourth stage of coaching expands on the insights and feedback that began in the first three stages. In this stage, the coach uses an array of leadership development tools and resources to help the leader learn new ways of thinking, feeling and behaving. A leader's learning style, whether experiential, conceptual, or observational, will help determine what methods will be most helpful.

Using a Leadership Log

New choices cannot occur without expanding awareness. The ability to hold a mirror to see oneself is a fundamental competency of developing respectful, effective leaders. One primary tool for learning to reflect and be proactive is a leadership log. The leaders are encouraged to keep a log of situations that feel both successful and challenging. They are encouraged to identify the following in their logs.

Leadership Log

- Describe the situation.

- Describe how you felt about the situation and why.

- Describe how you behaved.

- What were the consequences of the behavior?

- What other choices did you have?

The log provides rich examples for the coaching process. Leaders learn how to manage their emotions and what behaviors are effective. Coaches can offer support and resources that are directly applicable to the leader's everyday world.

In one example, a leader was astounded that an email sent back to a subordinate asking pointed questions about a project shut down the conversation between them. The leader felt the email was expressing interest, and that it was not a rejection of the project. The awareness log showed that he was excited about the project but also anxious to move it forward. The coaching opportunity here was to explore how emails are poor vehicles for capturing excitement and motivating others, because the nonverbal and emotional messages are missing. In addition, asking questions without directly communicating support and interest can create defensiveness in others. The leader then chose to meet with the project leader and has greatly reduced the role of email in crucial conversations.

Proactive Planning

Helping leaders be proactive in changing their behavior is another core strategy for coaching respectful leadership. In what situations can leaders anticipate using new behavior patterns and create different histories with those with whom they work? The list might include one-on-one meetings, plans for change, and presentations. What can leaders do to prepare for these contexts? What situations are most challenging to them? and What approaches may be more effective than those in the past? Being prepared can reduce the anxiety or tensions that may lead to disrespectful behavior. For example:

> When George met with his accounting staff, he often felt and reacted impatiently—the staff's focus on detail and their inability to give him a bigger picture of the budget was frustrating. As a result, he interrupted them and made sarcastic remarks about their profession. In addition, his accounting staff was female and perceived his behavior, when compared with male staff in other departments, as demeaning and sexist.
>
> The coaching focused on George's feelings, needs, and behavior in this situation. George realized his own culpability for the outcome of these meetings. He developed a clear strategy for the next meeting. First, he apologized for his behavior and clearly communicated what financial information he needed and why. He actively listened to questions and concerns and discovered that he had not comprehended the challenges of the software being used. He also expressed appreciation for his accounting staff's specific contributions to the

business. George and the accounting department manager planned to support the staff's need for new tools and helped establish mutual trust. In the meantime, the staff worked diligently to deliver the information George needed.

By encouraging them to reflect and experiment in tough situations, coaches help leaders see the array of possibilities for leadership. Leaders also begin to see how diversity, whether professional background, ethnicity, gender, or personality, can make a difference in how they and others react and in how to adapt to those differences. It is a shifting perspective that calls for the ability to know what is appropriate, when, and why. For example, global teams confront the impact of cultural norms on respectful behavior daily. Virtual teams working across global boundaries struggle with the inadequacy of electronic communication and the paucity of face time to work through conflict and decisions highly affected by cultural differences. By acknowledging the challenge of cultural differences, leaders can minimize the barriers and help teams adapt to disparate values and styles.

Developing Empathy and Sensitivity

Leaders who become attuned to themselves and empathetic toward others become increasingly sensitive to disrespectful behavior in others. Previously oblivious to common disrespectful behavior, they now find themselves reacting strongly. These "teachable moments" are wonderful opportunities for leaders to coach others, and when appropriate, share their own journeys. They also reveal the depth of the leaders' commitment to respect.

The experimenting stage of respectful leadership coaching helps the leader establish new awareness, attitudes, and practices. Generally, the focus is significantly less on decreasing disrespect and more on increasing effective, respectful leadership behavior.

Stage V: Sustaining the Transformation

As with most coaching processes, the success of coaching for respectful leadership depends on the leader's ability to sustain both the internal and external changes. The "unconscious" has become "conscious" both in terms of eliminating the targeted behavior patterns and of integrating new practices. As they reach the end of the coaching period, the coach and leader should ask the following questions: Has the leader learned to reflect on his or her behavior as well as to understand and connect with others in critical situations? Can he or she identify the emotional trigger points and biases that lead to dysfunctional behavior? Is he or she clear about the connection between leading respectfully and the success of the team or organization? Does he or she understand the concept so aptly articulated by Aristotle that being angry is easy, but to be angry at the right time, for the right reason, in the right way, is not easy? (Goleman, 1995).

As a result of the coaching process, leaders should experience success from their changed behavior. A leader's ability to notice the positive outcomes of his or her new behaviors is important for sustaining the transformation. These outcomes should become self-reinforcing and augmented by formal and informal assessments from others in the work environment. The coach can help the leader celebrate both the profound insights and the small, incremental changes that occur during the coaching process. Examples of success for individual leaders include the following:

- Helped the person identify the underlying issues and supported the ability to solve the problem;

- Facilitated more open discussion and trust by spending more time walking around and learning about employee concerns;

- Apologized for an action that had unintended consequences for someone's job;

- Facilitated a difficult change by acknowledging the team reactions and emotions before engaging them on how they could move forward;

- Facilitated open feedback on initiatives at a staff meeting;

- Stopped responding to emotional issues via email and picked up the phone;

- Found humor in themselves, rather than telling jokes that offended people;

- Greeted people every day and found authentic ways to regularly express appreciation for people's work;

- Balanced appreciation with challenging feedback; and

- Sponsored and participated in a major diversity initiative focused on global business partners.

How Long Does It Take?

How long it will take depends on the behavior patterns, the person, and the organizational climate. Most organizations want to begin to see some change in "disrespectful" behavior immediately because the cost for them is so high. Some leaders are able to quickly perceive why their behavior is inappropriate and apply their leadership acumen to making a change. For others, the "blind spot" is so difficult to see that regular coaching sessions over several months may be required to help long-lasting change take place. Organizations may want to know at the beginning how long and how much coaching is needed, but coaches should be honest that, until the data is shared and the coach can assess the leader's background and reaction, it is not possible to know.

When Does Coaching Fail?

Many factors contribute to why coaching may not help improve a leader's behavior besides the leader's denial of the feedback or his or her unwillingness to authentically engage in the process. They include, but are not limited to, the following:

- The leader has significant mental health issues, such as anxiety, depression, or other emotionally relevant problems. These concerns may warrant referrals to other resources.

- The coaching reveals other significant leadership deficiencies that undermine the leader's credibility and effectiveness.

- The leader's best efforts are not enough to re-establish trust and credibility with direct reports.

- The leader discovers that the job or organization is not a good fit for his or her professional or personal development.

The feedback that the coaching has not fulfilled the goals of the leader or organization can come from the organization, the leader, or the coach. If the coach believes that these dynamics are at play, he or she should consider sharing these hypotheses in a coaching session. Such observations usually take time to form and are most effectively explored when the coaching relationship is established and mutual trust has been established.

Evaluating Success

As at the beginning of the coaching process, the organization, leader, and coach all have a role in deciding when the coaching has been effective. Not every organization will make the commitment for all five stages of coaching. For some leaders and behaviors, the first two stages are sufficient education and development to initiate change. If a coach strongly believes that more coaching and support are indicated, it's important to communicate that reasoning to both the leader and the organization. The leader and organization can then decide whether to proceed.

Conclusion

Coaching for respectful leadership is an important focus for organizations and coaches. When leaders behave disrespectfully, they seriously undermine not only their own efficacy as leaders, but also the culture and values of the organizations they represent. This crisis of leadership can motivate leaders to stop their dysfunctional behavior and learn new ways to lead.

Coaches who engage leaders in addressing disrespectful behavior should be well-prepared. By facilitating helpful feedback, exploring emotional intelligence skills, and integrating leadership theory and knowledge, coaches can provide a safe, authentic climate for leaders to change.

References

Caruso, D.R., & Salovey, P. (2004). *The emotionally intelligent manager: How to develop and use the four key emotional skills of leadership.* San Francisco, CA: Jossey-Bass.

Cherniss, C., & Goleman, D. (Eds.). (2001). *The emotionally intelligent workplace: How to select for, measure, and improve emotional intelligence in individuals, groups and organizations.* San Francisco, CA: Jossey-Bass.

Cortina, L.M., Magley, V.J., Williams, J.H., & Langout, R.D. (2001). Incivility in the workplace: Incidence and impact. *Journal of Occupational Health Psychology, 6*(1), 64-80.

Druskat, V.U., & Wolff, S.B. (2001, March). Building the emotional intelligence of groups. *Harvard Business Review.*

George, B. (2007). *True north: Discover your authentic leadership.* San Francisco, CA: Jossey-Bass.

Goleman, D. (1995). *Emotional intelligence: Why it can matter more than IQ.* New York: Bantam Books.

Goleman, D., Boyatzis, R., & McKee, A. (2002). *Primal leadership: Realizing the potential of emotional intelligence.* Boston, MA: Harvard Business School Press.

Kellerman, B. (2004). *Bad leadership: Why it is, why it matters, and why it happens.* Cambridge, MA: Harvard Business School Press.

Lipman-Blumen, J. (1996). *Connective leadership: Managing in a changing world.* Oxford, UK: Oxford University Press.

Luft, J., & Ingham, H. (1955). The Johari window: A graphic model of interpersonal awareness. *Proceedings of the Western Training Laboratory in Group Development.* Los Angeles: University of California, Los Angeles.

Salisbury, J., & Dominick, B.K. (1994). *Investigating harassment and discrimination: A practical guide.* San Francisco, CA: Pfeiffer.

Salisbury, J., & Jaffey, F. (1995). Individual training for sexual harassers in the workplace. In M. Paludi (Ed.), *Ivory power: Sexual harassment on campus* (rev. ed.). Albany, NY: State University of New York Press.

Vardi, Y., & Weitz, E. (2004). *Misbehavior in organizations.* Mahwah, NJ: Lawrence Erlbaum Associates.

Jan C. Salisbury, *owner of Salisbury Consulting, is a consultant and trainer who specializes in organization development, leadership coaching, diversity issues, and emotional intelligence in the workplace. Serving public and private employers for over twenty-five years, she is the author of several professional articles and co-authored the book* Investigating Harassment and Discrimination: A Practical Guide *and is working on a new book,* Leading the Culture of Respect.

Exploring the Compromise of Trust When Using Email

William J. Shirey

Summary

This qualitative study was conducted to explore how people perceive and describe breaches of trust in email communication. Social learning and communication preference theories provide the theoretical basis for the study. Eleven interviews were conducted with experienced email users. The results of the study suggest that trust is sometimes compromised during routine email communication among workers, and that it is an area worth addressing in organizational training programs.

In the last fifteen years, email use has increased exponentially (Weber, 2004). With email transactions rapidly replacing traditional forms of communication (the written office memo, for example), designing information systems to encourage trust in mediated interactions has become a key concern (Riegelsberger, Sasse, & McCarthy, 2005). This study is unique because it seeks to understand how and why trust is compromised in organizations. After reviewing the theoretical basis for the study, this paper will address the methodology, discussion, and conclusions.

Defining Trust

For the purposes of this study, trust is defined as the reliance by a person upon other email users to recognize and protect the rights and interests of all others, as well as to avoid offensive material in email communication. Although there is an abundance of literature on trust, rarely does the literature address perceptions of how email communication can compromise trust.

Theoretical Basis and Variables

Bandura's Social Learning Theory

Bandura's (1977) social learning theory offers three variables (behavior, personal factors, and environmental factors) in a model to describe social learning. Bandura questioned the thinking of the 1970's that described behavior (B) as a function of the person (P) and the environment (E) or $B = f(P,E)$. His research focused on the idea that all three variables: behavior, the person, and the environment, operate as interlocking determinants of each other. This model of behavior is depicted in Figure 1.

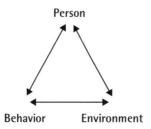

Figure 1. Bandura's Social Learning Model

Bandura concluded that psychological functioning from a social learning perspective is a continuous reciprocal interaction among personal, behavioral, and environmental determinants. In other words, behavior is viewed as affecting and being affected by the participant's cognitions, the environment, and the person-situation interactions (Davis & Luthans, 1980).

For example, if one were to examine the *person* and *environment* variables, the reciprocal relationship in the model depicts a situation in which a person is affected by the environment, and the environment is also affected by the person. Bandura provides the following example to help visualize this situation. Consider an experiment in which an animal is subjected to shock every minute unless the animal pushes a lever that forestalls the shock for thirty seconds. Those who do not learn how to control the shocks experience an unpleasant environment. In contrast, those who quickly learn how to control the shocks experience an environment free of punishment. Based on this illustration, one might ask, "Does the person affect the environment or does the environment affect the person?" Bandura argues that the person and the environment affect each other in a reciprocal relationship.

Bandura's model of social learning allows us to explore more deeply the complex relationships among people, their behavior, and the environment. This is particularly useful when examining how people perceive and describe breaches of trust in email communication. A person's understanding of trust will influence his or her behavior, which also influences the environment. While Bandura's social learning theory is helpful in examining trustworthy behavior among people in the organizational environment, Salmon and Joiner's communication theories provide insights into communication preferences that are useful in trying to explain how trust might be compromised in email communication.

Media Richness Theory

Media richness theory (Daft & Lengel, 1986) is the first of three communications theories used to describe channel preferences for face to face, telephone, email or written communication. The two variables associated with media richness theory are richness and equivocality. Communication richness can be described using a continuum on which face-to-face communication is considered the richest form of communication, followed by the telephone, email, and then written documents. Media richness theory posits that the content of the communicated message influences the choice of the communication channel. Equivocality refers to the existence of multiple and conflicting interpretations of information (ambiguity) within an organization (Daft & Lengal, 1986). Communication channels vary in their ability to process information that has conflicting interpretations. When equivocality is high, communication channels that are higher in richness (like face-to-face) are preferred due to the unique characteristics that promote a shared understanding (such as facial expression, body language, and voice tone). In contrast, when equivocality is low, and a shared understanding exists, leaner communication channels are adequate to convey information. Richness and equivocality are significant variables when examining trust in email communication. If members of an organization are careless in choosing their communication channel based on the content of the message, it can cause a breakdown in trust.

Media Features Theory

Media features theory (El-Shinnaway & Markus, 1998) is a second theory offered to describe communication channel preference. The two variables associated with media features theory are functionality and usability. Functionality refers to the ability of a communication channel to support a user to accomplish his or her work task. For example, if the requirement is for large amounts of numerical data to be communicated, it would be more functional to use email or a written document to ensure that the content is not compromised. Usability refers to the extent to which a communication channel allows a message to be transferred in a clear and readable format (Larcker & Lessig, 1980; Swanson, 1987). For example, it may be difficult to contact people in different countries and time zones face-to-face or even by phone; email may be more usable.

Both functionality and usability can be factors to consider when analyzing trust in communication. This is particularly true for organizational members who are not co-located. Email that functionally communicates based on its content, and email that is useable because it is responsive and timely, has the potential to significantly build trust.

Situational Determinants Theory

Situational determinants theory is the third communication theory (Salmon & Joiner, 2005). It has two variables: geographic uncertainty and task uncertainty. Geographic uncertainty involves the distance between people trying to communicate. Task uncertainty refers to the fact that tasks vary in complexity and ambiguity. Due to the differences in message complexity, Kettinger and Grover (1997) argue that the communication channel should match the task characteristics. In addition, distance between communication partners has been found to be positively associated with email use (Jarvenpaa, Rao, & Huber, 1988). Therefore, it is reasonable to assume that both geographic and task uncertainty can influence whether or not email is a preferred method of communication. Those who fail to consider the importance of geographic and task uncertainty in their communication choices risk losing the trust of their co-workers. The process of selecting a communication channel based on situational, media richness, or media features variables is an important factor in communication. It can be a critical determinant of whether trust is built or breached in relationships.

Methodology

Data Collection

In order to determine how people perceive and describe breaches of trust in email communication, data was required from relatively experienced email users who could identify factors that impacted trust when sending and receiving email in their professional work. Approximately ten to fifteen interviews were planned to gather sufficient data to recognize repetition from the interviews and to allow development of applicable themes.

An interview guide was developed with main questions designed to address how people perceive and describe breaches of trust in email communication. Main questions were related to each of four general areas: demographics, trust definition, social learning theory, and communication theories. Participants were selected based on geographic proximity, experience with email, and availability. Interviewees were predominantly government employees from the Department of Defense.

Each interview was tape-recorded and then transcribed for later analysis. Eleven total interviews were conducted and transcribed for analysis. This was considered sufficient based on the redundancy of the data during the sampling process (Patton, 2002).

Data Analysis

Data was organized by studying each of the transcribed interviews and highlighting expressions relevant to building or compromising trust, as well as the preferences and processes associated with email communication. Each statement relevant to trust and email communication was then clustered into common categories or themes. For example, data gathered from participants on their personal definitions of trust was considered important because it provided insight into how participants experienced a compromise of trust in email communication.

Data analysis was accomplished by reviewing interview transcripts and coding important quotes. These quotes were coded as follows: definitions of trust, offensive emails, behavior that decreases trust, channel preferences, and effects of trust on the organizational environment. From these codes, four themes emerged that appeared to be correlated with breaches in trust.

Misrepresentation

Misrepresentation occurs in a number of ways and is generally not intentional. However, by far, the most prevalent cause of misrepresentation was related to the forwarding of email. A root cause of this phenomenon was identified by several interviewees as laziness. In other words, people did not take the time to ask for permission to forward another's email, nor did they re-write the email to more accurately convey the desired message. One interviewee described the phenomenon like this:

> "There's a temptation not to apply judgment and thought when you can just punch a button and send it to fifteen people in the hope that one of them may be interested. . . . I don't know if you need this or not, but here it is. There is a lot of garbage out there floating."

Therefore, the inherent characteristics of email that allow other people's messages to be sent easily to others, combined with laziness, can easily result in a compromise of trust and the misrepresentation of others.

In addition, misrepresentation occurs when parts of an email message are cut and pasted into a new message that is then void of the important context needed to communicate accurately. Worse yet, misrepresentation can occur when an email is forwarded without permission and the person forwarding the email editorializes the comments of another. Take this example from one of the interviews involving a military officer forwarding an email from a co-worker to a general officer (edited to protect confidentiality):

> "We basically just forwarded it up to the general [four star level] and left that original message with Major so-and-so's name [from a different organization] at the bottom, [and said in the email] FYI boss, we're getting this from _____ [the Major's organization]. Well, it turns out that General _____ [four-star] rolled in on General _____ [three-star commander of the Major's organization] with both guns. In other words, we did not expect that to happen and now we've got our buddy's name at the bottom of this and so there's an email trail with General _____ [three-star], this guy's boss, with his name at the bottom of it, and we're kind of uh oh. Wish we had that to do over again. This was one where we didn't have any wrong intentions but . . . this guy's probably going to be careful not to send us that type of information again."

Virtually every interview described a situation where trust was compromised due to misrepresentation involved with the forwarding of another's email. This behavior is often not addressed in organizational training. As one respondent pointed out, "I think rarely do we openly talk about email policy, email expectations in organizations. . . . Rarely do we set . . . a good set of guidelines . . . that help steer people in how to use email effectively."

Message Quality

A second theme associated with trust and email communication was the quality of the information in the message. This was the broadest and most complex of all the constituents. Several issues were associated with email content such as accuracy, appropriateness, timeliness, and the perceived integrity of the person sending the email.

1. *Accuracy*. The importance of accuracy was vividly described in an interview with a gentleman who routinely communicates at high levels using email to pass classified information. He said, "I work with very sensitive information and the boss [four-star general] has to be able to trust that I have the accurate data, [that] I'm not just shooting from the hip . . . [that] I got it from an ambassador or State Department representative." Another participant captured this point by saying:

> "We trust leaders based on the quality of their emails. . . . We tend to trust leaders when we get emails that appear that [to have been] thought through. . . . where they are understandable, where there seems to be a quality component built into the emails. I think leaders develop trust with followers through that same mechanism."

Therefore, the quality of the email, and particularly the accuracy of the information, is critical to building trust between email recipients.

2. *Appropriateness.* Appropriateness of the message was also a factor related to trust. Emails characterized as offensive or unwanted compromise trust. What might be offensive can vary among people. However, this study found several common categories of offensive email. Email that included messages that were pornographic, racist, or off-color were generally considered offensive. Several participants tried to help define where one might draw the line on what is offensive or not. One stated that, "The rule I use is if you can't show it to your mother, don't put it in an email." Another suggested he considered emails offensive under the same criteria as "if I was sitting face-to-face with someone." He then offered some examples, "Vulgarity, profanity, an affront to my faith, I find those offensive emails." One of the most graphic examples of how offensive email can breach trust came from a female participant who had received a pornographic email (female nudity) from a male acquaintance. She said:

> "I was really astonished because it was extremely inappropriate … and I think my words were somewhere along the lines of 'What was he thinking sending this to me? Did he think that I would appreciate this?' I was just shocked. At that point I didn't trust anything else sent from that person. Any time I opened something up [from him], I either deleted it [immediately] or opened it up when no one was looking, just because I never knew what it was going to be."

Clearly, because this material was offensive, this was an email that significantly impacted the relationship and the trust between these two workers. Interestingly, most participants in the study found emails with data of no relevance or value (such as "spam") offensive as well. One participant highlighted the differences between data, information, and knowledge. He said, "Data is something that happens to be available. Data becomes information when it has some kind of relevancy to the organization. Information becomes knowledge when it's not only relevant but when there's some value component associated with it." Every participant in the study had strong negative feelings about irrelevant email, whether they were forwarded from those they knew or received from unknown sources.

3. *Timeliness.* The timeliness (or lack thereof) of an email message can also influence trust. One interviewee captured an important characteristic of email, "[It] has a time stamp on it and lets [others] know you tried to contact them as soon as [possible]." As a result, for those communicating across time zones and geographic boundaries, even if they cannot be contacted quickly, email provides a mechanism to show others you attempted to inform them in a timely manner. One participant said, "I trust those who make the attempt to notify me soonest, who notify me when there's a change, when there's something that impacts me, either directly or indirectly, that increases my trust of that person."

In contrast to the positive aspects of timeliness, there is a negative aspect associated with the ability to respond quickly with email that can impact quality. Participants in the study highlighted the dangers of pushing the send button too quickly when responding to an email message that may have caused feelings such as anger, frustration, hurt, or anxiety. One interviewee described this phenomenon and offered a technique to avoid breaching trust by sending a poorly timed email of questionable quality:

> "The technique I use if I'm irritated or mad when I write the email, I write it but I don't send it and I leave it in the draft box and then go back and read it. If I'm still mad, I leave it in the draft box, and I go back and read it. And finally, when I'm calm I go back and read it and nine times out of ten, I delete it."

Someone prone, (due to personality, emotional state, or other factors) to immediately send the email described above, would undoubtedly risk a compromise in trust. Environments that promote very responsive email communication might be vulnerable to emails that risk quality for the sake of timeliness. This threat was articulated by one participant in the study who had obviously considered this phenomenon:

> "I can sit here on email and reach the same audience with misspellings, inappropriate phrasing, subject-verb disagreement, and I wind up looking like an idiot in the process with the push of a button. I do say that would not enhance any one else's trust in my abilities to communicate data in the future."

While the responsive attributes of email provide timely ways to increase trust, the data suggests users must be disciplined to balance responsiveness with quality content in the email message.

4. *Integrity.* The last aspect relating to email message content is the perceived integrity of the one sending the message. Aside from the basic truthfulness of the message, if the content of the message is viewed as overly opinionated, incomplete, or not accounting for both sides of an issue, it can be viewed as deceitful in nature and not trustworthy. One interviewee pointed out the importance "to be very careful to caveat what's fact versus what is opinion." An important characteristic of email is that it allows one to clarify thoughts during message preparation; and, in a step-by-step process, think through an issue, write it down, and then modify what was written to ensure clarity. Participants in the study highlighted the importance of offering a complete picture, not being deceitful, and offering a perception of openness, honesty and candor.

Related to integrity and openness is the behavior of those who send emails well above the level of their supervisors. Although this behavior could be associated more with the email process than the actual content of the email, both the content and process can be potentially deceitful. One interviewee characterized this phenomenon as "violating what we in the military would call the chain of command [and people] do so very easily at no immediate personal expense because they don't have to walk past the boss's office to go to their boss's boss." This type of behavior has the potential to compromise the trust between a follower and leader.

Vulnerability

The third theme was vulnerability, or the fear of retribution felt by those sending emails. It was clear from the research that participants valued relationships with supervisors who were viewed as protective and caring. This type of leadership positively effects email communication with followers. One interviewee described such a trustworthy leader by saying, "Protection from the leader builds trust. Knowing you could go to the leader and he or she will have your best interests at heart. [Knowing that the leader] was caring for you." It is not surprising that the data suggests a protective, caring leader will have more open and honest communication with followers. In contrast, another participant pointed out, "If I trust my boss to get and use accurate data, I will do that. If I don't trust the boss, or if I think he's going to hold it 'against' me, then maybe I won't deliver the ugly baby, then we'll put some lipstick on it first." This interviewee highlighted the reluctance to communicate certain information ("ugly baby") to his boss without first masking it. Another participant was reluctant to communicate at all with an untrustworthy supervisor. He offered the following example:

> "I've had bosses who emailed where I was reluctant to respond because the boss wasn't very trustworthy and what I emailed tended to just backfire on me. So if my boss sent something out that says he wants a response, I might just kind of lie low."

The data confirms that vulnerability and fear of retribution are related to trust in email communication. Supervisors who are protective and caring promote team building, camaraderie, and a transparent, open communication environment.

Channel Preference

A fourth theme was channel preference or the mode of communication used to pass information. These channels include: face-to-face, phone, email, and traditional written document communication. Choosing an inappropriate communication channel for the situation can cause a breach in trust. One respondent captured what was a predominant theme with regard to conditions where email communication would not be appropriate:

> "Face-to-face communication, of course, is preferred any time there's a measure of some type of need for sensitivity, whether that's [a] correction for

performance deficiency, for example, anything that has to do with a personal issue of that person, [it] should be done face-to-face, never [by] email, because there's just too much nonverbal information that is also being passed that cannot be seen."

Another interviewee shared a graphic example of how poor judgment, with respect to channel preferences, can breech trust in an organization. This situation was in the context of receiving supervisor feedback on work performance:

"Usually I get a kind of cryptic email and I might get a follow-on cryptic phone call, and I have requested the last three years, requested in writing, a face-to-face evaluation. I still have not received it. It's a lack of integrity. I don't trust him [the supervisor] because I don't think he has the integrity to tell me what he's thinking [face-to-face]."

Face-to-face communication was also the predominant choice when dealing with multiple or conflicting interpretations of an issue. In addition to non-verbal cues, face-to-face offers some other advantages in this context, as captured by one participant:

"I think face-to-face [is better] because [it] gives you the opportunity for rapid exchange of information that you don't have in any of the other [communication] mechanisms. That doesn't mean that all face-to-face communication eliminates confusion, but I think there's a greater probability that in open, honest, kind of trustworthy, face-to-face communication it is a little bit easier to avoid some of the pitfalls and confusion that can be generated in other forms."

Another participant agrees that face to face is preferred when dealing with conflicting views; however, he addresses the influence of emotion and the potential inefficiency of going back and forth with email communication:

"Where something could easily be misinterpreted, I find it's better to talk. In areas where I know it [is] going to create a conflict, where I know a person is probably going to disagree, it's just easier to pick up a phone and have it out. I know it's going to create some emotion so let's just go ahead get the issues on the table; otherwise you can get into a back and forth with the email. Just pick up the phone and talk to each other."

While the preponderance of participants in the study preferred face-to-face communication as a trust-building channel when dealing with conflict, there were a few who argued that a written document or email could be more effective. One lawyer interviewed stated:

"If people are just talking, they don't express themselves the same way that they write. If you make somebody write it down, just write the words down, it gives you a document to work from. That's what I do in my legal profession. We work off writings, and only writings."

The logic of writing down one's thoughts, and clearly thinking through the issue before responding certainly has value. The situation will dictate a channel preference offering the best chance to build trust. However, participants suggested that "[a] relationship is enhanced regarding the trust when you can supplement [email communication] with face-to-face when possible." In situations where people are geographically separated, email with a follow-up phone call might also reduce conflict and increase trust.

Data Synthesis

Bandura's (1977) social learning model can be applied to this study in the context of the reciprocal relationship between the variables of person, behavior, and the environment. Brown, Trevino, and Harrison (2005) propose social learning theory as a basis for understanding ethical leadership. In their study, they describe how leadership involves influence and how trustworthy leadership can promote ethical behavior. For example, one might argue that a trustworthy person promotes trustworthy behavior, which promotes a trustworthy environment. Similarly, a trustworthy environment promotes trustworthy behavior, which promotes trustworthy people.

To illustrate, one participant offered the following example of how her environment affected behavior with respect to communication channel preference within the organization:

> "A trusting relationship was built when you would take the time to walk across the hall to talk as opposed to just send emails. Some of this may be related to a person's personality type, whether he's extroverted or introverted, and that may be a factor. It might be part of the organizational culture. At George Washington University the culture goes back eighteen years or so. That culture started from telephone and face-to-face communication so there may be more of an inclination to communicate that way to build trust."

In the environment described above, communicating entirely by email might not be the fastest way to gain trust within the organization.

Bandura's model can also be used as a framework for synthesizing the four themes (misrepresentation, message quality, vulnerability, and channel preference). For example, a person who exhibits behavior in email communication that misrepresents others because of sloppy forwarding techniques risks developing an untrusting relationship with co-workers and contributes to a less trusting environment. Using another constituent with the model, one might argue that a person who feels vulnerable with respect to sending emails to his supervisor will exhibit behavior (less likely to send emails) that will influence the environment (less open).

The message quality and channel preference themes might also be viewed in light of the behavior and environment variables. For example, one who writes emails that are completely accurate, applicable, and timely can be a model for trust and influence within the environment. In contrast, in the context of the channel preference themes, if a supervisor consistently disciplines followers or provides performance feedback with email (as opposed to face-to-face communication), such leader behavior risks compromising trust and influencing the environment negatively.

Although each theme might not directly apply to each of Bandura's variables, the model provides a useful tool to consider how the themes might influence an organization. To illustrate, if an organization has an environment where large quantities of email are passed on a regular basis that produce little valuable information, one might consider what behavior might be causing the phenomenon. The root source of the emails might be a person forwarding without realizing the data was not useful. Such a person should be more disciplined to spend time reviewing the quality of emails before they are sent out to large addressees.

In addition to social learning theory, communication preference theory can be viewed in light of the four themes. For example, vulnerability might play a significant role if a person is geographically separated from her supervisor and is working on a complex task. The situational determinant variables of geographic uncertainty and task uncertainty require strong communication via phone or email in the absence of face-to-face communication. Therefore, vulnerability needs to be low to encourage success when both geographic and task uncertainty are high.

Another illustration of how communication theory might be synthesized with themes involves the correlation between message quality and media richness theory. According to the theory, if equivocality is high (more complexity and ambiguity) then more richness (face-to-face or phone communication) is required. However, the data from the study indicates that if message quality is high, even in an environment with high ambiguity, a leaner communication channel (like email) may be adequate. In fact, a few participants in the study preferred written communication when multiple interpretations of an issue were present. One of these participants stated:

> "Written or email communication is preferable because it allows you to clarify your thoughts, it gives the ability to modify what was written, and it involves the step-by-step process where you can think through the issue and think through what you want to put down."

In general, message quality and misrepresentation were two themes not addressed in the communication theories. The data from this study strongly shows that poor message quality and misrepresentation due to inappropriate forwarding of emails are significant factors in reducing trust.

Discussion and Conclusions

This qualitative study took data from eleven interviews and consolidated it into four themes that describe factors associated with the compromise of trust in email communication. These themes (misrepresentation, message quality, vulnerability, and channel preference) were analyzed in the context of Bandura's (1977) social learning theory and communication preference theories (media richness, media features, and situational determinants). Misrepresentation, inherent in the process of forwarding emails, and message quality, associated with accurateness of the information sent, applicability, timeliness, and the perceived integrity of the person sending the email, were considered significant factors in the compromise of trust. Vulnerability can also be a trust factor, and generally results in restricting the frequency of emails and the openness associated with the message. Channel preference is a factor in breaches of trust when an inappropriate communication mode is used for a given situation. Communication preference theory and social learning theory offer a framework to examine the appropriateness of email communication to either build or breach trust within an organization.

Looking first at misrepresentation, email forwarding has a significant influence on trust and often results in people feeling violated due to comments taken out of context. The root cause of this phenomenon appears to be either a perceived need to act quickly or laziness. Therefore, it is proposed that misrepresentation is a factor in compromising trust when email channels are used; and misrepresentation is affected by the sender's perceived time available as well as lethargy. In a larger sense, such a proposition will likely be influenced by other social learning variables such as the environment or a person's personality.

This study suggests that message quality variables (accuracy, appropriateness, timeliness, and integrity) are related to trust in email communication. Accuracy and integrity are probably the most significant of the variables, followed by appropriateness and timeliness. Further research is required to determine how these variables are correlated with message quality and how message quality is correlated with trust.

While vulnerability and channel preference are also important determinants of trust in email communication, the data gathered from this study is not sufficient to suggest any new theory.

The definition initially used to describe trust was too narrow. That definition focused more on using email in a way that protected the rights and interests of others. However, participants in the study viewed trust associated with email in other ways that may be important to consider in the future. Specifically, participants broadened the definition of trust by highlighting the importance of accuracy, reliability, integrity, openness, and loyalty.

The results of this study suggest that trust is sometimes compromised during routine email communication among workers and is an area worth addressing in organizational training programs. As communication technology continues to advance at an exponential rate, it will be important for organizations to ensure that trust between workers is not compromised with modernization.

References

Bandura, A. (1977). *Social learning theory.* Upper Saddle River, NJ: Prentice-Hall.

Brown, M.E., Trevino, L.K., & Harrison, D.A. (2005). Ethical leadership: A social learning perspective for construct development and testing. *Organizational Behavior and Human Decision Processes.*

Daft, R.L., & Lengel, R.H. (1986). Organizational information requirements, media richness and structural design. *Management Science,* pp. 554–571.

Davis, T.R., & Luthans, F. (1980). A social learning approach to organizational behavior. *The Academy of Management Review, 5*(2).

El-Shinnaway, M., & Markus, M. L. (1998). Acceptance of communication media in organizations: Richness of features? *IEEE transactions of professional communication.* pp. 242–253.

Jarvenpaa, S.L., Rao, V.S., & Huber, G.P. (1988). Computer support for meeting of groups working on unstructured problems: A field experiment. *MIS Quarterly,* pp. 645–666.

Kettinger, W.J., & Grover, V. (1997). The use of computer-mediated communication in an inter-organizational context. *Decision Sciences, 28*(3), 513–556.

Larcker, D.F., & Lessig V.P. (1980). Perceived usefulness of information: A psychometric examination. *Decision Sciences,* pp. 121–134.

Patton, M. Q. (2002). *Qualitative research and evaluation methods* (3rd ed.). Thousand Oaks, CA: Sage.

Riegelsberger, J., Sasse, M.A., & McCarthy, J.D. (2005). *The mechanics of trust: A framework for research and design.* University College London, UK. Department of Computer Science.

Salmon, S., & Joiner, T.A. (2005). Toward an understanding of communication channel preferences for the receipt of management information. *Journal of American Academy of Business, 7*(2), 56–63.

Swanson, E. B. (1987). Information channel disposition and use. *Decision Sciences,* pp. 131–145.

Weber, R.M. (2004). Beam me up (and out of this e-mail/virus mess). *Journal of Financial Service Professionals, 58*(6).

William J. Shirey, Ph.D., *is president of ISE Consulting, an organization development firm helping organizations to manage change through strategic planning, executive coaching, and improved leader-follower communication. Prior to ISE Consulting, Shirey was a senior strategic planning analyst with Lockheed Martin and served in the Air Force as a fighter pilot and staff officer. He has a B.S. in management from the U.S. Air Force Academy and a Ph.D. in organizational leadership from Regent University.*

Managing Free Agents

Mohandas Nair

Summary

A free agent (freelancer/contract worker) brings focused, specialized input into an organizational system. Working independently, a free agent can be more original and creative, unfettered by any structured framework that can restrict the effort of full-time employees. This calls for a need to manage free agents differently so that their independence is not compromised and yet they are made to feel that they belong in the organization.

The Human Spirit

Free agents, also called freelancers or contract workers, are typically independent, creative, and spontaneous; they have unique thoughts and experiences. They have amazing capability, which they demonstrate only when they are allowed to work on their own. They like to make their own choices and decisions, working on matters of interest to them. Thus, to get the best out of such an individual, you will need to provide an organizational environment that will enable his or her spirit to soar.

Understandably, regular employees are limited: they have to work according to rules, follow procedures, and report to bosses who squash their individuality. Their creativity is constrained. Their efficiency and effectiveness are compromised.

Working Within a Structured Environment

All employees work in a constraining environment. Initially, they fight and struggle to retain their individuality, but ultimately succumb to larger forces. Adaptation reduces the stress they feel related to loss of freedom, but it still damages their capacity to perform at high levels. They can rarely, if ever, give their best.

Others fail to adjust. They may continue with the organization, disillusioned and dissatisfied with their circumstances. Others flit from organization to organization looking for a place in which they can feel self-actualized. A few break free to become free agents.

Enabling Freedom Within Constraints

"Aware" organizations implement various processes to get the most out of their human resources. Good strategies and processes have enabled speedier adjustment and adaptability of the full-timers. Other organizations use monetary and other incentives to retain and get some extra output from their people. Most organizations are fortunate in that the majority of people are not aware of what is in the way of giving their best. They blame themselves: no proper education, experience, attitude, etc. Although there can be some truth in this, an organization can find ways to help individuals maximize their effectiveness.

The Free Agent

The free agent may not be completely free in his or her ability to make things happen exactly as he or she desires. However, the free agent has the benefit of being in charge of his or her own time. By being able to plan and schedule their own activities to a great extent, free agents can work at a comfortable pace and adjust to circumstances. They can more easily manage social and family commitments, which can have a significant impact on any worker's output.

Adjusting in a Constraining Environment

Not every employee wants to become a free agent. The majority are content to work within the confines of a system. They have grown accustomed to taking orders within that structure. Thus, working in an organization may even be comfortable for people. But even if they don't recognize the fact, they are constrained, risk averse, and shy away from making critical decisions. Not having to take responsibility helps them to tune out after office hours. Having a job is necessary. For some there is no urge to self-actualize on the work front. For others, there may be longing, but as they are risk averse, they prefer to work within the safe confines of an organization.

The Free Agent's Strengths

Free agents are not pressured to look for the first solution to a problem. They may find the process of problem solving itself fulfilling. They want to learn new concepts and skills in their areas of interest and thus develop expertise in their fields. They can then help others achieve objectives.

Truly excellent free agents derive passion from their work. They put forward their best efforts when provided with personally fulfilling assignments. Drudgery for rewards is not their style. Fulfillment comes from doing something that is meaningful.

Managing the Free Agent

To tap the enormous potential of free agents, an organization should welcome them without burdening them with unnecessary routines, procedures, and other roadblocks. This will not be easy, as they may have to interact with others who may not be happy with their presence. Here are some thoughts on how the organization could provide an environment that would enable a free agent to flourish.

Treat Free Agents as Members of the Organization

Organizations accept "full time" employees as part of the organization. Their loyalty is not questioned, and they are automatically invited to all functions. They are made to feel that they are a part of the organization and are privy to whatever happens there. Free agents somehow do not enjoy this status. They may not have access to necessary information. Their loyalty to the organization is not assumed. It is thought that they will not pull their weight in a crunch situation.

Instead, free agents could be treated as being part of the organization, be included in events and have access to information. This could have a positive impact in the free agent's feeling more loyalty and commitment to the organization. A loyal person will go all out to deliver excellent results. This, combined with the expertise and independent thinking of the free agent, could bring excellence in output. A free agent who is kept at a distance may fulfill only his or her contract with the organization, but may not have the desire to do anything more.

Induct Free Agents into the Organization

Induct the free agent into the organization in the same way as any full-time employee. Provide information on the organization's vision, mission, long-term plans, and operational issues. Link them with significant people they will be interacting with. Talk to them about the organization's credo and values and how the organization does what it does. Touch on issues like quality, ethics, and excellence. Have a senior person conduct an orientation session. Be open to all questions and demonstrate the organization's enthusiasm for having them on board.

Don't Differentiate Free Agents from Employees

Try not to differentiate between free agents and full-time employees. This could include providing commuting facilities, access to the cafeteria, gymnasium, and the like. They should be part of the office celebrations and be presented with awards for exceptional performance. Of course, free agents should be subject to the same disciplinary measures and work within the organizational norms.

Include Free Agents in Meetings

Involve free agents in meetings in which their point of view is useful. Help them to break the ice with new members in the organization so that there is cooperation and synergy in group work.

Bring Former Employees Back as Free Agents

Check whether valued former organizational members could be inducted as free agents. They could go to work immediately, being familiar with the organization and duties of the job, and loyalty may not be an issue.

Give Employees the Chance to Become Free Agents

Observe full-time employees with drive and the desire to strike out on their own. Check whether they want to work as free agents. This will enable the organization to retain these employees and at the same time give them the satisfaction of being able to strike out on their own. The risks involved in becoming free agents is thus less for these people, and they would be indebted to the organization and feel great loyalty.

Provide Orientation for Free Agents

Assist free agents to connect smoothly with all organizational processes. They are primarily there to provide their expertise. They need the support of the organization's internal members to check on how their ideas will be incorporated. Key organizational members can form a bridge for ideas to become embedded into organizational processes.

Affirm Confidentiality with Free Agents

On the issue of confidentiality, leaders may feel that confidentiality is a greater issue with free agents, but the organization is as vulnerable to losing information through its full-time employees, especially when they quit and join a competitor. Free agents, because they want to be given more assignments, are likely to keep issues confidential in their own interests. Full-time employees who leave may never come back. They have little to worry about. Free agents can be asked to sign confidentiality agreements if there is any concern.

<u>Conclusion</u>

Free agents can provide focused, specialized services when an organization desires them. The organization can get the best of both worlds when they provide free agents with the independence to work on their own and also give them a feeling of being part of the organization. Under these circumstances, free agents will likely feel compelled to provide their best efforts to achieve organizational goals.

Mohandas Nair *is a management educator and a free agent. He is a teacher, trainer, writer, and facilitator of learning. He is a B. Tech (Mech.) from IIT Kharagpur, India, has a diploma in training and development and has thirty years of experience in industry and consultancy in industrial engineering and human resources development. He has published two books, written numerous articles, and facilitated many management development programs.*

Managing Talent Management Takes Talent
A Guide to Setting Up the Process
Andy Beaulieu

Summary

Talent management is a business process for (1) identifying current employees who might one day qualify for a significant leadership role and (2) taking planned, deliberate steps to prepare them to move into such a role. This article is focused heavily on the first of those two pieces—sometimes also called succession planning. The outcome of that component of talent management is a robust assessment of succession candidates and an alignment of individuals against specified, future roles. For it to be effective, however, talent management must include extensive leadership development activities to prepare those future leaders for upward movement when the opportunity presents itself.

The Talent Management Process

This article outlines the key components of a talent management process. Your organization may elect to customize these steps to keep the process simple or to make it more robust. You may also want to link it to other related systems you already have in place, such as performance management, development planning, and training.

The steps to building and executing an effective talent management process include the following:

- Define purpose, goals, and scope.

- Assemble an oversight committee.

- Set policy.

- Develop operational parameters.

- Develop and conduct the assessment.

- Compile and organize the data.

- Conduct organizational reviews.

- Implement development plans.

- Assess process effectiveness.

Each of these steps is covered below.

Define Purpose, Goals, and Scope

Perhaps the most important step in the successful use of any business process is to outline its purpose and goals. These help set expectations and align the organization around what is to be accomplished.

To accomplish this step, work with the *top leader* of the organization to address the following questions:

- What are the greatest needs of the organization related to future leadership?

- What challenges do we face related to our future leadership needs?

- How effective have we been recently in overcoming these challenges and meeting our needs?

- What changes, either external (industry, technology, regulatory, etc.) or internal (strategy, current leadership population), will affect the leadership makeup of this organization in the future?

- What do we hope to accomplish through this process?

- What is the scope of leadership positions that should be included in the process?

- How will we know whether we are successful? What will be different? What would we see happening—or not happening—as a result of this process?

- Specifically, what goals/metrics might we set to guide the process and measure its success?

The results of this exploration should be formulated into a "charter" for the oversight committee (see below) as well as a communication to the broader organization (depending on your approach to publicizing this activity; see the Policy section for more details).

Assemble an Oversight Committee

An oversight committee, formed of leadership representatives from most of the key business areas, should be formed to help guide the initial approach to talent management. Once the process is developed and in place, ongoing oversight may be placed within the organization's regular structure. For instance, human resources may own the talent management process on an ongoing basis, reporting up to leadership as needed.

The oversight committee should include leaders from the major business areas. These individuals will set policy for talent management, develop and oversee the process, ensure cooperation from their own areas, and help address any issues that may arise. Be aware that these individuals will probably not be allowed to see all the data that eventually is collected, but this should become clear when they work through the policy questions listed below.

At its first meeting, the oversight committee should decide when/how often it will meet, how it will make decisions, and any other working guidelines needed to support its effectiveness as a team. It may take a few longer meetings up-front to develop the talent management process, after which the committee might meet weekly to review progress and address critical questions and issues.

Set Policy

Talent management can be a sensitive topic that can instigate controversy on multiple levels. Some of the issues can be predicted, discussed in advance, and documented as "policy." Others may need to be settled as they arise. The following list of questions should be considered:

- Who will have access to talent management data?

- How will employees be informed of their ratings and nominations?

- How will development occur to help prepare nominees for future leadership roles?

- Are the organization's current leadership development programs adequate?

- Who can override nominations? (For example, if an employee is nominated as a successor to another position, can another leader override that nomination if he/she deems it is not appropriate?)

- How will developmental activities be funded?

- How will data security be maintained?

- How will policy decisions be communicated?

- How will future questions/issues around policy be raised to this group and decided?

Once the topics above have been covered, the organization might feel ready to "get started." The remaining topics below will take the organization through a prescribed process of developing and conducting the assessment, reviewing the data and its implications, and planning and carrying out any immediate and longer-term activities. This process should be understood and validated by the oversight committee and adjusted as necessary to accommodate preferences and link with existing systems and schedules. A realistic timeline should be created, recognizing that the steps listed above may take four to six months to complete in a sizable organization, especially the first time. A schedule that is too ambitious can undermine the efforts of all involved when key deadlines start to slip.

Develop Operational Parameters

To guide the design of the talent management process, the oversight committee needs to specify a number of operational parameters. The top leader should previously have outlined the scope of leadership positions that should be included in the process. Taking its cue from this direction, the committee needs to specify the following:

- Key positions for which successors will be identified

- Specific employees who will be assessed as possible successors

In many cases, talent management is applied to roles within the top three or four levels of the organization. For example, you may decide to include the top leader, his/her six direct reports, and all those reporting to those six direct reports. Or you may start with this type of definition, but then deselect certain positions (e.g., a high-level individual contributor who reports to the president, but is not considered a "leader") for whom successors do not need to be identified. In the end, a definitive list should be produced so there is no confusion about which positions are being addressed. The following information should be included in the list of "succession positions":

- Position reference number
- Position title
- Current incumbent
- Current manager
- Business unit

Among the selected positions, the oversight committee should identify those for which a "pooled" list of possible successors could be maintained, rather than developing separate lists. For instance, if there are four different "regional VP sales" positions, representing four different regions, it might make more sense to maintain a separate pool of candidates. The oversight committee should review the list of "succession positions" and make decisions about which ones could be pooled. Note that there would be separate pools for each grouping of positions. Once the "succession positions" are identified, the committee must identify all those individuals who will be considered as possible successors to all those positions. Generally, it is recommended that you go down one level or grade below the lowest level of succession positions. Other individuals may be added, but for equity reasons it is probably best not to exclude any individuals unilaterally. If they are not qualified for upward movement, the assessment of these individuals would serve to preclude them from arriving as high-ranked successors.

The data needed for talent management must be collected through some type of special assessment. Most talent management processes use a few key parameters as the basis for rating individuals and making talent management decisions. Key parameters for the oversight committee to discuss and designate include:

- Contribution and potential ratings
- Willingness to relocate
- Succession nominations

Contribution is a factor used in many talent management systems to identify the performance of the individual over the past few years. It is intended to present a more steady, long-term view than the annual rating for performance. *Potential* is a factor not generally used in other performance systems. It indicates the individual's perceived ability to succeed at a higher level of leadership.

For both variables, a simple, three-point scale may be used. Definitions for three such anchors are provided below:

Contribution

- High: Consistently achieves quality results that meet or exceed expectations.

- Medium: Generally achieves expected results.

- Low: Is struggling to achieve expected results.

Potential

- High: Is ready to move up and succeed at the next level of leadership.

- Medium: With further development, should be able to move up to the next level.

- Low: Is well placed at this time.

Willingness to relocate is simply an indication of whether the person would relocate to take on a new role in the future. It is not a binding decision at this point (some employees would go for the right opportunity or to a desired geographic location), but it helps leadership know how to treat the individual.

Succession nominations are used in talent management processes to earmark individuals for specific future moves, should those positions become available. Given the list of leadership positions for which future successors are desired, individuals being assessed can be "nominated" against those positions. Later in the process, those nominations are compiled and reviewed, with an eye toward weeding out the less viable nominations and then ranking those who remain. Specifying succession nominations permits targeted development and preparation. However, some other approaches to talent management may identify future moves more broadly.

Develop and Conduct the Assessment

The variables outlined above are captured in a sample instrument, provided in Exhibit 1 at the end of this article. It is an assessment form that can be customized for your organization, and it references the "succession position list" which you will need to compile.

Steps involved in preparing for the talent management assessment include the following:

- Determine assessment roles and process, such as:

  - Who will complete the assessments?

- When will the assessments be due?

- Who will ensure the completion of all assessments within each business area by the deadline?

- Who will compile all the incoming data?

- Develop the assessment instrument.

- Test the assessment instrument and make any adjustments.

- Conduct the assessment.

Typically, each individual in the talent management pool is assessed by his/ her current manager—including identifying succession nominations. However, those nominations are reviewed later and may be overridden by a unit leader at a later date. At that time the remaining succession nominees are ranked against one another to identify the best candidates.

While many organizations will give an assessment instrument a "quick look" before starting, I recommend that you conduct at least a small test to ensure that the questions are interpreted correctly so that the resulting data is more likely to be consistent.

When you are ready, the assessment should be conducted according to the process and a timeline you have developed.

Compile and Organize the Data

The assessment data must be compiled and organized for ease of access. Often spreadsheets are employed for this purpose, but more sophisticated tools certainly exist at every price point. At a minimum, the following "cuts" of data should be compiled:

- How was each person rated?

- What are the average ratings for each business unit?

- What are each person's succession nominations?

- Who are each position's succession nominees?

- Where are the "red flags":

  - Positions with few or no nominees

  - Highly rated (potential) candidates with few or no nominations

  - Business units with low average contribution and/or potential ratings

One other analysis common to talent management is the "C-P Matrix." It is used to analyze collective strengths and weaknesses across an entire organizational unit. The C-P Matrix consists of a grid wherein the two variables—and their respective three-point scales—are mapped together to form a "nine-box" matrix. The counts of employees falling into each of the nine boxes may be shown; in some organizations, the actual names are provided. More important are the implications on individuals falling into the various boxes, and the percentage of the organization in the "green zone" (high-high, medium-high, and high-medium) versus those in the "red zone" (low-low, low-medium, and medium-low). Individuals in the "top box" (high potential, high performance) should receive special developmental attention and, when ready, should be strategically "moved up"—even if it means moving someone out of a position to make room. The aforementioned three-point scale used to measure an individual's contribution and potential is the foundation for the C-P Matrix.

Conduct Organizational Reviews

Talent management often culminates in "organizational reviews" at the organizational unit level, plus the top level. The leaders of the various organizational units each review their own data and prepare for the meeting with the top executive. The top executive meets with each of the leaders separately, for as long as a whole day with each, to review the data and make succession decisions. These formalized reviews reinforce the importance of the process, as well as drive a schedule for completing the work each year. While leadership development should be ongoing, the talent management process is often an annual activity aimed at keeping the data and plans current.

At the *organizational unit level*, the leader works with the human resources professional managing this process plus his/her oversight committee member. The goals of this interaction include the following:

- Review the data.

- Validate nominations to positions within each area.

- Review average ratings to assess the strength of his/her organization.

- Prepare the leader to conduct his/her review with the top level executive.

The unit leader must review all the data of his/her organization to ensure its validity. Sometimes the ratings, which may have been submitted by lower-level managers, need to be adjusted to create equity across the whole unit. The succession nominations of his/her employees may also have to be adjusted.

Another activity at this phase is the review and validation, or adjustment, of succession nominations to the unit leader's own positions. Some of these nominations will have come from outside the unit, and not all of them will be appropriate. Using his/her knowledge of the requirements of the positions, the unit leader should rank the nominations to place the best candidates in the front of the line, reject any nominations that would not be appropriate, and possibly even solicit additional nominations when needed.

The leader should also review the distribution of his/her employees' contributions and potential ratings. This review may produce conclusions that compel the leader to initiate developmental activity—or even to initiate changes in key positions. One of the grittier outcomes of talent management is the realization of incumbent leadership weaknesses and the action around resolving them with personnel changes.

Out of all this review, the unit leader should be prepared to conduct a similar discussion with the top executive, justifying decisions and agreeing to further action as needed.

The *top-level* review often looks like a series of meetings, many lasting more than a half-day, each attended by the top-level executive and one of his/her direct reports (the unit-level leaders), assisted by human resources. The goals of these meetings are to:

- Review succession nominations to positions at the top two to three levels.

- Make succession and development decisions.

- Identify weaknesses in the current organization, and agree to remedies.

Some of the issues raised in these meetings would have been discussed before, but the process tends to drive decisions that may have been lingering. The action items arising out of these meetings should be documented and should become goals of the unit leader. Some of the decisions may have to be implemented right away, such as the removal of an incumbent who is not performing at a sufficient level to make room for a succession candidate to step into a bigger role.

Resulting from the series of review meetings will be action items for immediate and longer-term follow-up. It is critical to the integrity of the talent management process for these actions to occur and to be attributed to the process.

However, while they serve to drive the process and concentrate activity, the review meetings are not the only opportunity for succession decisions to be made. Certainly, throughout the year as leadership opportunities arise, the succession nominees should be tapped. Nothing kills a talent management process more quickly than a series of external hires to key leadership opportunities.

Implement Development Plans

The most critical element of talent management is the development of future leaders. Developmental activities may be focused on preparing for specific roles or be more generalized. Many articles and books have been published on the topic of leadership development, but one of the best is *The Lessons of Experience* by Morgan McCall, Jr., Michael Lombardo, and Ann Morrison. The authors outline the case for forms of development beyond classroom training. In fact, formal training is cited in their research as one of the least influential approaches for developing leaders. Development plans arising out of your talent management process should emphasize stretch projects, shadow assignments, job rotations, stressful situations, do-or-die challenges, and the like. Involve top executives in the development of others through coaching, mentoring, and sponsorship roles. For maximum impact, make it demanding—and real.

Assess Process Effectiveness

Early on, the top leader identified the goals of the talent management process. Although at this point the long-term impacts are not known, some early indicators—plus a broader sense of accomplishment—should be apparent.

For any process to remain vital, it must change and improve over time. Collect feedback from stakeholders and change the talent management process to accomplish the most critical emerging needs.

In the same vein, the many activities undertaken as a result of your talent management will exhibit a variety of results. For instance, some types of developmental activities will work better than others. Feedback and "lessons learned" about these activities should be collected and discussed, in order for the most successful to be replicated to the greatest degree possible. Success stories could be collected, not only for their promotional value, but for their ability to inspire and guide future participants in search of direction and hope.

The Results of Talent Management

The "war for talent" is not an over-hyped scare tactic by consultants pushing the next big trend. Organizations are reporting an increasing scarcity among the leadership ranks, thus driving the need to "grow from within." Organizations with a reputation for superior talent management report a "first choice advantage" when it comes to combing through the ranks of MBA candidates.

More concretely, the benefits of a robust talent management process may include:

- Lower attrition among high-potential future leaders, as they are less likely to be attracted by "a few extra dollars" when they know what their organization has in store for them in the future.

- Lower "cost to fill" key leadership positions that are filled internally rather than through more costly, external processes.

- Reduced instance of "bad fit"—that high-level new hire who clashes with the culture and struggles in the role from day one, only to disappear within a few, painful months.

- Improved leadership capability, leading to improved business performance and execution.

Thus the benefits of talent management are many, and the imperative becomes clearer every day.

References

Charan, R., Drotter, S., & Noel, J. (2001). *The leadership pipeline: How to build the leadership-powered company.* San Francisco, CA: Jossey-Bass.

McCall M., Jr., Lombardo, M., & Morrison, A. (1988). *The lessons of experience.* New York: Lexington Books.

Andy Beaulieu's *consulting practice, Results for a Change, achieves organization change using a results-first approach. His leadership development program, Extreme LD™, pits future leaders in a race against time to deliver bottom-line business results and achieve their stated development objectives within a thirteen-week time limit. In private practice since 2004, he has completed significant projects with clients such as Bank of America, Marriott International, T. Rowe Price, and World Wildlife Fund.*

This is his eighth contribution to a Pfeiffer Annual. He consults to organizations on leadership talent management and development planning. A free demonstration copy of his MS Excel®-based Succession Planner software may be found at www.businessperform.com.

Exhibit 1. Sample Talent Management Process Guide

Date:

Employee Name:

Employee Title:

Manager Name:

Manager Title:

Organization: Circle one: <include list of organizational units here>

Ratings

Contribution Rating: Select the rating that best describes this employee's overall contribution to business results over the past three years:

- High
- Medium
- Low

Potential Rating: Select the rating that best describes this employee's ability to succeed at a higher level of leadership:

- High
- Medium
- Low

Relocation Preference

At this time, does this person appear to be willing to relocate?   Yes   No

Succession Nominations

Referencing the attached list of "Succession Positions" (those positions for which we want to identify, track, and groom individuals to step into if the opportunity arises), indicate those for which this person might be a strong candidate. Recognize that other leaders may have the right to review nominations and cull the list to only the most qualified candidates.

    1.

    2.

    3.

    4.

    5.

    6.

    Please return your completed forms to <person responsible> by <date needed>.

Looking on the Bright Side
Conceptual Frameworks for Positive Performance

Martha C. Yopp and Michael Kroth

Summary

More and more research and popular literature is showing that positive, healthy work environments result in a highly motivated workforce and increased organizational success. Management consultants must become increasingly able to utilize frameworks that enable healthy, generative work environments in order to best support their organizations' goals. The workforce is becoming a more important source of competitive advantage relative to other traditional sources such as technology, economies of scales, and financial resources. Organizational commitment, job satisfaction, and higher performance seem to be the result when employees believe their organizations support them. A positive emotional climate also contributes to organizational success. Much has been reported about the beneficial results of positive work environments, but how to achieve them is still a challenge for most leaders and organizational consultants today. In this article, we will describe four positive approaches to building organizational capacity: (1) asset mapping, (2) building on strengths, (3) appreciative inquiry, and (4) Kroth's Seven Principles for Motivating Work.

Asset Mapping

Asset mapping is often used in community planning but can also be a tool for organization development. It entails identifying the resources of an organization, both tangible and intangible, in the belief that every organization should focus on what can be maintained and improved, rather than on deficits that need to be overcome.

Assets come in many forms, including people, product lines, infrastructure, culture, natural resources, competitive advantage, or location. They include not only the competencies of employees and volunteers, but also social networks and enduring relationships, political and financial capital, and buildings. Assets may be as intangible as the community perception of corporate goodwill and contribution or as tangible as the coal or silver that comes out of a mine. These resources are listed, just as when making an inventory. From that, strategies can be developed to capitalize on them. Asset mapping is positive, realistic, and inclusive (Kerka, 2003).

Asset mapping is an affirming alternative to the typical approach, which focuses on deficits, what is wrong, and what must be fixed. Most consultants are familiar with problem identification, needs assessment, and problem solving. The first step always seems to be figuring out what is wrong with the organization and its people—and then trying to figure out what to do about it. This kind of scarcity approach can create hopelessness and despair in people and the overall organization because from the start they are on the defensive, feeling as if they are a part of an inquisition rather than a process for renewal. It is then a struggle to turn that around and refocus people on the strengths they have and how those are welcomed, desired, and needed for organizational success. Assets are positive components within an organization. One model for asset-mapping involves three layers (Wold, 2005).

The first layer looks at the skills and talents of the people within the organization. Skill and talent inventories may lead to strategies for working smarter, not harder. The abilities of employees give organizations the opportunity to move faster, think more strategically, endure longer, and fight harder. The second layer requires listing all the relational assets within the organization and how they are linked to the external environment. These are part of the organization's social capital. Strong, cohesive relationships are powerful and deserve organizational nurturing and support. The third layer involves mapping the physical or tangible resources of the institution, such as money or infrastructure.

Asset mapping offers a positive approach to organizational planning, based on the assumptions that all organizations are rich in different types of resources and that people care about the organization and are willing to act to support positive change. Asset mapping can be a potent instrument. It draws people into finding their strengths, it kindles energy, and it can change the future of a group or organization. Assets that are not identified and mobilized are likely to underperform, never achieve their true potential, or add little value to organizational efforts. That is why mapping is only the starting point for maximizing organizational resources. They must be invested in, added to, and developed so that they can earn the returns necessary to increase organizational capacity in other arenas. This synergetic approach to building the potential strengths of the organization should continually revitalize not only the leadership but every other aspect of the organization (Wold, 2005).

Building on Strengths—People

Using asset mapping as a conceptual framework for positive change aligns with positive approaches for leading and developing people. Human resource development scholars and practitioners have concentrated on trying to figure out how to maximize human capital for years, developing ever more thoughtful and successful ways to train, develop, and utilize people in the work environment. Marcus Buckingham's approach is closely related to asset mapping. In his book, *Now, Discover Your Strengths* (2001), he writes about the misguided assumption that somehow the traditional fixation on identifying, analyzing, and correcting weaknesses will make organizations strong.

Buckingham believes that finding faults reveals very little about strengths. Strengths, he says, have individual patterns. Furthermore, for people to be successful in a chosen career, they must ascertain those strong suits and capitalize on them. Effective leaders create environments that help employees cultivate and enhance their unique powers. "The great organization must not only accommodate the fact that each employee is different," he says, but "it must capitalize on these differences" (Buckingham, 2001, p. 5). Buckingham states compellingly that most organizations' basic assumptions about people are wrong. Each employee has unique strengths and weaknesses. Trying to identify and correct weaknesses does not work. Identifying strengths and capitalizing on them does. He believes that two assumptions guide successful managers of people:

1. Each person's talents are enduring and unique.

2. Each person's greatest room for growth is in the area of his or her greatest strength.

These two assumptions explain why great managers focus on outcomes, treat employees differently, and spend the most time with their best people. Buckingham thinks great managers build on the strengths of employees in other ways. For example, he believes that they:

- Know and value the unique abilities and even the eccentricities of their employees and how to turn a person's particular talent into performance.

- Succeed when they identify the differences among people, challenging each to excel in his or her way.

- Consider a strength to be not necessarily something one is already good at, but could be. It may be something to which he or she has not yet been exposed. It may be a predilection, something a person finds satisfying and looks forward to doing again and again, therefore becoming better at over time. A weakness, on the other hand, is something a great manager knows drains energy, even when the person is competent.

- Recognize that the most powerful motivator for employees is recognition, not money.

(Buckingham, 2005)

Appreciative Inquiry

Also on the path of positive thinking is the concept of appreciative inquiry (AI), which looks at organizational successes and encourages positive change. Appreciative inquiry was developed by David Cooperrider and his mentor Suresh Srivastva in the 1980s (Cooperrider & Srivastva, 1987). Businesses, organizations, and individuals have adopted its strengths-based philosophy and methodology for organizational improvement. It has become one of the most popular approaches to organizational intervention and has been discussed in many venues. We will cover it briefly here, but encourage consultants and leaders to learn more about this powerful tool for positive change.

AI is the exploration of what is best in people, organizations, and the world. It strives to discover what gives life to organizations or people when they are at their best and feel alive. The process is to ask questions, often through storytelling, that help the organization to understand and move toward its positive potential. As with asset mapping, instead of starting with problems or weaknesses, AI involves imagination, innovation, focus on achievements, and learning from peak moments. It seeks to discover the core of positive change and is built upon the belief that humans and human systems grow in the direction of the questions they ask—either negative or positive.

The principles of AI are applied using the 4-D cycle. This gives us a framework to implement the process, although no two applications of the process are the exactly the same. Cooperrider and Whitney (2000) briefly summarize the 4-Ds:

1. *Discovery:* The Discovery phase mobilizes a whole system inquiry into the positive change core.

2. *Dream:* The Dream phase creates a clear, results-oriented vision in relation to discovered potential and in relation to questions of higher purpose.

3. *Design:* The Design phase involves creating possibilities of the "ideal organization," an organization design that people feel is capable of focusing on a positive core.

4. *Destiny:* The Destiny phase strengthens the positive capability of the whole system, enabling it to build hope and momentum around a deep purpose and to create processes for learning, adjustment, and inventiveness (pp. 6–7).

The AI process has been used in multiple settings with varying types of organizations, including government, for-profit, and not-for-profit organizations, and in over one hundred countries.

Kroth's Seven Principles for Motivating Work

Kroth's principles are another positive approach to organization development. Michael Kroth lays out seven principles, based on research, theory, and practice that contribute to a healthy, highly motivating work environment, which any manager can practice. In his book, *The Manager as Motivator* (2006), he organizes these into what he calls "setting the environment" and "crossing the Rubicon."

"Setting the environment" entails everything that supports lasting motivation and instills effort beyond set goals or reward systems. Four factors develop this "beyond-the-call-of-duty" motivation:

- *Principle One:* Organizational commitment motivates powerfully.

- *Principle Two:* The more you care, the more they will care.

- *Principle Three:* The more you know about people, the more you will know what to do.

- *Principle Four:* Do what you love, the motivation will follow.

Kroth's shorthand for these are *committing, caring, understanding,* and *enjoying.* These provide the climate for positive motivation, in contrast with toxicity, treating employees like dirt, saying one thing and doing another, micromanagement or abandonment, and being unfair.

What Kroth calls "crossing the Rubicon" comes from Julius Caesar's crossing in 49 B.C., upon threat of death. When Caesar crossed, committing an irrevocable act, he reportedly said "the die is cast." In the same way, there is a tangible difference between what happens when setting goals and what happens once committed to them. The principles comprising "crossing the Rubicon" are:

- *Principle Five:* Belief in personal capability enables goal setting and goal pursuit.

- *Principle Six:* Great goals get people going.

- *Principle Seven:* Willpower is the engine for goal pursuit.

The manager's practice for Principle Five is to be an "expectancy" manager, because people who believe in their own capabilities set higher goals, dedicate more effort to them, and endure longer. The manager's practice for Principle Six is to master the art and science of goal setting, because setting the right kind of goals increases performance. The manager's practice for Principle Seven is to use strategies to strengthen and support willpower, because the achievement of significant goals requires stick-to-it-iveness when obstacles or diversions arise.

These seven principles provide the basis for a healthy and highly motivating work environment. Without the first four principles, goal setting and pursuit may be draconian and create a situation in which employees do only what they have to do, and nothing beyond that. Enduring, positive performance requires leaders to practice all seven of the principles.

Conclusion

Asset mapping, building people from strengths, appreciative inquiry, and Kroth's seven principles are all frameworks for developing positive performance from employees that lasts. They are not the only approaches, but they provide leaders and consultants with four methodologies to create work environments that will attract and retain employees and, while they work there, produce the most results in a healthy and affirming organization.

References

Buckingham, M. (2005, March). What great managers do. *Harvard Business Review.*

Buckingham, M., & Clifton, D.O. (2001). *Now, discover your strengths.* New York: The Free Press.

Cooperrider, D.L., & Srivastva, S. (1987). Appreciative inquiry in organizational life. *Research in organizational change and development* (Vol. 1, pp. 129–169). Greenwich, CT: JAI Press.

Cooperrider, D.L., & Whitney, D. (2000). A positive revolution in change: Appreciative inquiry. In D.L. Cooperrider, Jr., P.F. Sorenson, D. Whitney, & T.F. Yeager (Eds.), *Appreciative inquiry: Rethinking human organization toward a positive theory of change* (pp. 3–27). Champaign, IL: Stipes Publishing.

Kerka, S. (2003). Community asset mapping. *Eric Clearinghouse on Adult, Career, and Vocational Education: Trends and Issues Alert, 47.*

Kroth, M.S. (2006). *The manager as motivator.* Westport, CT: Praeger.

Wold, C. (Ed.) (2005). *Creating a value-added community.* St. Paul, MN: Northwest Area Foundation.

Martha C. Yopp *serves as the director of the University of Idaho Center for Economic Education. She is a professor of business education and adult/organizational learning and leadership at the University of Idaho and has been published in numerous journals on topics including the successful program planning and design of adult education programs and effective training and development activities. Her experience has been diverse, including working for five years as the assistant to United States Supreme Court Justice William O. Douglas.*

Michael Kroth, Ph.D., *is the author of* The Manager as Motivator *and the co-author of* Transforming Work: The Five Keys to Achieving Trust, Commitment, and Passion in the Workplace. *He is an assistant professor at the University of Idaho in adult/organizational learning and leadership. He is the leadership field editor for ASTD's* In-Practice *online newsletter, a member of the National Speakers Association, and a past member of the ASTD International Program Advisory Committee.*

Coaching for Behavioral Change

Marshall Goldsmith

Summary

My mission is to help successful leaders achieve positive, long-term, measurable change in behavior. The process described in this article is being used by coaches around the world for this same purpose. When the steps in the process are followed, leaders almost always achieve positive behavioral change, not just as judged by themselves, but as judged by pre-selected, key co-workers. The process has been used with great success by both external coaches and internal coaches.[1]

Our "Pay for Results" Behavioral Coaching Approach

Our coaching network (Marshall Goldsmith Partners in collaboration with Hewitt Associates) provides coaches for leaders around the world. All of the behavioral coaches who work with us use the same general approach. We first reach an agreement with our coaching clients and their managers on two key variables: (1) the key behaviors that will make the biggest positive change in increased leadership effectiveness and (2) who the key stakeholders are who can determine (six to eighteen months later) whether this change has occurred.

We then are paid only after our coaching clients have achieved a positive change in key leadership behaviors as determined by key stakeholders.

I believe that many behavioral coaches are paid for the wrong reasons. Their income is largely a function of "How much do my clients like me?" and "How much time did I spend in coaching?" Neither of these is a good metric for achieving a positive, long-term change in behavior.

---

[1]For a study on the effectiveness of this process with internal coaches in GE Financial Services, see Leveraging HR: How to Develop Leaders in "Real Time," in M. Effron, R. Gandossy, & M. Goldsmith (Eds.), *Human Resources in the 21st Century*. Hoboken, NJ: John Wiley & Sons, 2003.

In terms of liking the coach, I have never seen a study that showed that clients' love of a coach was highly correlated with their change in behavior. In fact, if coaches become too concerned with being loved by their clients, they may not provide honest feedback when it is needed.

In terms of spending clients' time, my clients are all executives whose decisions often impact billions of dollars. Their time is more valuable than mine, so I try to spend as little of their time as necessary to achieve the desired results. The last thing they need is for me to waste their time!

Knowing When Behavioral Coaching Won't Help

Since we use a "pay only for results" process in behavioral coaching, we have had to learn to qualify our coaching clients. This means that we only work with clients we believe will benefit from our coaching process.

We refuse to work with leaders who don't care. Have you ever tried to change the behavior of a successful adult who had no interest in changing? How much luck did you have? Probably none! We only work with executives who are willing to make a sincere effort to change and who believe that this change will help them become better leaders. Our most successful coaching clients are committed to being role models for leadership development and their companies' values.

Some large corporations "write people off." Rather than fire them, they engage in a pseudo behavioral coaching process that is more "seek and destroy" than "help people get better." We only work with leaders who are seen as potentially having a great future in the corporation. We only work with people who will be given a fair chance by their management. We refrain from working with leaders who have been "written off."

There are several different types of coaching. We only do behavioral coaching for successful executives, not strategic coaching, life planning, or organizational change. I have the highest respect for the coaches who do this kind of work. That is just not what our network does. Therefore, we only focus on changing leadership behavior. If our clients have other needs, we refer them to other coaches.

Finally, I would never choose to work with a client who has an integrity violation. We believe that people with integrity violations should be fired, not coached.

When will our approach to behavioral coaching work? If the issue is behavioral and the coaching client is given a fair chance and is motivated to improve, the process described in this article will almost always work. If these conditions do not exist, this process should not be used.

Involving Key Stakeholders

In my work as a behavioral coach, I have gone through three distinct phases.

In phase one, I believed that my clients would become better because of me. I thought that the coach was the key variable in behavioral change. I was wrong. We have recently completed research with over 86,000 respondents on changing leadership behavior.[2] We have learned that the key variable for successful change is not the coach, teacher, or advisor. The key variables that will determine long-term progress are the people being coached and their co-workers.

In phase two, I spent most of my time focusing on my coaching clients. I slowly learned that a motivated, hard-working client was more important than a brilliant coach! I learned that their ongoing efforts meant more than my clever ideas. My results improved!

In phase three (where I am now), I spend most of my time not with my coaching client but with the key stakeholders around my client. By my doing this, my clients results have dramatically improved.[3]

I ask key stakeholders to help the person I am coaching in four critically important ways:

1. "Let go of the past." When we continually bring up the past, we demoralize people who are trying to change. Whatever happened in the past happened. It cannot be changed. By focusing on a future that can get better (as opposed to a past that cannot), the key stakeholders can help my clients improve. (We call this process feed forward, instead of feedback.[4])

2. "Be helpful and supportive, not cynical, sarcastic, or judgmental." As part of our coaching process, my clients involve key co-workers and ask them for help. If my clients reach out to key stakeholders and feel punished for trying to improve, they will generally quit trying. I don't blame them! Why should any of us work hard to build relationships with people who won't give us a chance? If my clients' co-workers are helpful and supportive, my clients experience increased motivation and are much more likely to improve.

3. "Tell the truth." I do not want to work with a client, have him or her receive a glowing report from key stakeholders and later hear that one of

---

[2]H. Morgan & M. Goldsmith. (2004, Fall). Leadership Is a Contact Sport. *Strategy+business*.

[3]This process is explained in more detail in "Recruiting Supportive Coaches: A Key to Achieving Positive Behavioral Change," in M. Goldsmith, V. Govindarajan, B. Kaye, & A. Vicere (Eds.), *The Many Facets of Leadership*. Upper Saddle River, NJ: Prentice Hall, 2003.

[4]"Try Feed Forward, Instead of Feedback" originally published in *Leader to Leader*, Summer 2002.

the stakeholders said, "He didn't really get better, we just said that." This is not fair to my client, to the company, or to me.

4. "Pick something to improve yourself." My clients are very open with key stakeholders about what they are going to change. As part of our process, our clients ask for ongoing suggestions. I also ask the stakeholders to pick something to improve and to ask my client for suggestions. This makes the entire process two-way instead of one-way. It helps the stakeholders act as "fellow travelers" who are trying to improve, not "judges" who are pointing their fingers at my client. It also greatly expands the value gained by the corporation in the entire process.[5]

Steps in the Behavioral Coaching Process

The following steps provide an outline of our behavioral coaching process. Every coach in our network has to agree to implement them. If the coach follows these basic steps, our clients almost always improve!

1. *Involve the leaders being coached in determining the desired behavior in their leadership roles.* Leaders cannot be expected to change behavior if they don't have a clear understanding of what desired behavior looks like. The people we coach (in agreement with their managers) work with us to determine desired leadership behavior.

2. *Involve the leaders being coached in determining key stakeholders.* Not only do clients need to be clear on desired behaviors, but they need to be clear (again in agreement with their managers) on key stakeholders. There are two major reasons why people deny the validity of feedback: wrong items or wrong raters. By having our clients and their managers agree on the desired behaviors and key stakeholders in advance, we help ensure their buy-in to the process.

3. *Collect feedback.* In my coaching practice, I personally interview all key stakeholders. The people I am coaching are all potential CEOs, and the company is making a real investment in their development. However, at lower levels in the organization (which are more price sensitive), traditional 360-degree feedback can work very well. In either case, feedback is

---

[5]For a great description of the impact of co-workers' focusing on their own improvement, read "Expanding the Value of Coaching: From the Leader to the Team to the Organization," in H. Morgan, P. Harkins, & M. Goldsmith (Eds.), *The Art and Practice of Leadership Coaching.* Hoboken, NJ: John Wiley & Sons, 2005.

critical. It is impossible to be evaluated on changed behavior if there is not agreement on what behavior to change!

4. *Reach an agreement on key behaviors for change.* As I have become more experienced, my approach has become simpler and more focused. I generally recommend picking only one or two key areas for behavioral change with each client. This helps ensure maximum attention to the most important behavior. My clients and their managers (unless my client is the CEO) agree on the desired behavior for change. This ensures that I won't spend a year working with my clients and have their managers determine that we have worked on the wrong thing!

5. *Have the coaching clients respond to key stakeholders.* The person being reviewed should talk with each key stakeholders and collect additional "feed forward" suggestions on how to improve on the key areas targeted for improvement. In responding, the person being coached should keep the conversation positive, simple, and focused. When mistakes have been made in the past, it is generally a good idea to apologize and ask for help in changing the future. I suggest that my clients listen to stakeholder suggestions and not judge the suggestions.

6. *Review what has been learned with clients and help them develop action plans.* As was stated earlier, my clients have to agree to the basic steps in our process. On the other hand, outside of the basic steps, all of the other ideas that I share with my clients are suggestions. I just ask them to listen to my ideas in the same way they are listening to the ideas from their key stakeholders. I then ask them to come back with a plan of what they want to do. These plans need to come from them, not from me. After reviewing their plans, I almost always encourage them to live up to their own commitments. I am much more of a facilitator than a judge. I usually just help my clients do what they know is the right thing to do.

7. *Develop an ongoing follow-up process.* Ongoing follow-up should be very efficient and focused. Questions like, "Based on my behavior last month, what ideas do you have for me next month?" can keep a focus on the future. Within six months, conduct a two-to-six item mini-survey with key stakeholders. They should be asked whether the person has become more or less effective in the areas targeted for improvement.

8. *Review results and start again.* If the person being coached has taken the process seriously, stakeholders almost invariably report improvement. Build on that success by repeating the process for the next twelve

to eighteen months. This type of follow-up will assure continued progress on initial goals and uncover additional areas for improvement. Stakeholders will appreciate the follow-up. No one minds filling out a focused, two-to-six-item questionnaire if they see positive results. The person being coached will benefit from ongoing, targeted steps to improve performance.

The Value of Behavioral Coaching for Executives

While behavioral coaching is only one branch in the coaching field, it is the most widely used type of coaching. Most requests for coaching involve behavioral change. While this process can be very meaningful and valuable for top executives, it can be even more useful for high-potential future leaders. These are the people who have great careers in front of them. Increasing effectiveness in leading people can have an even greater impact if it is a twenty-year process, instead of a one-year program.

People often ask, "Can executives really change their behavior?" The answer is definitely yes. If they didn't change, we would never be paid (and we almost always get paid). At the top of major organizations, even a small positive change in behavior can have a big impact. From an organizational perspective, the fact that the executive is trying to change anything (and is being a role model for personal development) may be even more important than what the executive is trying to change. One key message that I have given every CEO I coach is "To help others develop—start with yourself!"

Marshall Goldsmith, Ph.D., *is a world authority in helping successful leaders become even better—by achieving positive change in behavior for themselves, their people, and their teams. He was recently named by the American Management Association as one of the fifty great thinkers and leaders who have impacted the field of management over the past eighty years. Dr. Goldsmith has a Ph.D. from UCLA. He has been asked to teach in the executive education programs at Dartmouth, Michigan, MIT, Wharton, Oxford, and Cambridge Universities. He is the co-author or editor of nineteen books, including* The Leader of the Future *(a BusinessWeek best-seller),* Global Leadership: The Next Generation, *and* The Art and Practice of Leadership Coaching.

The Seven Habits of Highly Effective Facilitators (with Thanks to Stephen R. Covey)

Judith R. Holt

Summary

Since it was published twenty years ago, *The Seven Habits of Highly Effective People* has been read and incorporated into the public consciousness. Stephen Covey synthesized the wisdom of many self-help gurus into a relatively short book, applicable to people in all walks of life. This article elaborates on the specific application of Covey's principles to the art, science, and practice of facilitation.

When Stephen Covey published his book about "habits" of highly effective people, the experts in management and management consulting rushed to declare it revolutionary. Well-known management gurus such as Rosabeth Moss Kanter, Tom Peters, Ken Blanchard, Norman Vincent Peale, Roger Staubach, and Dr. Denis Waitley praised its universal and effective messages.

> "It is solid wisdom and sound principles."
> **Richard M. Euro,** author of *Life Balance and Teaching Children Values*

It's difficult to believe that it has been twenty years since we first began thinking about Covey's principles. "First things first" has become the mantra of many. Covey posits that habits are acquired, repetitive behavior patterns. As Aristotle said, "We are what we repeatedly do. Excellence, then, is not an act, but a habit." Covey's book is a sure and tested roadmap to excellence.

Some time ago, I thought about the application of these habits with respect to facilitation and was delighted to discover how well they apply themselves to my business. There is much, much more to Covey's book than I will attempt to cover here. If you haven't read it—and truly thought about its principles and ideas—you will only have scratched the surface of its wisdom by reading this article.

Inside-Out

Covey begins his exploration of the *Seven Habits of Highly Effective People* with a discussion about paradigms. Most of us are familiar with this term from the 1960s, when it was introduced by Kuhn's (1962) theory that "almost every significant breakthrough in the field of scientific endeavor is first a break with tradition, with old ways of thinking, with old paradigms" (Covey, 1989, p. 29).

But Covey carries this further by explaining that we have personal paradigms and how these influence the way we see the world and react to it. We have all experienced paradigm shifts in our lives. Perhaps we experienced a paradigm shift when we voted for the first time and realized that we were participative members of our society. Or maybe we needed to shift our paradigm when we were given a promotion—we had to see ourselves in new roles.

Some shifts in paradigms are instantaneous, and some occur over time. But we first have to shift how we think about things before we can react to or act upon anything. Covey says that we need to shift our paradigms to a "new level of thinking" that is a "principle-centered, character-based, 'inside-out' approach to personal and interpersonal effectiveness" (Covey, 1989, p. 42). By understanding and integrating the seven habits of highly effective people as shifts to our paradigms, we can transform our professional lives.

Habit 1: Be Proactive

As a facilitator, you constantly practice the habit of being proactive, although you may not realize it. As you are developing the agenda for a meeting or an intervention, you are the one who will offer ideas, present concepts, and take the initiative. You make the suggestions and bring creativity to the engagement.

But Covey's definition of proactive refers to your personal actions—the initiative and responsibility to make things happen by changing yourself. He elaborates on the concept of our "Circle of Concern" (Covey, 1989, p. 83), things in which we have no particular mental or emotional involvement such as the national debt or other circumstances over which we have no control. He compares that with our "Circle of Influence," over which we have control and about which we can do something.

As a facilitator, one of your jobs is to focus your efforts and the efforts of the people in your care on those areas in which you (and they) can make positive changes. That is why you are being hired.

Habit 2: Begin with the End in Mind

At a deep level, you need to decide what your destination will be—the destination of your life—and design your everyday activities to reach it.

On a daily basis, every time you develop an agenda or plan a meeting or structure an intervention, begin with the end in mind. Ask yourself, "What does the customer want to achieve?" "What is the deliverable?" "What should the outcome be?" By concentrating on the end product, you can structure the activities to achieve it.

When I work with a client, I ask, "What do you want to have in your hand at the end of this effort?" In other words, I begin by assisting my client to think of the end product.

Habit 3: Put First Things First

The natural outcome of beginning with the end in mind is to "put first things first." In the facilitation world, you usually structure an agenda with the icebreaker at the beginning. Break the ice, get folks comfortable, and only then introduce the subject.

Covey says that everything is created twice: there is a "mental or first creation, and a physical or second creation to all things" (Covey, 1989, p. 99). This is especially true for facilitators. You will need to design the activities you intend to conduct before presenting them. You will have to think through all the steps, issues, personalities, consequences, and outcomes in order.

Putting first things first requires the ability to delay gratification. When you work through a process step-by-step to achieve the outcome you desire, it is essential to know what should happen first.

Habit 4: Think Win/Win

Covey writes that "win/win is not a technique; it's a total philosophy of human interaction" (Covey, 1989, p. 206). In fact, "The alternative paradigms are win/lose, lose/win, lose/lose, win, and win/win or no deal" (Covey, 1989, p. 206) I'm sure you have seen many examples of each as you worked with groups.

Most people operate from the win/lose paradigm. Our sports are directed from that paradigm. Most contests are of a "there is only one winner" sort. You even see families that pit children against each other. Covey describes these scenarios and their impact on our lives in great detail.

Of all the habits of effective facilitators, I believe this is the most important. There are many examples of how we can structure our meetings, our processes, and our outcomes to create win/win solutions. When you create ground rules for your engagement, you are creating opportunities for everyone to contribute fully. An ice-breaker activity, for example, is meant to create a comfortable atmosphere for the participants. Every time you intervene, you are inviting everyone to be included. Brainstorming, the nominal group technique, and consensus building are all ways to allow for a win/win.

Perhaps the only exception is a voting process, so use a vote only to poll the group, not for a final decision. Consensus—the "I can live with it" definition—is a form of win/win.

Habit 5: Seek First to Understand, Then to Be Understood

Covey begins his discussion of this habit by saying, "Most people do not listen with the intent to understand; they listen with the intent to reply" (Covey, 1989, p. 239). How many meetings have you facilitated when you could easily discern that a "discussion" between two participants was really a "debate"? That is, each speaker was only listening to the other in order to construct his or her rebuttal. A situation like that is when the skills and abilities of a facilitator are needed most.

Covey describes four levels of listening:

- Ignoring—not really listening at all

- Pretending—not really listening, but giving the impression that we are

- Selective listening—only hearing the parts of the conversation we want to hear

- Attentive listening—paying attention to and understanding the message

Covey adds a fifth level: "the highest form of listening, empathic listening" (Covey, 1989, p. 240), listening with the intention to understand what the other person is really saying. In my facilitation practice, I call this "listening with my gut." It's the ability to get myself out of the way to be able to really hear and understand the meaning and intention and emotion of the message. It's only when you truly understand what someone is saying that you can respond in a way that enables the other person to understand your reply.

We must be sure that we understand what our clients are saying. We have to understand their needs, their intentions, their problems, their hopes, and their desired outcomes. All the probing questions that I use when I am interviewing a client prior to a meeting are meant to help me listen empathically. Only when I truly understand the client can I help him or her understand my vision of how I can help.

"Knowing how to be understood is the other half of Habit 5, and is equally critical in reaching win/win solutions" (Covey, 1989, p. 255). At this point the other habits can begin to join together as a whole: Be proactive when you begin with the end in mind to put first things first as you design a win/win strategy for your client once you have listened to and understood him/her!

Habit 6: Synergize

Covey brings it together in one coherent philosophy under Habit 6. He says, "The exercise of all of the other habits prepares us for the habit of synergy" (Covey, 1989, p. 262).

Our traditional definition of synergy means the whole is greater than the sum of its parts. Covey elaborates on synergy in communication, education, management, leadership, and personal relationships.

When we apply synergy to facilitation, it brings an element of surprise. We know that the sum of the parts will be different from and more than we anticipate, but we don't really know how those differences will manifest themselves. Surrendering to the synergy of a group means trusting the group to find itself in a new place.

I believe we are most successful as facilitators when the group no longer requires our intense assistance and intervention. My goal is to get a group start and then to get out of their way! It's like driving a car down a highway. But once the car is heading in the right direction and at the appropriate speed, you only need to make minor adjustments.

There is joy in being a part of the synergy of a group. It is wonderful to watch a group move through the Drexler/Sibbet Team Performance™ Model to reach the point of "high performance" (Johansen, 1991, p. 25) and to know that I was responsible (to a smaller or larger degree) for their success!

Habit 7: Sharpen the Saw

Sharpening the saw means taking time to increase your knowledge and hone your skills. It's easy to become complacent and satisfied in a profession when you are successful and when you have been doing the same thing for a number of years. We may begin to think that there are only so many different ways to structure a strategic planning session or a team-building session or that there are only so many ways your participants will challenge you. Covey challenges us to look at ourselves from four dimensions of renewal and take the time to pay attention to all of them:

- Physical: Exercise, Nutrition, Stress Management

- Mental: Reading, Visualizing, Planning, Writing

- Social/Emotional: Service, Empathy, Synergy, Intrinsic Security

- Spiritual: Value Clarification & Commitment, Study & Meditation

(Covey, 1989, p. 288)

Sharpening the saw means investing in ourselves to bring new meaning into our lives, to increase our value to our clients, and to enhance our business practice.

Conclusion

Reading and understanding Covey's book can have a transformational impact on your personal life as well as your facilitation practice. There is so much wisdom in *The Seven Habits of Highly Effective People* that I have only scratched the surface. The *direct application* of Covey's principles to the business of facilitation is amazing.

So I challenge you to sharpen your saw when you begin your next engagement with the end in mind as you put first things first by seeking first to understand your client and then to be understood as you work to bring them to a win/win place in synergy!

References

Covey, S.R. (1989). *The seven habits of highly effective people.* New York: Simon and Schuster.

Johansen, R. (1991). *Leading business teams.* Reading, MA: Addison-Wesley.

Kuhn, T. (1962). *The structure of scientific revolutions.* Chicago, IL: The University of Chicago Press.

Judith R. Holt, CPF, CMF, *is a management consultant specializing in collaborative technology facilitation, training, and systems leasing in Washington, D.C. Holt is an International Institute for Facilitation (INIFac) "Certified Master Facilitator" and an International Association of Facilitators (IAF) "Certified Professional Facilitator" with sixteen years' experience in strategic planning, process analysis/reengineering, decision support, and team building. She has a bachelor of science degree in mathematics with minors in physics and education from Radford University in Radford, Virginia.*

New Accountabilities
Non-Financial Measures of Performance
Ajay M. Pangarkar and Teresa Kirkwood

Summary

Mention the word "performance" and many managers immediately shift their thinking to measures related to some type of financial result. This is how many managers are formally trained. They believe measuring performance through financial accountability provides the most relevant and simplest way to demonstrate progress and productivity.

It is true that financial outcomes are tangible, immediate, and relevant, but their strength lies in measuring short-term objectives. In recent years, however, corporate America has had its share of downfalls relating to the manipulation of financial performance measures, so much so that shareholders and the public are demanding that performance measures deliver a longer-term outlook and be independent from financial outcomes. This outcry has led organizations down a more enlightened path developing and including more non-financially based measures. This article will compare financial-based performance measure challenges and examine the need for non-financial accounting.

The Challenges of Financial-Based Performance Measures

The challenges with financial-based performance measures are two-fold. First, financial measures are often overused and extensively relied upon. Managers of companies face a tremendous amount of pressure to perform and to demonstrate results quickly. The most convenient method to show their results is through financial metrics. These measurements are fast and familiar for managers. They also provide a very narrow focus of the organization's impact in the marketplace. Secondly, financial-based measures do not reflect true performance drivers against intangible outcomes. For example, how does a manager quantify customer satisfaction or intellectual capacity in a financial context? In several organizational studies, there is an over-emphasis of financial metrics such as shareholder value, profitability, and expense reduction over non-financial measures such as customer satisfaction, quality, and innovation.

The Growing Need for Non-Financial Accountability

In recent years, many companies are finding that measuring performance based on financial results is at times relevant, but they also find it necessary to have a more inclusive and holistic approach to performance measurement. It is increasingly important that performance be directly linked to the strategic objectives of the organization. Financial performance metrics provide results related to short-term outcomes. But when dealing with organizational strategy, a long-term approach is required and maximizes the impact of non-financial performance measures.

Many non-financial factors have demonstrated that they contribute to and have a lasting impact on a company's market value. Since these non-financial measures are more forward looking and are linked to operational activities, they help to focus a manager's efforts and better evaluate employee performance.

The current economic environment is placing increasing importance on intangible factors such as employee knowledge, continuous process improvement, innovative capabilities, and intellectual capital. In recent years, strategic frameworks have developed "dashboards" for management to balance financial and non-financial performance indicators. The most common type of framework is the "balanced scorecard." It translates corporate strategy through performance measures, allowing managers to make more appropriate decisions.

Why are non-financial measures gaining prominence within the business environment over financial metrics? It is because these measures provide a direct correlation with strategic objectives. Most financial measures focus on short-term accountabilities and leave out intangible factors that directly affect the customer, supplier, and employee. The same financial results lead to situations narrow in focus and set up adversarial environments based on irrelevant data. Financial measures can also be manipulated to meet the outcomes desired by the party reporting them.

Numbers are not the most complete or appropriate measure to demonstrate organizational performance. They do not address non-financial factors that help organizations attain their strategic objectives, leading to improved financial performance. Take for example a company expanding product research and development. This non-financial objective goes against traditional financial performance measures, negatively affecting financial indicators, increasing expenses, and reducing bottom-line results. Yet, the company may attain its long-term objective of becoming a market leader in its product space, resulting in improved financial performance.

Managers can no longer use financial measures as the holy grail of organizational accountability. They must integrate non-financial measures to communicate objectives, assist in the effective implementation of strategic plans, and provide incentive to address long-term strategy.

The success drivers for many industries lie in intangible assets such as human capital and innovative capability, rather than traditional measures of hard assets as represented in a company's balance sheet. Non-financial measures are the qualitative value of the firm's intangible assets in indirect relationship to quantitative results. Many studies examine how non-financial performance measures of intangible assets lead to differences in U.S. companies' stock market values. Commonly, measures related to innovation, management capability, employee relations, quality, and brand recognition contribute to a company's overall value. Because they leave out these intangible assets, financially oriented measures can lead managers to make poor and risky decisions.

The Benefits of Non-Financial Measures

There is considerable evidence demonstrating that non-financial measures are also good indicators of a company's financial performance. Financial results traditionally do not take into account or capture long-term benefits, even when trying to maximize financial performance. Under current accounting convention, expenses and costs are declared in the period in which they are incurred, so they often reflect poor performance. But if the expenditures are justified, future profitability will be improved, along with other intangible benefits. For example, let's say you want to extensively develop your employee skills base and foster a more cohesive workplace. This would require a significant investment in training, coaching, and other methods of support. In the near term, this would negatively affect a company's financial performance, but the longer-term non-financial benefit would result in innovative ideas and products, leadership in market presence, increased productivity, and improved reputation through reduction in errors and defects. These intangible results would lead to many financial benefits, increased demand and sales for products, increasing profit margins, and increased future cash flow, to name a few.

An additional benefit non-financial measures offer is the ability to balance factors within and beyond your control. External such as market changes are wild cards in performance measurement. The greatest benefit of non-financial factors is the focus on actions that are within the control of the organization. What does this mean for you and your company? It means that (1) the company is less susceptible to external changes, (2) managers are able to focus on issues directly related to strategic objectives, and (3) both employees and managers can evaluate and improve their performance.

Limitations to Non-Financial Performance Measures

Resistance

Changing the rules for evaluating performance in an organization is a challenge. Financial-based measures are an ingrained way of measuring performance. New forms of performance evaluation are often met with skepticism, especially as organizations introduce "flavors of the month." The first hurdle for integrating non-financial-based measures is resistance from all levels of the organization.

Costly and Time-Consuming

Another major drawback is the perceived time and expense needed. Too often the cost and time involved in developing a performance management system can exceed expected benefits. Excessive development and implementation time, incorrect selection and inconsistent application of measures, and significant time involved in selling the solution to employees often leave systems orphaned.

Performance measurement is linked to results rather than to constant evaluation. In theory this makes complete sense, but too many organizations make any performance measurement process an exercise in futility, continually discussing, evaluating, and reporting performance results, rather than capitalizing on those results. With increasing competitive pressures and changing economic conditions, there is no time for extensive discussion of performance results. If your performance evaluation metrics, especially non-financial ones, require a significant amount of time, then you might want to rethink your performance criteria and how they are evaluated. Begin by reducing the indicators used; then minimize reporting processes and reduce the number of meetings to discuss outcomes.

Confusion

Consistency is crucial if any type of performance measurement system, financial or non-financial, is to be effective. Too many times managers attempt to balance existing performance measures with new, non-financial-based measures. This not only takes more time but also causes confusion among those using the measures.

No Common Base for Measurement

A significant disadvantage of the use of non-financial measures is the need for a common base for measurement. Non-financial performance data can be measured in many ways and it is important to ensure that there is a common measure and a common understanding of that measure. Each organization sets measures in a way unique to its needs. Some develop measures in relation to strategic priorities and rank their importance to the overall objectives through a weighted average approach, whereas others assign subjective measures.

Your goal is to minimize randomness and subjectivity, making the measures tangible and relevant to your organization. To minimize resistance and reduce skepticism from employees, it is essential to link them to the non-financial measures you implement. Too often managers adopt a non-financial measure without demonstrating the relationships between the measure and any tangible indicator of performance such as shareholder value, market share, or earnings per share. A weak correlation to a tangible result could lead to a dead end.

Too Many Indicators

Another mistake often made is attempting to implement too many indicators. More is not necessarily better and can lead to a dilution of the information and a loss of data integrity. As an example, Bell Canada Enterprises (see Figure 1) developed a structured approach, clearly knowing their strategic objective and understanding that business is built on customer experiences. Their performance strategy differentiates between internal and external factors and clearly defines relevant key performance indicators, linked back to the strategic objectives and tangible results. When measuring the performance of call center representatives, for example, Bell Canada utilizes leading indicators such as revenue per person hour.

What Drives Performance?

To develop effective performance measures, begin by understanding your organization's objectives and values. These contribute to the overall success of the organization and help to translate your strategic vision into specific actions.

Although this seems like common sense, managers still tend to develop measures that are irrelevant or overly complex. Begin by understanding what you are attempting to address strategically. Bell Canada Enterprises, for example, links its performance to customer experiences and satisfaction. Once you have identified the organizational values, you can develop performance drivers that directly link back to the overall objectives and, hence, link to financial-based results.

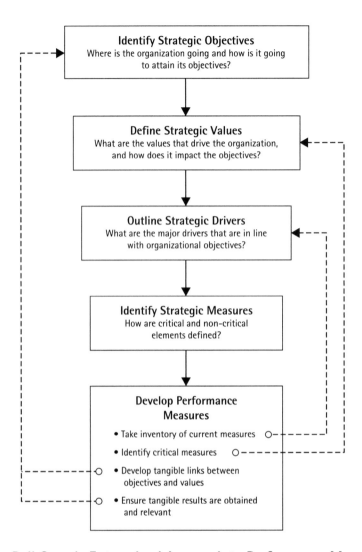

Figure 1. Bell Canada Enterprises' Approach to Performance Measurement

Another way to develop performance measures is to benchmark with competitors, suppliers, and industry clients. Benchmarking can also involve an internal comparison of historical performance. Caution is required, as comparing performance measures from one organization to another can lead to significant discrepancies because objectives and cultures vary.

One of the most reliable methods of measuring non-financial performance is through the relationship of intangible measures to numerical data-driven performance. At Bell Canada Enterprises, performance indicators of call center representatives are based on the customers' experience, but the results are based on average call handle time and first call resolution.

Keeping Performance Measures Simple Keeps It Real

Usually, larger organizations tend to develop more complex non-financial measures. Take inventory of your non-financial indicators and identify those which are effective. It is important to begin from the top (strategic orientation and objective) and work your way down to the value drivers of the organization. Discard all measures that do not deliver any value and develop new metrics addressing issues critical to advancing the organization toward its goals. Two things are important to remember during this process: (1) not all performance indicators have to be identical for each task and (2) simplicity in your measures is usually most effective.

The next step is to integrate the measures through transparent and easily accessible processes facilitating reporting and evaluation. The choice of performance measures should not be taken lightly, as they will impact all levels of the organization and employee performance.

Each non-financial performance measure is as unique as each organization seeking to implement an effective performance management process. As direct and simple as financial performance measures can be, they do not reflect organizational strategy entirely. The true value of non-financial measures is in the selection of appropriate objectives related directly to organizational strategy. But keep in mind that any performance management solution is a dynamic process and choices made today may not reflect the direction taken tomorrow. Your performance management process must evolve along with your organizational strategy and changes in the environment.

Ajay M. Pangarkar, CTDP, and Teresa Kirkwood, CTDP, *are partners at CentralKnowledge.com. At CentralKnowledge, they align learning strategy and performance with business and strategic objectives. They are the authors of* Linking Learning Strategy to the Balanced Scorecard *(Pfeiffer, in press) and* Building Business Acumen for Trainers *(Pfeiffer).*

Leadership and Idiosyncrasy Credit
The IC Model and Its Implications for Leadership Practice
Ingo Winkler

Summary

What makes leaders and leadership effective? This question is one of the most basic in leadership research and practice. Consequently, a lot of leadership research is focused on the antecedents of leadership effectiveness. So it is no surprise that leadership theories comprising normative conclusions are more prominent, such as charismatic/value-based leadership (House, 1977; House & Shamir, 1993), leader-member exchange theory (Graen, 1976; Graen & Uhl-Bien, 1995) and OB-Mod (Luthans & Kreitner, 1985). Other approaches that focus on the description and explanation of leadership aspects, such as the attribution theory of leadership (Calder, 1977; Mitchell, Green, & Wood, 1981) and the idiosyncrasy model of leadership (Hollander, 1958; Hollander & Julian, 1970) are somewhat neglected these days. It is useful, however, to examine these more descriptive leadership theories for their normative content.

This article will focus on the idiosyncrasy model (IC model) of leadership, first developed by Edwin Hollander (1958). It will show that the model has several consequences for our understanding of leadership. Finally, five implications for leadership practice will be deduced.

The Idiosyncrasy Model of Leadership

Leadership and Status

The IC model of leadership (Hollander, 1958, 1960, 1980, 1992, 1993, 2004) builds the awareness that leadership is a product of shared interpersonal perceptions. Every member of a group has a certain degree of status. Within the IC model, status is considered to be a result of interaction and is referred to as an idiosyncrasy credit (Hollander, 1958), defined as the "positively disposed impressions" an individual acquires from other group members (Hollander, 1958, p. 120; Hollander, 1960, p. 247). This group-awarded credit allows for idiosyncratic behavior to a certain degree before group sanctions are applied (Hollander, 1958).

According to the model, group members ascribe credit to other members of the group based on perceived competence, for example, contributions to the group's main task, conformity, and maintaining existing group norms (Hollander, 1993). Competence includes such aspects as the control of scarce resources, the access to important information, or the ability to deal with critical situations (Yukl, 1994). Conformity is defined as the level to which group members comply with existing norms of a group. If the group member's performance is positively perceived by the others, and if this member behaves according to group norms, the individual's acceptance rises and the person gains a certain level of credit. "Where an individual fails to live up to expectancies, i.e., non-conforms, he (or she) loses credits" (Hollander, 1958, p. 120).

Eventually the individual reaches a certain threshold at which time it becomes appropriate in the eyes of the other group members to assert influence (Hollander, 1960). Consequently, high-idiosyncrasy-credit group members are allowed to assume leadership and to influence others. The research literature on idiosyncrasy credit also focuses on the different criteria for influencing the accumulation of idiosyncrasy credit, for example, intelligence (Hollander, 1978), personal characteristics (Kenny & Zaccaro, 1983), gender (Geis, Boston, & Hoffman, 1985), number of verbal statements (Stein & Heller, 1983), or seniority (Insko, Gilmore, Moehle, Lipsitz, Drenan, & Thibaut, 1982).

Thus, according to the IC model, leaders in work groups receive their legitimacy, that is, the basis for their attainment of the leader status (Hollander, 2006), out of their so-called high-idiosyncrasy credit. Their high-idiosyncrasy credit means high status within the group and serves as a long-term base to legitimize leadership. As a consequence, the accumulation of high-idiosyncrasy credit in the past results in the ascription of leadership and allows the group member to influence others in the future.

Nonconformity of Leaders

If we consider leader behavior, we often observe non-conformity. For example, leaders introduce new objectives and tasks or change the member structure. Subsequently, leaders often do not comply with existing group norms in order to introduce innovations. According to the IC model, such behavior should result in a loss of credit and, thus, accorded status. Because of their high-idiosyncrasy credit, however, leaders are granted permission to show idiosyncratic behavior before group sanctions are applied. "Once a fund of credits has been accumulated, the leader is in a position to be innovative and can depart from normal group practice to a certain degree" (Bryman, 1986, p. 8). Moreover, once an individual is assigned to be in the lead, the other group members expect innovative behavior from him or her. Being the leader in a group also means deviating from existing norms to a certain degree in order to move the group forward. However, innovative actions, that is, nonconformity, of a leader must be in line with expectations associated with the leadership role (Hollander, 2006). They cannot deviate in any way they want (Hollander, 1961). Instead, because they are expected to assume leadership, they are only allowed to act differently in a manner that is consistent with their high-status roles (Hollander, 1958, 1961). Additionally, nonconformity is related to group success. If leaders deviate from existing group norms to bring in innovations but fail to contribute to the group's main objective, they will be blamed for the failure and, consequently, will lose credit (Alvarez, 1968; Hollander, 1960).

Elected Versus Appointed Leaders

Hollander and Julian (1970) demonstrate that election and appointment of a group leader produce differing evaluations by followers. As shown, legitimacy of a group leader is the result of a complex process of social interaction. Correspondingly, the ability to influence others differs between leaders who are elected by the group members and leaders who are formally appointed (Hughes, Ginnett, & Curphy, 1996; Yukl, 1994). Elected leaders have a larger latitude to deviate from existing norms, as they have proven themselves to the group with past performance and demonstrations of conformity (Goldman & Fraas, 1965; Hollander & Julian, 1970, 1978). Appointed leaders could not draw on former performance, as they are new to the group. Consequently, their status derives only from the formal position and maybe reputation. They are often in a weak position because their initial legitimacy is low (Hollander, 1993).

Critical Review of the IC Model

The IC model, in the first place, significantly enhances our understanding of leadership emergence. It explains how leadership develops out of the interaction process among group members. Second, the model describes how leadership roles, once established, are reproduced and changed. Thus, it allows for process-based studies of leadership. Third, subject to the link between idiosyncrasy credit and leadership, the IC model illustrates why the same behavior by different group members results in diverse effects. Although it is sometimes stated that the model lacks empirical results as most studies use laboratory settings (Yukl, 1994), the IC model of leadership is absolutely able to explain leadership in real groups.

Implications for Leadership Practice

The IC model does not say how leadership ought to be. Rather it describes how leadership emerges and operates in relatively non-coercive situations in which power is not absolute but depends on the context and the individuals involved (Hollander, 2006). Nevertheless, it delivers a base for a set of implications for leadership practice, which are outlined below:

1. Leadership in a given work group is not solely set up on formal positions. Rather, it emerges from the interaction process of the group and the accorded status of the group members. Hence, leadership roles can differ from formal positions, and group members (e.g., the most experienced) other than the officially assigned leader may assert influence and get in the lead.

2. Leadership emergence and maintenance depend on followers. Without the acceptance of followers, group leaders have no legitimacy and, therefore, are not able to lead. This fact is often neglected in leadership research and practice, which tend to be leader-centered. However, without the acceptance and support of followers, leaders, even with the power of their formal positions, can hardly achieve anything.

3. A group member can only assume leadership if he or she has high status. As a result, if a group member has leadership ambitions and is willing to assert influence, this individual has to show performance and conformity in order to achieve the high status. A high-status degree serves as a legitimate base for taking over leadership. Consequently, if individuals are willing to get in the lead they have to show patience and develop their leadership base. According to the IC model, this is the only possible way to gain long-term leadership acceptance.

4. Once a group member is accepted as leader and decides to assume leadership this person cannot rest on his or her high status. Preferably, leaders of a group have to maintain their legitimate base by showing further performance and conformity with group norms. Furthermore, a group leader must lead, that is, must take on the leadership role and the associated behavior. Group members expect leaders to show authority and make decisions (Estrada, Brown, & Lee, 1995). If a group member with assigned leadership fails to fulfill these expectations, his or her idiosyncrasy credits,

and hence status, will decrease, and this individual will run the risk of being stripped of the leadership role.

5. Within organizations, group leaders are frequently appointed, not elected. Appointed leadership, however, means that the leader's acceptance among the group members is limited. So even if new leaders are ambitious and highly motivated to introduce changes, appointed leaders have to take their time in order to learn about group norms and group structure. Knowing these norms and adhering to them is a key factor in accumulating status in the group. Appointed leaders will be able to successfully introduce innovations only as high-status members of the group.

Conclusion

The IC model delivers explanations for leadership emergence and effects of leadership. It is rather descriptive and focuses on complex interaction processes in groups and reciprocal evaluations of group members. It has several implications for leadership practice. For example, the important role of followers for leaders could be clarified, and advice for appointed leaders could be deduced.

The analysis of the IC model for its normative content shows that descriptive leadership approaches are not just interesting for academics, but also relevant for leadership practice.

References

Alvarez, R. (1968). Informal reactions to deviance in simulated work organizations: A laboratory experiment. *American Sociological Review, 33,* 895–912.

Bryman, A. (1986). *Leadership and organizations.* London: Routledge & Kegan Paul.

Calder, B.J. (1977). An attribution theory of leadership. In B.M. Staw & G.R. Salancik (Eds.), *New directions in organizational behavior* (pp. 179–204). Chicago, IL: St. Clair.

Estrada, M., Brown, J., & Lee, F. (1995). Who gets the credit? Perceptions of idiosyncrasy credit in work groups. *Small Group Research, 26*(1), 56–76.

Geis, F.L., Boston, M.B., & Hoffman, N. (1985). Sex of authority role models and achievement by men and women: Leadership performance and recognition. *Journal of Personality and Social Psychology, 49*(12), 636–653.

Goldman, M., & Fraas, L.A. (1965). The effects of leader selection on group performance. *Sociometry, 28,* 82–88.

Graen, G.B. (1976). Role-making processes within complex organizations. In M.D. Dunnette (Ed.), *Handbook of industrial and organizational psychology* (pp. 1202–1245). Chicago: Rand McNally.

Graen, G.B., & Uhl-Bien, M. (1995). Relationship-based approach to leadership: Development of leader-member exchange (LMX) theory of leadership over 25 years: Applying a multilevel multi-domain perspective. *Leadership Quarterly, 6*(2), 219–247.

Hollander, E.P. (1958). Conformity, status, and idiosyncrasy credit. *Psychological Review, 65*(2), 117–127.

Hollander, E.P. (1960). Competence and conformity in the acceptance of influence. *Journal of Abnormal & Social Psychology, 61*(3), 361–365.

Hollander, E.P. (1961). Some effects of perceived status on response to innovative behavior. *Journal of Abnormal and Social Psychology, 63*(2), 247–250.

Hollander, E.P. (1978). *Leadership dynamics: A practical guide to effective relationships.* New York: Macmillan.

Hollander, E.P. (1980). Leadership and social exchange processes. In K.J. Gergen, M.S. Greenberg, & R.H. Willis (Eds.), *Social exchange: Advances in theory and research* (pp. 103–118). New York: Plenum.

Hollander, E.P. (1992). The essential interdependence of leadership and followership. *Current Directions in Psychological Science, 1*(2), 71–75.

Hollander, E.P. (1993). Legitimacy, power, and influence. In M. Chemers & R. Ayman (Eds.), *Leadership theory and research: Perspectives and research directions* (pp. 29–48). San Diego, CA: Academic Press.

Hollander, E.P. (2004). Idiosyncrasy credit. In G.R. Goethals. (Ed.), *The encyclopedia of leadership* (pp. 695–700). Greater Barrington, MA: Berkshire/Sage.

Hollander, E.P. (2006). Influence processes in leadership-followership: Inclusion and the idiosyncrasy credit model. In D.A. Hantula (Ed.), *Advances in social and organizational psychology: A tribute to Ralph Rosnow* (pp. 293–312). Mahwah, NJ: Lawrence Erlbaum Associates.

Hollander, E.P., & Julian, J.W. (1970). Studies in leader legitimacy, influence, and innovation. In L.L. Berkowitz (Ed.), *Advances in experimental social psychology* (pp. 33–69). New York: Academic Press.

Hollander, E.P., & Julian, J.W. (1978). A further look at leader legitimacy, influence, and innovation. In L.L. Berkowitz (Ed.), *Group processes* (pp. 153–165). New York: Academic Press.

House, R.J. (1977). A 1976 theory of charismatic leadership. In J.G. Hunt & L.L. Larson (Eds.), *Leadership: The cutting edge* (pp. 189–205). Carbondale, IL: Southern Illinois University Press.

House, R.J., & Shamir, B. (1993). Toward the integration of transformational, charismatic and visionary theories of leadership. In M. Chemers & R. Ayman (Eds.), *Leadership theory and research: Perspectives and research directions* (pp. 81–108). San Diego, CA: Academic Press.

Hughes, R.L., Ginnett, R.C., & Curphy, G.J. (1996). *Leadership: Enhancing the lessons of experience.* Chicago, IL: Irwin.

Insko, C.A., Gilmore, R., Moehle, D., Lipsitz, A., Drenan, S., & Thibaut, J.W. (1982). Seniority in the generational transition of laboratory groups: The effects of social familiarity and task experience. *Journal of Experimental Social Psychology*, *18*, 557–580.

Kenny, D.A., & Zaccaro, S.J. (1983) An estimate of variance due to traits in leadership. *Journal of Applied Psychology*, *68*(4), 678–685.

Luthans, F., & Kreitner, R. (1985). *Organizational behavior modification and beyond: An operant and social learning approach.* Glenview, IL, London: Scott, Foresman and Company.

Mitchell, T.R., Green, S.B., & Wood, R.E. (1981). An attributional model of leadership and the poor performing subordinate: Development and validation. In T.G. Cummings & B.M. Staw (Eds.), *Research in organizational behavior* (pp. 197–234). Greenwich, CT: JAI Press.

Stein, R.T., & Heller, T. (1983). The relationship of participation rates to leadership status: A meta-analysis. In H.H. Blumberg, A.P. Hare, V. Kent, & M.F. Davies (Eds.), *Small groups and social interaction (Vol. 1)* (pp. 401–406). Chicester, UK: John Wiley & Sons.

Yukl, G.A. (1994). *Leadership in organizations.* Englewood Cliffs, NJ: Prentice Hall.

Ingo Winkler *has worked in the academic field for eight years. Currently he holds the assistant professor position in organizational studies at Chemnitz University of Technology, Germany. His research interests cover several areas of organizational behavior and human resource development, such as inter-firm collaboration, organizational change, leadership theory, and new forms of employment.*

Job Analysis
Its Critical Role in Human Capital Management
Leonard D. Goodstein and Erich P. Prien

Summary

In this article, the authors present a six-step human capital life cycle, which they use to illustrate the hiring and retention process. In particular, they emphasize the importance of job analysis, a key factor that impacts all of the remaining steps in the cycle and that is the cornerstone of an effective hiring process.

Identifying the right person to fill a job vacancy has always been difficult. In the United States, the aging, culturally diverse, and heterogeneous work force has increased that difficulty, and a globally competitive economy makes searching for competent workers an even more formidable task. The rise of the Internet and the virtual avalanche of resumes employers receive in response to each job posting make the task of finding suitable candidates yet more laborious.

Still, hiring the wrong people poses serious risks to all businesses—from the smallest to the large, multinational corporation. Indeed, the costs of a hiring mistake are estimated to be from one-half to ten times an individual's annual salary. The expense of hiring mistakes must be controlled by using a systematic and consistent approach to identifying and hiring competent and suitable people.

Hiring a competent and suitable individual to fill a position is a true win-win proposition—for both the new employee and the employer. Recruiting competent people for positions in which they can succeed, feel good about what they are doing, and experience the positive regard of their co-workers is highly reinforcing to everybody. New employees should experience a boost in their sense of self-worth and self-esteem. They should begin to feel secure and bring greater focus and energy to their work as job satisfaction increases. This growing sense of achievement and capability, in turn, leads to greater increases in motivation, to further achievement, and to a greater sense of competence.

For the employer, hiring such people is equally important. First, it saves money by raising productivity, lowering personnel turnover, and reducing supervisory problems. Further, personnel conflicts and problems decline sharply, as does the turnover of new hires, all of which result in considerable savings in additional hiring costs and downtime. Proper selection processes significantly reduce the risk of litigation for negligent or discriminatory hiring practices. An organization succeeds when its hiring process places people in jobs that allow them to utilize their abilities, capabilities, and skills. Finally, from a societal point of view, good selection also provides genuine equal opportunity to all people and helps our economy grow by increasing productivity and reducing job dissatisfaction.

Despite the many benefits of hiring the right candidate to fill a job vacancy, doing so is not easy for most organizations. In our experience, one of the most important reasons for this difficulty is that all too many supervisors and managers do not have a clear understanding of the competencies necessary for success in a particular job and how to assess those competencies. If you do not know what you are looking for, it is difficult to find it!

It is important to place job analysis in a proper context, one that illuminates its importance in the management of an organization's most important asset, its human capital.

The Human Capital Life Cycle

We believe that the ideal human capital life cycle is best understood as involving six more or less discrete steps. All too often employers do not differentiate these steps clearly and thus do not follow them, leading to poor-quality outcomes. The six steps approach employee recruitment, selection, and hiring as the initial aspects of an employee life cycle, one that is concerned with employees throughout their employment careers. The six steps are

- Job analysis
- Recruitment
- Screening
- Final selection
- Job orientation
- Training and development

Additional phases of human capital management appear later in work life as employees move through a career and into retirement, but we will concern ourselves only with these initial six steps, ones that build on the job analysis and universally affect virtually all employees and most jobs. Beginning with job analysis, we will review each of these steps briefly.

Job Analysis

It is not possible to overestimate the importance of a competent job analysis in the human capital process. It is the step on which the entire employee life cycle hinges and thus should be regarded as one of the most important professional responsibilities of both the human resource staff who must conduct thorough job analyses and of their managers who must initiate and oversee the process (Wilson, 2007.)

Simply stated, the purpose of a job analysis is to provide an in-depth understanding of the competencies required for success in order to select appropriate candidates. A job competency is a behavior, or set of behaviors, necessary to accomplish a specific work task or achieve a specific goal. These competencies can range from the most simple, such as filing, operating a punch press, or answering callers politely and warmly, to the most complex, such as neurosurgery or getting along with a difficult supervisor.

The importance of using comprehensive job analyses in selecting among candidates is strongly supported by empirical research. This research (e.g., Campion, Palmer, & Campion, 1997; Campion, Pursell, & Brown, 1988) clearly shows that, when the hiring process was based on a careful job analysis, the prediction of job success is greatly increased and that it is possible to identify correctly those candidates most likely to succeed. This line of research also supports the conclusion that much of the early research on the problems in predicting job success was seriously flawed by one critical omission—the lack of job analyses that identified the characteristics necessary for success on that job. And it is crucial that there be consensus among those actually performing the job analysis (Peiser & Yaakov, 2004.)

Further, there is considerable evidence (summarized in Ployhart, Schneider, & Schmitt, 2006) that effective staffing procedures based on careful job analyses provide organizations of all sizes with a sustained competitive advantage. It becomes difficult, if not impossible, to argue that conducting competent job analyses is not the foundation of all human resource management and the deployment of human talent.

Recruitment

In job postings for recruiting candidates, the job analysis should be used to specify the knowledge, skills, and abilities (requirements) of successful candidates. Although this will probably not reduce the flood of resumes that recruiters currently experience with every job posting, it does serve two important purposes. First, it provides a template for screening the mass of resumes. Which of these resumes clearly indicates that the sender possesses the requirements necessary for success? For example, to what extent has the applicant tailored the resume to fit the articulated set of requirements in the job posting? How carefully has the resume been prepared? How often have there been job changes? What is the nature of the self-described accomplishments? What are the specific skills required for *this* job? (Reiter-Palmer, Young, Strange, Manning, & James, 2006).

Second, an accurate and sufficiently detailed posting will serve as a template that gives a measure of protection against charges of discriminatory hiring. The degree to which the applicant does not meet the specific requirements set forth in the job posting is critical in any defense against discriminatory hiring practices, providing that it can be shown that these requirements are actually related to on-the-job success, a topic to which we return later.

If the initial recruitment process includes some interviewing, the recruiter needs to remember that this interview has two purposes. One is to sell the job to attractive candidates, those who appear to have the necessary set of requirements. The other is to verify that the applicant does meet the requirements. This means that the recruiter must understand both the job and the candidate well enough to probe for the validity of the information contained in the resume. The recruiter must know enough about the job to test for the presence or absence of the required skills and knowledge.

One of the dangers of conducting initial interviews of this type is that the recruiter may view the purpose solely as selling the candidate on the job. Organizations should be careful not to reward recruiters for the number of candidates they promote to the screening process. Rewarding recruiters for the number of candidates who make it through the screening process to the final selection stage is far wiser.

Screening

Most hiring organizations do not make a clear distinction between screening and selection, which means that the organization is putting too much time, effort, and energy into examining too many inappropriate candidates. By screening, we mean the identification of those few applicants who appear most likely to possess the requirements for advancement to the selection process. We would argue that the optimal number of such candidates who should be advanced to the final selection process is between three and five. Elsewhere we have provided a comprehensive model for the use of psychological tests in such screening (Goodstein & Prien, 2006).

Final Selection

The final selection among the best three to five candidates will ordinarily involve a series of interviews with different key supervisors and managers in the organization. All too often the final selection process tends to be unplanned, which leads to non-functional redundancy in the topics addressed. We strongly recommend that the persons who will be conducting the interviews meet prior to the first interview and develop an interview plan based on the job analysis; for example, decide who will ask what questions, decide which issues need to be covered by more than one interviewer, and so forth. Such planning greatly increases the database developed by the interview process, and also makes the candidate feel that, if this is a sample of management behavior, the organization is well managed.

In addition, an in-depth follow-up and verification of each candidate's education, work history, and background should occur in order to determine whether the candidate possesses the essential requirements. Our experience revealed that there are too many cases of falsified educational records, non-existent jobs, bankruptcies, convictions for a variety of offenses, and other misdeeds, none of which were included in the resume, of course. Research has shown that in most resumes as many as one-third of all the so-called "facts" are simply not true. Each of these issues needs to be carefully checked.

This final step of the selection process that we are advocating requires time and effort, but it has the capacity to pay rich dividends in the kind of employee it yields. Indeed, the same can be said of the entire hiring process that we have described thus far. There is a clear rule at work here, "Hire hard, and manage easy!" The reverse, however, seems to be more often the rule.

Job Orientation

Most descriptions of the initial human capital management process do not include job orientation as part of this process, but we insist that they should do so. Most frequently, orientation involves simply turning the new hire over to the human resources staff, who spend their time explaining the various company benefit programs and having the new hire fill out the necessary forms. While these are important ingredients of any orientation program, they are not the issues that are paramount to most new employees.

What new employees really want to know and should be told is how to succeed on the job and how to avoid getting in difficulties early on. Two questions we often suggest the supervisor should answer as if the new employee were asking them are, "If your best friend were to come to work here, what bit of advice would you offer about how to succeed?" and "What could I do in the short run that would cause me to fail?" This is clearly the advice that one would give to a close friend or relative, but is often very difficult for a new employee to obtain. And this advice should be based on the data developed through the job analysis.

In our judgment, the hiring process does not end with the final selection decision. After that decision is made, every organization should want the successful candidate to succeed. A job orientation that provides psychological support as well as administrative support enhances the likelihood of that success, as does having a training and development plan in place for the new employee, one based on the job analysis.

Training and Development

Once the new employee is oriented and working toward becoming successful, the issue of the employee's needs for further training and development become important. When a new employee is hired as a trainee, the importance of a training and development plan should be obvious, and a plan ready to be implemented should be available. Indeed, virtually all new employees will have training and development needs—needs that the job analysis and the selection process should have highlighted.

Because there are no perfect new hires, each will pose some kind of unique needs for further training and development, and it is at this early stage that these needs should be addressed. While obviously other training and development needs will surface over time, the new hire offers a unique opportunity for training and development. What are this new hire's specific training needs? Where could a training program, a course, some coaching, or mentoring early on make a real difference in performance and enhance the possibilities for long-term success? Further, this kind of effort on the part of organization is likely to make a real difference in the attitude of the new employee. "Someone up there really wants me to succeed!"

Conclusion

That the job analysis is the cornerstone of every employee life cycle process should be obvious—and that it affects applicants, new hires, employees, and employers. In every instance, the job analysis is the core of the process, from identifying what requirements are necessary to developing training and development plans for individual employees as well as in supporting and mentoring them to become successful parts of a well-functioning organization (Ployhart, Schneider, & Schmitt, 2006).

In summary, we have sketched out a human capital management process that provides a context for understanding the important role that competent job analyses play in that process. It is our hope that this will revive the focus of the HR community to this most critical aspect of managing our human capital.

References

Campion, M.A., Palmer, D.K., & Campion, J. (1997). A review of structure in the selection interview. *Personnel Psychology, 50,* 655–702.

Campion, M.A., Pursell, E.D., & Brown, B.K. (1988). Structured interviewing: Raising the psychometric properties of the employment interview. *Personnel Psychology, 41,* 25–42.

Goodstein, L.D., & Prien, E.P. (2006). *Using individual assessment in the workplace: A practical guide for HR professionals, trainers, and managers.* San Francisco, CA: Pfeiffer.

Peiser, C., & Yaakov, M. (2004). Job analysis by consensus: A case study. *Man and Work, 13,* 26–43.

Ployhart, R.E., Schneider, B., & Schmitt, N. (2006). *Staffing organizations: Contemporary practice and theory.* Mahwah, NJ: Lawrence Erlbaum Associates.

Reiter-Palmer, R., Young, M., Strange, J., Manning, J., & James, J. (2006). Occupationally specific skills: Using skills to define and understand jobs and their requirements. *Human Resources Management Review, 16,* 356–375.

Wilson, M.A. (2007). A history of job analysis. In L.L. Koppes (Ed.), *Historical perspectives in industrial and organizational psychology.* Mahwah, NJ: Lawrence Erlbaum Associates.

Leonard D. Goodstein, Ph.D., *is a Washington, D.C.-based consulting psychologist who specializes in providing consultation in personality assessment, especially in the workplace, as well as executive coaching. He is a principal with Psichometrics International, LLC, a developer and marketer of online pre-employment tests.*

Erich P. Prien, Ph.D., *is a Memphis, Tennessee-based industrial and organizational psychologist specializing in the development, standardization, and application of psychological tests, especially in the workplace. He is the founder and president of Performance Management Press.*

Contributors

A.P. Arora
Professor, Marketing Research
Management Development Institute
Sukhrali, Gurgaon, Haryana
India
  91-124-4013050,59
  email: aparora@mdi.ac.in

Halelly Azulay
TalentGrow
1719 Lorre Drive
Rockville, MD 20852-4138
  (301) 760-7179
  fax: (301) 230-2237
  email: Halelly@TalentGrow.com
  URL: www.TalentGrow.com

Andy Beaulieu
Results for a Change, LLC
13036 Mimosa Farm Court
Rockville, MD 20850
  (301) 762-6780
  email: andy@resultsforachange.com
  URL: www.resultsforachange.com

Tim Buividas
Corporate Learning Institute
1195 Summerhill Drive
Lisle, IL 60532
  (630) 971-5075
  fax: (630) 971-5076
  email: tbuividas@corplearning.com

Richard L. Bunning
Senior Consultant
Phoenix Associates (UK) Ltd.
57 Higher Lane
Rainford, Merseyside WA11 8AY
United Kingdom
  00.44.1744.88.4430
  email: Richard@Phoenix-erope.biz

Ann T. Chow
Metropolitan Detroit Bureau of School
  Studies, Inc.
391 Education
Wayne State University
Detroit, MI, 48202
  (313) 577 1729
  fax: (313) 577 8278
  email: annchow@wayne.edu

Phyliss Cooke, Ph.D.
Adjunct Faculty
Capella University
1935 Harton Road
San Diego, CA 62123
  (858) 569-5144
  fax: (858) 569-7318
  email: Phyliss6@earthlink.net

Michael Dulworth
President and CEO
Executive Networks, Inc.
291 Geary Street, Suite 310
San Francisco, CA 94102
  (415) 399-9797, ext. 803
  email: mdulworth@executivenet
  works.com
  URL: www.executivenetworks.com

Daniel Eckstein, Ph.D.
1923 Greentree
23 Elkins Lake
Huntsville, TX 77340
  email: danielgeckstein@yahoo.com
  URL: www.leadershipbyencourage
  ment.com

Audrey Ellison
Mosaic Marketing on the Bay
2 Adalia Avenue, Suite 402
Tampa, FL 33606
  (813) 250-0278
  email: ae@mosaicmktgbay.com

Susan K. Gerke
Gerke Consulting & Development
28782 Jaeger Drive
Laguna Niguel, CA 92677
  (949) 831-7088
  fax: (949) 831-0502
  email: sgerke@sbcglobal.net

Marshall Goldsmith, Ph.D.
P.O. Box 9710
Rancho Santa Fe, CA 92067-9710
  (858) 759-0950
  fax: 858-759-0550
  email: Marshall@MarshallGoldsmith
  .com

Jeanette Goodstein, Ph.D.
4815 Fox Hall Crescent, NW
Washington, DC 20007
  (202) 333-3134
  fax: (202) 333-8519
  email: LENG@aol.com

Leonard D. Goodstein, Ph.D.
Independent Consultant
4815 Fox Hall Crescent, NW
Washington, DC 20007
  (202) 333-3134
  fax: (202) 333-8519
  email: LENG@aol.com

Dr. K.S. Gupta
E-3, Block 2
Samhita Square
Basavanagar Main Road
Vibhutipura
Bangalore-560037
India
  09916927146
  email: ksgupta37@hotmail.com
  email: ksgupta37@gmail.com

Rajen K. Gupta
Professor, Organization Development
Management Development Institute
Sukhrali, Gurgaon, Haryana
India
  91-0124-4560183,126
  email: rgupta@mdi.ac.in

Judith R. Holt, CPF, CMF
JRH Associates, Inc.
P.O. Box 11244
Alexandria, VA 22312-0244
  (703) 354-6776
  email: jrholt@jrhassoc.com

Teresa Kirkwood
CentralKnowledge
214 Lamarche
Laval, Quebec H7X 3M7
Canada
   (450) 689-3895
   fax: (450) 689-3895
   email: teresa@centralknowledge.com

Nancy S. Kristiansen
Training by Design Consulting
Saint Joseph's College of Maine
278 Whites Bridge Road
Standish, ME 04084
   email: nancyk@leadershipforlearning
   .com
   email: nkristiansen@sjcme.edu
   URL: www.leadershipforlearning.com
   URL: www.sjcme.edu/masterbusad
   min/mbanew.html

Michael Kroth, Ph.D.
Assistant Professor
University of Idaho
322 E. Front Street, Suite 440
Boise, ID 83702
   (208) 364-4024
   fax: (208) 364-4078
   email: mkroth@uidaho.edu

Vera Litcheva
Corporate Learning Institute
1195 Summerhill Drive
Lisle, IL 60532
   (630) 971-5075
   fax: (630) 971-5076
   email: vlitcheva@thechicagoschool.
   edu

James L. Moseley, Ed.D.
Administrative and Organizational
   Studies Division
Instructional Technology Program
College of Education
Wayne State University
395 Education
Detroit, MI 48202
   (313) 577 7948
   fax: (313) 577 1693
   email: moseley@wayne.edu

Mohandas Nair
A2 Kamdar Building
607, Gokhale Road (South)
Dadar, Mumbai – 400 028
India
   (91 22) 2422 6307
   email: mknair@vsnl.net
   email: nair_mohandas@hotmail.com

Julie O'Mara
O'Mara and Associates
2124 Water Rail Avenue
North Las Vegas, NV 89084
   (702) 541-8920
   email: Julie@omaraassoc.com
   URL: www.omaraassoc.com

Ashish Pandey
Research Leader
Pragati Leadership Institute
310, Beaver Grandeur
Prune, Maharastra
India
   91-020-27290173
   email: Ashishp75@rediffmail.com

Ajay M. Pangarkar
CentralKnowledge
214 Lamarche
Laval, Quebec H7X 3M7
Canada
  (450) 689-3895
  fax: (450) 689-3895
  email: info@centralknowledge.com

Sheryl D. Peck, Ph.D.
Director, Leadership Development
Suntiva Executive Consulting
7600 Leesburg Pike, Suite 305E
Falls Church, VA 22043
  (703) 462-8473
  fax: (703) 462-8477
  URL: www.suntiva.com

David Piltz
The Learning Key, Inc.
1093 General Washington Memorial
  Boulevard
Washington Crossing, PA 18977
  (215) 493-9641
  (800) 465-7005
  fax: (215) 493-9642
  email: dpiltz@thelearningkey.com

Dr. Robert C. Preziosi,
Professor and Faculty Chair of HRM
Huizenga School
Nova Southeastern University
3301 College Avenue
Davie, FL 33314
  (954) 262-5111
  fax: 954-262-3965
  email: Preziosi@huizenga.nova.edu

Erich P. Prien
10 S. Main Street, Apt. 1308
Memphis, TN 38103
  (901) 523-0682
  email: pmptest@accessllc.net

Alan Richter, Ph.D.
QED Consulting
41 Central Park West
New York, NY 10023
  (212) 724-3335
  email: alanrichter@qedconsulting
  .com
  URL: www.qedconsulting.com

Sara Keenan Rohling
2915 Brook Drive
Falls Church, VA 22042
  (571) 594 3591
  email: srohling@suntiva.com

Lou Russell, CEO
Russell Martin & Associates
6329 Rucker Road, Suite E
Indianapolis, IN 46220
  (317) 475-9311
  fax: (317) 475-0028
  email: lou@russellmartin.com

Jan C. Salisbury, President
Salisbury Consulting
2450 Bogus Basin Road
Boise, ID 83702
  (208) 336-07703
  fax: (208) 342-0987
  email: jansalisbury@cableone.net

William J. Shirey, Ph.D.
110 Tuckahoe Trace
Yorktown, VA 23693
  (757) 329-6537
  email: iseconsulting@cox.net

Steve Sphar, J.D.
2870 Third Avenue
Sacramento, CA 95818
  (916) 731-4851
  email: sphar4@earthlink.net

Kris Taylor
4710 South 100 East
Lafayette, IN 47909
  (765) 404-8950
  fax: (765) 448-9124
  email: kris@ktaylorandassoc.com

Sivasailam "Thiagi" Thiagarajan
4423 East Trailridge Road
Bloomington, IN 47408
  (812) 332-1478
  email: Thiagi@thiagi.com
  URL: thiagi.com

Sacip Toker
Administrative and Organizational
  Studies Division
Instructional Technology Program
College of Education
Wayne State University
369 Education
Detroit, MI 48202
  (313) 577 4648
  fax: (313) 577 1683
  email: saciptoker@wayne.edu
  email: saciptoker@gmail.com

Karon West
West Consulting Group
258 Glengrove Avenue West
Toronto, Ontario M5N 1W1
Canada
  (416) 484-4549
  fax: (416) 482-1790
  email: wcg@total.net

Dr. Ingo Winkler
Chemnitz University of Technology
Reichenhainer Str. 39/612
09126 Chemnitz
Germany
  0049 371 531 4159
  email: ingo.winkler@wirtschaft
  .tu-chemnitz.de

Martha C. Yopp, Ed.D.
Professor
University of Idaho
322 E. Front Street, Suite 440
Boise, ID 83702
  (208) 364-9918
  fax: (208) 364-4078
  email: MYopp@uidaho.edu

Contents of the Companion Volume, *The 2009 Training Annual*

**Talent Management Topics

Editor's Choice

Inventories, Questionnaires, and Surveys

How to Use the CD-ROM

System Requirements

PC with Microsoft Windows 98SE or later
Mac with Apple OS version 8.6 or later

Using the CD with Windows

To view the items located on the CD, follow these steps:

1. Insert the CD into your computer's CD-ROM drive.

2. A window appears with the following options:

    Contents: Allows you to view the files included on the CD-ROM.

    Software: Allows you to install useful software from the CD-ROM.

    Links: Displays a hyperlinked page of websites.

    Author: Displays a page with information about the Author(s).

    Contact Us: Displays a page with information on contacting the publisher or author.

    Help: Displays a page with information on using the CD.

    Exit: Closes the interface window.

If you do not have autorun enabled, or if the autorun window does not appear, follow these steps to access the CD:

1. Click Start → Run.

2. In the dialog box that appears, type d:\<\\>start.exe, where d is the letter of your CD-ROM drive. This brings up the autorun window described in the preceding set of steps.

3. Choose the desired option from the menu. (See Step 2 in the preceding list for a description of these options.)

In Case of Trouble

If you experience difficulty using the CD-ROM, please follow these steps:

1. Make sure your hardware and systems configurations conform to the systems requirements noted under "System Requirements" above.

2. Review the installation procedure for your type of hardware and operating system.

It is possible to reinstall the software if necessary.

To speak with someone in Product Technical Support, call 800–762–2974 or 317–572–3994 M–F 8:30 A.M.–5:00 P.M. EST. You can also get support and contact Product Technical Support through our website at www.wiley.com/techsupport.

Before calling or writing, please have the following information available:

*   Type of computer and operating system

*   Any error messages displayed

*   Complete description of the problem.

It is best if you are sitting at your computer when making the call.

Pfeiffer Publications Guide

This guide is designed to familiarize you with the various types of Pfeiffer publications. The formats section describes the various types of products that we publish; the methodologies section describes the many different ways that content might be provided within a product. We also provide a list of the topic areas in which we publish.

FORMATS

In addition to its extensive book-publishing program, Pfeiffer offers content in an array of formats, from fieldbooks for the practitioner to complete, ready-to-use training packages that support group learning.

FIELDBOOK Designed to provide information and guidance to practitioners in the midst of action. Most fieldbooks are companions to another, sometimes earlier, work, from which its ideas are derived; the fieldbook makes practical what was theoretical in the original text. Fieldbooks can certainly be read from cover to cover. More likely, though, you'll find yourself bouncing around following a particular theme, or dipping in as the mood, and the situation, dictate.

HANDBOOK A contributed volume of work on a single topic, comprising an eclectic mix of ideas, case studies, and best practices sourced by practitioners and experts in the field.

An editor or team of editors usually is appointed to seek out contributors and to evaluate content for relevance to the topic. Think of a handbook not as a ready-to-eat meal, but as a cookbook of ingredients that enables you to create the most fitting experience for the occasion.

RESOURCE Materials designed to support group learning. They come in many forms: a complete, ready-to-use exercise (such as a game); a comprehensive resource on one topic (such as conflict management) containing a variety of methods and approaches; or a collection of like-minded activities (such as icebreakers) on multiple subjects and situations.

TRAINING PACKAGE An entire, ready-to-use learning program that focuses on a particular topic or skill. All packages comprise a guide for the facilitator/trainer and a workbook for the participants. Some packages are supported with additional media—such as video—or learning aids, instruments, or other devices to help participants understand concepts or practice and develop skills.

- *Facilitator/trainer's guide* Contains an introduction to the program, advice on how to organize and facilitate the learning event, and step-by-step instructor notes. The guide also contains copies of presentation materials—handouts, presentations, and overhead designs, for example—used in the program.

- *Participant's workbook* Contains exercises and reading materials that support the learning goal and serves as a valuable reference and support guide for participants in the weeks and months that follow the learning event. Typically, each participant will require his or her own workbook.

ELECTRONIC CD-ROMs and web-based products transform static Pfeiffer content into dynamic, interactive experiences. Designed to take advantage of the searchability, automation, and ease-of-use that technology provides, our e-products bring convenience and immediate accessibility to your workspace.

METHODOLOGIES

CASE STUDY A presentation, in narrative form, of an actual event that has occurred inside an organization. Case studies are not prescriptive, nor are they used to prove a point; they are designed to develop critical analysis and decision-making skills. A case study has a specific time frame, specifies a sequence of events, is narrative in structure, and contains a plot structure—an issue (what should be/have been done?). Use case studies when the goal is to enable participants to apply previously learned theories to the circumstances in the case, decide what is pertinent, identify the real issues, decide what should have been done, and develop a plan of action.

ENERGIZER A short activity that develops readiness for the next session or learning event. Energizers are most commonly used after a break or lunch to stimulate or refocus the group. Many involve some form of physical activity, so they are a useful way to counter post-lunch lethargy. Other uses include transitioning from one topic to another, where "mental" distancing is important.

EXPERIENTIAL LEARNING ACTIVITY (ELA) A facilitator-led intervention that moves participants through the learning cycle from experience to application (also known as a Structured Experience). ELAs are carefully thought-out designs in which there is a definite learning purpose and intended outcome. Each step—everything that participants do during the activity—facilitates the accomplishment of the stated goal. Each ELA includes complete instructions for facilitating the intervention and a clear statement of goals, suggested group size and timing, materials required, an explanation of the process, and, where appropriate, possible variations to the activity. (For more detail on Experiential Learning Activities, see the Introduction to the *Reference Guide to Handbooks and Annuals*, 1999 edition, Pfeiffer, San Francisco.)

GAME A group activity that has the purpose of fostering team spirit and togetherness in addition to the achievement of a pre-stated goal. Usually contrived—undertaking a desert expedition, for example—this type of learning method offers an engaging means for participants to demonstrate and practice business and interpersonal skills. Games are effective for team building and personal development mainly because the goal is subordinate to the process—the means through which participants reach decisions, collaborate, communicate, and generate trust and understanding. Games often engage teams in "friendly" competition.

ICEBREAKER A (usually) short activity designed to help participants overcome initial anxiety in a training session and/or to acquaint the participants with one another. An icebreaker can be a fun activity or can be tied to specific topics or training goals. While a useful tool in itself, the icebreaker comes into its own in situations where tension or resistance exists within a group.

INSTRUMENT A device used to assess, appraise, evaluate, describe, classify, and summarize various aspects of human behavior. The term used to describe an instrument depends primarily on its format and purpose. These terms include survey, questionnaire, inventory, diagnostic survey, and poll. Some uses of instruments include providing instrumental feedback to group members, studying here-and-now processes or functioning within a group, manipulating group composition, and evaluating outcomes of training and other interventions.

Instruments are popular in the training and HR field because, in general, more growth can occur if an individual is provided with a method for focusing specifically on his or her own behavior. Instruments also are used to obtain information that will serve as a basis for change and to assist in workforce planning efforts.

Paper-and-pencil tests still dominate the instrument landscape with a typical package comprising a facilitator's guide, which offers advice on administering the instrument and interpreting the collected data, and an initial set of instruments. Additional instruments are available separately. Pfeiffer, though, is investing heavily in e-instruments. Electronic instrumentation provides effortless distribution and, for larger groups particularly, offers advantages over paper-and-pencil tests in the time it takes to analyze data and provide feedback.

LECTURETTE A short talk that provides an explanation of a principle, model, or process that is pertinent to the participants' current learning needs. A lecturette is intended to establish a common language bond between the trainer and the participants by providing a mutual frame of reference. Use a lecturette as an introduction to a group activity or event, as an interjection during an event, or as a handout.

MODEL A graphic depiction of a system or process and the relationship among its elements. Models provide a frame of reference and something more tangible, and more easily remembered, than a verbal explanation. They also give participants something to "go on," enabling them to track their own progress as they experience the dynamics, processes, and relationships being depicted in the model.

ROLE PLAY A technique in which people assume a role in a situation/scenario: a customer service rep in an angry-customer exchange, for example. The way in which the role is approached is then discussed and feedback is offered. The role play is often repeated using a different approach and/or incorporating changes made based on feedback received. In other words, role playing is a spontaneous interaction involving realistic behavior under artificial (and safe) conditions.

SIMULATION A methodology for understanding the interrelationships among components of a system or process. Simulations differ from games in that they test or use a model that depicts or mirrors some aspect of reality in form, if not necessarily in content. Learning occurs by studying the effects of change on one or more factors of the model. Simulations are commonly used to test hypotheses about what happens in a system—often referred to as "what if?" analysis—or to examine best-case/worst-case scenarios.

THEORY A presentation of an idea from a conjectural perspective. Theories are useful because they encourage us to examine behavior and phenomena through a different lens.

TOPICS

The twin goals of providing effective and practical solutions for workforce training and organization development and meeting the educational needs of training and human resource professionals shape Pfeiffer's publishing program. Core topics include the following:

Leadership & Management

Communication & Presentation

Coaching & Mentoring

Training & Development

e-Learning

Teams & Collaboration

OD & Strategic Planning

Human Resources

Consulting

What will you find on pfeiffer.com?

- The best in workplace performance solutions for training and HR professionals

- Downloadable training tools, exercises, and content

- Web-exclusive offers

- Training tips, articles, and news

- Seamless on-line ordering

- Author guidelines, information on becoming a Pfeiffer Affiliate, and much more

Discover more at www.pfeiffer.com